W9-CAE-491

DATE DUE

SEP 2 5 2015	
OCT 0 5 2018	
WITHDRAWN	

BRODART, CO.   Cat. No. 23-221

Heredity *and* Environment *in* 300 Adoptive Families

Heredity *and* Environment *in* 300 Adoptive Families

The Texas Adoption Project

Joseph M. Horn
and
John C. Loehlin

ALDINETRANSACTION
A Division of Transaction Publishers
New Brunswick (U.S.A.) and London (U.K.)

Copyright © 2010 by Transaction Publishers, New Brunswick, New Jersey.

This book is printed on acid-free paper that meets the American National Standard for Permanence of Paper for Printed Library Materials.

Library of Congress Catalog Number: 2009023281
ISBN: 978-0-202-36345-5
Printed in the United States of America

Library of Congress Cataloging-in-Publication Data

Horn, Joseph M.
    Heredity and environment in 300 adoptive families : the Texas adoption
project / Joseph M. Horn and John C. Loehlin.
        p. cm.
    Includes bibliographical references and index.
    ISBN 978-0-202-36345-5
        1. Adoption--Texas--Case studies. 2. Parent and child--Texas--Case studies. 3. Parents--Texas--Case studies. I. Loehlin, John C. II. Title. III. Title:
Heredity and environment in three hundred adoptive families.

HV875.56.T4 H67 2010
362.73409764--dc22

                                                                2009023281

Contents

Preface

This book describes a thirty-five-year study of three hundred families who adopted a child from a Texas home for unwed mothers during the years 1963 to 1971. (These children are thus now adults.) The study was initiated and directed by Joseph M. Horn, at the time a fresh young University of Minnesota PhD on the Psychology faculty of the University of Texas at Austin. He soon recruited two of his colleagues, John Loehlin and the late Lee Willerman, to assist him in the study. The rest, as they say, is history.

The present book sketches the history of the project and brings together its many findings—currently scattered through various articles in professional journals—plus a few hitherto unpublished results reported here for the first time. We conclude with a discussion of the implications of these findings for two groups of people: first, for those directly concerned in one way or another with adoptions; and second, for those of us—surely most of us—who wonder from time to time about the differences among the individuals around us. This is because an adoption study lets us separate the two things that parents provide children: their genes and their family environments. In adoptive families, one set of parents provides the former and another set of parents provides the latter.

We have tried to write this book so as to make it accessible to general readers. For this reason, we have minimized the number of direct citations in most parts of the text—if present, they take the form of (author's surname, date), which should let you find them in the reference list at the back of the book if you wish. Otherwise, notes at the beginnings of chapters provide sources for material covered in that chapter. The book contains many numerical tables, but we have tried to keep them simple, and have provided an introduction to them at the beginning of Chapter 2. Finally, there is a glossary of technical terms at the back of the book, preceding the references.

It remains in this preface to acknowledge the many people and institutions who have contributed in one way or another to this particular scientific enterprise.

First, and most critical, are the members of the three hundred adoptive families that participated in the study. Although for reasons of confidentiality we cannot name them, we want to assure each participating member of each one of the families that we deeply value the time and effort that he or she contributed to the project.

Next, we are grateful for the institutional support we have received. The original study was financed by the National Institute of Mental Health, through its grant MH2480. The separate mail study and the ten-year follow-up were supported by the National Science Foundation, through grants BNS7902918 and BNS8209882. Later phases of the project were supported by the Pioneer Fund. We are grateful to its presidents Harry F. Weyher, Jr., and J. Philippe Rushton for their help. Our institutional home, the Psychology Department of the University of Texas at Austin, has supported us and continues to support us in many ways. And finally, the Methodist Mission Home of San Antonio has played a central and essential role in the research. We are grateful to its three successive presidents, Spencer Stockwell, Harold Burkhardt, Jr., and Larry Watson for their wholehearted support of the study. In particular, without Dr. Stockwell's foresight in gathering data on the birth mothers, this book would simply not exist. We are also grateful to the Home's consulting psychologist, Arthur G. Bouton, who contributed in a major way to the testing; and to many members of the Methodist Mission Home staff, including Lillian Smith, Bertha Cardwell, Bea Pearce, Dorothy Johnson, Mona McDonald, Mildred Miller, and others, who helped in contacting the adoptive families, providing data from the files, and in other ways.

Many individuals at the University of Texas played important roles in the project. Administrative Assistants Carol Weegar and Carol Shirley worked successively to keep things moving; later, Jody Ernst took on that task in addition to doing her dissertation work on the project and carrying out some of the home interviews. Many graduate students in the Psychology Department were involved in the project at one time or another; among those (in addition to Jody) were Richard Arnold, Jeremy Beer, Richard Bouton, Ralph Carney, Marilyn Erickson, Mary Green, Nancy Lawson, Ashleigh Merritt, Marsha Peterson, Gerald Turner, and David Vaughan. Finally, a number of undergraduate research assistants participated in various ways, including data entry, assistance with mailings, and rating of interviews. Among these were Jennifer Clemens, Jessica Cundiff, Eliot Davis, Cindy Fong, and Jeane Yo.

In addition, we are grateful to the numerous psychologists across the state who assisted with the testing of the families. In addition to Arthur

Bouton from the Methodist Mission Home, they include Kyle Babick, B. R. Barrington, Philip Dunbar, Alan Fisher, Richard Fullbright, Kathy Galvin, Neil Holliman, Jan Lander, Bert Levene, Barbara Leventon, Charles Mahone, Beatrice Matheny, Charles Middleton, Linda Montoya, Robert Nicholson, Nick Norton, Herb Stewart, William Whitehead, and Douglas and Shirley Winslow.

On a more personal level, we thank our wives, Joan and Marj, and our children, Tom and Karen, and Jennifer and James, for their tolerance and support throughout the long days and years of the project.

Finally, we would like to dedicate this book to the memory of Lee Willerman, a superb colleague and brilliant idea man, whose name, were he still with us, would be on its title page.

—JMH & JCL, 2009

1

A Brief History and Overview of the Project

This book is an account of a thirty-five-year research project involving three hundred families, each of whom adopted at least one child at birth from a Texas home for unwed mothers, the Methodist Mission Home of San Antonio. The book weaves together (1) information about the birth parents of the adopted children, gathered by the Home prior to the birth of the child in question; (2) information about the adoptive parents, gathered by our research team early in the study; and (3) information about the children in these families—the adopted child and others—gathered by the project at several points during their lives until adulthood.

1. Why Carry Out (or Read about) an Adoption Study?

Children adopted at birth have two sets of parents: both influential, but in different ways. The birth parents provide their adopted-away child with its genetic endowment but do not participate in shaping the child's environment. The adoptive parents do not contribute at all genetically but are in charge of directing the child's development through environmental means. If adopted children grow up to resemble the birth parents they have never even seen, the clear inference is that hereditary factors have had some influence. The Texas Adoption Project (TAP; Horn, et al., 1979) was designed to investigate this possibility across a range of human characteristics.

The question of the relative influence of the parents who provide the genes and the parents who provide the rearing environment is of direct concern to persons involved with adoptions: the adoptees themselves, members of families who adopt a child, and professionals who deal in one way or another with the adoption process. To what extent may an adopted child be expected to resemble one or the other set of parents in various respects?

But it is also a question of interest to anyone who wonders about the differences among individuals—the tremendous variation we all observe among the abilities, personalities, and life outcomes of the people we encounter. To what extent do these differences reflect differences among the genes of these individuals? To what extent do they reflect differences among the family environments in which they grew up? To what extent do they depend on other factors, such as unique combinations of genes and environments or sheer accident?

This book will not provide final answers to all such questions. No single study could. But it will provide many intriguing pieces of relevant evidence. We will not attempt to describe these in detail here: that is the task of the chapters ahead. But we can hint that the genes will play an appreciable role in our story, although not always a simplistic one; that there will be some surprises concerning how family environments operate; and that, at the end, ample mystery will still be left as to why humans grow up to be the fascinatingly varied individuals they are.

2. Previous Adoption Studies

There have been a number of previous studies that have used adoptive families to tease out genetic and environmental contributions to the differences among individuals. Readers who are not immediately concerned with this background may want to skip ahead to the next part of this chapter, "The Texas Adoption Project—Beginnings," and return to review historical matters later if desired.

Most of the early adoption studies focused on IQ. The classic studies of Barbara Burks (1928) in California and Alice Leahy (1935) in Minnesota demonstrated a substantial contribution of the genes to individual differences in IQ; a study by Freeman, Holzinger, and Mitchell (1928) in Chicago emphasized environmental contributions. An Iowa study by Skodak and Skeels (1949) suggested both a substantial environmental effect on average IQ and a large genetic contribution to individual differences.

Studies that are more recent have also used the adoption design to address issues of heredity and environment with respect to IQ. These include a study by Schiff and colleagues (1978) in France, which compared small groups at two extremes: children born of low-status parents but adopted in infancy into high-status homes, and half-siblings of these children who remained with their low-status mothers. There was a substantial average difference between the groups, suggesting environmental effects on average IQ. Three Minnesota studies, by Fisch, et al. (1976) and Scarr and Weinberg (1976; 1978) obtained low IQ correlations between unrelated adoptive siblings and larger correlations between biological ones, suggesting substantial genetic effects on individual differences in intelligence. The recent and ongoing Colorado Adoption Project shares with our own study the advantage of having measured IQs for birth mothers, and goes beyond it in having measured IQs for a subgroup of the genetic fathers of the adoptees, plus extensive measurements of the adoptive family environment. The results of this study to date have been reported in numerous articles and in a series of four books (Plomin & DeFries, 1985, 1988; DeFries, et al., 1994; Petrill, et al., 2003). They suggest that genes have an increasing importance with age in accounting for individual differences in IQ.

The adoption studies have placed considerably less emphasis on personality than on IQ, but there has been some. A British study (see Eaves, et al., 1989, pp. 125ff) included measures of extraversion and neuroticism for adoptive relatives, as did a Minnesota study (Scarr, et al., 1981). In general, the results are suggestive of a moderate role for the genes, and a minimal role for shared family environment, but individual correlations are sometimes erratic; the sample sizes are small enough for this to be attributable to sampling fluctuation (see Loehlin, 1992, p. 32). The Colorado study measured several personality traits (Plomin, et al., 1998); at age 16 there was little evidence of either the genes or family environments contributing substantially to individual differences. The authors speculate that this may be due to personality having a substantial component of its genetic effects non-additive, that is, due to gene combinations rather than individual genes: the latter constitute the major factor accounting for biological family resemblance in typical adoption studies.

This argument receives support from a special kind of adoption study, the comparison of identical twins reared together and apart. The most famous example of this is the Minnesota study by Thomas Bouchard and his colleagues (e.g., Tellegen, et al., 1988), but there have also been studies in England (Shields, 1962), Finland (Langinvainio, et al., 1984) and Sweden (Pedersen, et al., 1988). In general, these studies agree with the ordinary adoption studies in finding very little evidence of the effect of shared family environment—the separated identical twins are nearly as similar as twins reared together; but the estimates of genetic effects are higher from separated identical twins than from adoption studies—identical twins are genetically identical and share gene configurations as well as individual genes.

The majority of studies of adopted children are not primarily concerned with individual differences, but with average levels of achievement or psychological problems in adoptees relative to children growing up in families in the usual way with their biological parents. There have been many such studies. Wierzbicki (1993) reviewed 66 studies of adoption outcomes, and van IJzendoorn, et al. (2005) reviewed 62 studies of adoptees focusing on IQ or school performance. Studies such as these are mostly concerned with whether adopted children do as well as children growing up in comparable biological families (not quite, although most fall in the normal range), or whether adoptees do better than comparable children left behind and reared by their biological mothers (on the whole, considerably better). Studies of this kind suggest that adoptive family environments are having an effect on the abilities, personalities, and adjustment of the adopted children. Why these environments apparently do not produce much in the way of lasting family resemblance is a topic to which we will return in later chapters of this book.

3. The Texas Adoption Project—Beginnings

The Search for a Cooperating Agency

While straightforward in conception, adoption studies often face two serious practical difficulties. First, results that inspire confidence require relatively large numbers of adopted children and adoptive parents who will cooperate with investigators over a considerable span of time. Second, agencies handling adoptions do not often make and record detailed assessments of the birth parents' psychological status. Indeed, some of them see difficulties in placing children with adoptive families if such potentially negative information were to be generated. Could we locate an adoption agency who handled a large number of adoptions each year and who would be willing to share information and allow us to gather test data? In 1970 a search of all adoption agencies in Texas was begun. Using a list of approved agencies provided by the Texas Department of Human Services, a series of visits was initiated. At first results were not encouraging; visits in Dallas, Ft. Worth, and Houston showed that agencies were either not cooperative or had inadequate records. However, in San Antonio things were different.

The Methodist Mission Home (MMH) proved to be the ideal setting for the initiation of the TAP. Under the leadership of Dr. Spencer Stockwell, the MMH had been utilizing a wide range of objective psychological tests for guidance counseling over almost two decades. The number of unwed mothers served reached a peak of 321 in 1969 alone. Extensive files, including coded names and last known addresses, were being maintained on the thousands of girls and adoptive parents who had been clients over the years.

Of particular interest were the intelligence and personality tests given to the unwed mothers while they were in residence awaiting the birth of their child. These tests allowed us to take the measure of biological mother characteristics that are not usually available to investigators. It became obvious that if we could obtain the cooperation of the families who adopted these children we would have a good opportunity to correlate each biological mother to her biological but adopted-away child (an index of biological influences) and, at the same time, comparisons between adopted children and their adopted parents (an index of environmental effects) could be obtained using the same tests.

The way the MMH handled adoption also contributed to its suitability as a source for our sample of mothers and their adopted-away children. If the children have a long exposure to their birth mothers before adoption, both environmental and genetic influences from the mother are operating in the child's development. This can reduce the power of an adoption study to do the very thing it was designed to do, namely, separate genetic and environmental influences. Fortunately, all MMH adoptive placements were completed within a few days following birth, thereby reducing the possibility that the adoption design has been compromised.

Another way the usefulness of adoption studies can be reduced is if the children are placed for adoption with relatives or with adoptive parents who have been selected because they are similar to the biological parents. Again, we were fortunate in that the few adoptions by relatives were identified in the records and could be excluded from the sample. Also, the only measure of biological mother—adoptive parent similarity used in selecting adoptive parents was said to be physical similarity. At one time, the agency thought if the children were physically like their adoptive parents the potentially uncomfortable questions about lack of resemblance sometimes noticed by neighbors and schoolmates might be reduced to a minimum. This concern was waning during the years from which we selected our sample and less importance was attached to physical resemblance over the years. In any event, given the generally very low correlations between measures of physical similarity and our psychological traits of interest, the threat this would provide to the integrity of the adoption design would be minimal. As we will see later, the issue of the selective placement of children in families proved to be somewhat more complicated, but this gave us a promising start.

About the Methodist Mission Home

Two histories of the MMH have been published. The first, Stockwell (1966), was written by the man who was the director of the agency at the time we made our initial contact. Spencer Stockwell was excited to find some investigators who were interested in the wealth of information he had made sure was available in the MMH files. He became a vigorous advocate for our study, agreeing to make home visits to the adoptive parents and securing their cooperation for further testing. The second history, Richardson (1988), was written at a time when the number of unwed mothers served by the agency was at a historically low number as a result of legalized abortion and the popularity of unwed mothers rearing their own children. However, this second history does give some details concerning the criteria used by MMH in selecting which families would receive a child through the agency during the time our adopted parents completed their adoptions.

Covering the period of Stockwell's directorship, Richardson has the following description of requirements for prospective adoptive parents:

> The rigid requirements for adoptive families continued for sometime such as; neither [member of the] couple smokes, neither uses alcohol, neither has been divorced and only one child would be permitted. These rigidities were debated at most Board meetings and the restrictions have been modified until today. The first are; 1) both be over 24 and under 42; 2) that they be legally married at least three years; 3) that they be church members and have been active in a local church for at least one year; and 4) that they may not have more than one child. (Ch. 5, p. 3)

In the course of getting to know the people who actually did the investigations of the couples wanting to adopt, we learned that other criteria were also sometimes used in the selection process. Foremost among these was clear evidence of employment stability. This did not require an above average income, for some poorer families were chosen, but what did seem to be a requirement was a good work history with a steady source of income. Similarly, each family's self-reported history was examined for evidence of marital stability and an absence of behavioral problems such as alcoholism, mental illness, and criminality. We know these investigations were thorough because in our later interviews with adopted parents they sometimes referred to how intensive they were. One parent, a building contactor, claimed he could borrow a million dollars easier than he could get approval for adoption. Some of the other information used in the selection process included home visits and interviews, letters of reference from ministers and employers, and psychological test data on the birth mothers.

One more factor that influenced who could use the adoption services of the MMH was the ability to cover the expenses incurred in caring for the unwed mother and her child and in providing agency services. Both the parents of the unwed mother and the adopting parents were expected to contribute support for room, board, testing and counseling, and birth expenses. One result of this and the other requirements noted above was that both sets of parents tended to be above average in socioeconomic class. This advantage carried over to the unwed mothers and their children. Intellectual assessments carried out on the unwed mothers prior to the birth of their children showed them to be average or slightly above in intelligence test scores, while later testing showed the adopted-away children to be above the population average.

The Birth Mothers

All the birth mothers admitted to the MMH during the time of our study had been promised that their identities would be kept in confidence and that no attempt would be made in the future to locate or contact them. This security was maintained throughout our study.

As mentioned above, the MMH was extraordinary in its information gathering and records keeping. In addition, under Dr. Stockwell's guidance, the agency sought to generate new information about the women under their care so that the best advice could be given concerning their future mental health, education, and vocational choices. Using the results from all these tests, we were able to construct a reasonable profile of the women who were to form the nucleus of the TAP.

One commonly administered test at the MMH was the Minnesota Multiphasic Personality Inventory (MMPI), a test used among clinical psychologists to assist in diagnosis. This widely used assessment has published norms available that allow us to look for ways in which our sample might be similar to or different from the general population. The MMPI contains eight scales that can be used to detect psychopathological tendencies. These are: Hypochondriasis, Depression, Hysteria,

Psychopathic Deviation, Paranoia, Psychasthenia, Schizophrenia, and Hypomania.

Horn, et al. (1975) compared all the MMPI test scores available for unwed mothers from two years of admissions to the MMH with two additional samples of young women: 12th grade girls and married pregnant women. These comparisons revealed that being pregnant, whether married or not, seemed to increase tendencies to Hypochrondriasis, Depression, and Hysteria. Being an unwed mother, on the other hand, seemed to come with elevated tendencies on the other scales, with the scores on Psychopathic Deviation, Schizophrenia, and Hypomania showing the most increases.

What do these results indicate? First, what they do not say. These MMPI scale elevations do not mean the girls should be labeled as sick. These are average scores over the group, and many individuals score in the normal range for the general population. However, some do have very high scores and these girls may be at a significant risk of passing on to their children some of the same tendencies, if the tendency has a genetic component to it. The TAP would seem to be well suited to answer questions like this. Because we followed the adopted children well into their adulthood, we can compare each grown-up child to his or her biological mother.

The Adoptive Families

By examining the files, we soon came to understand the many different sources of useful information that might be tapped. In addition to the standard adoption design where adopted-away children are compared to their birth parents for signs of genetic influences and then to their adoptive parents for environmental indications, the adoptive families contained other persons whose presence could be used to provide confirmation of these initial estimates. In families with more than one adopted child, there are adopted siblings, who have no common genetic background, and can be used to measure the power of just the environment to make siblings alike. If environmental influences are very strong, adopted siblings ought to resemble one another just as much as biological siblings do. This provides a check on the estimate of the power of environment from comparisons of adopted children to their adoptive parents.

Some adoptive families contained one or more natural born children from the same parents who adopted children from the MMH. Comparing the natural children's resemblance to their biological parents against the resemblance of these same parents to their adopted children reared in the same family provides checks for estimates of both genetic and environmental influences. Strong genetic factors would be at work if the natural children showed an appreciable resemblance to their biological parents while this resemblance was weak or nonexistent between the adopted children and these same parents. Strong environmental factors would be indicated if there were an equivalent degree of resemblance between these parents and their natural and adoptive children.

Because of the value of these multiple estimates for both genetic and environmental influences, we were pleased to find that a majority of our prospective adoptive families had more than one child, either adopted or biological. It is also fair to say that we regarded these larger families as especially valuable and worked hard to secure their participation.

Getting Started

A thorough inspection of the MMH files revealed that girls who were admitted to the home between 1963 and 1971 seemed to be the best cohort from which to choose our initial sample. Most of these girls had been administered IQ tests as well as other tests, and most of their adopted-away children were now old enough to be administered the same or comparable tests. We matched the unwed mother files with the files of the family who adopted her child. This allowed us to verify that each unwed mother's child was with a family who we had a reasonable chance of being able to contact and attempt to gain their cooperation. Some of these families had kept in close contact with MMH through the years by sending cards and letters describing how their adopted child was developing. These families seemed like reasonable prospects. Other families had less frequent contact but were included if they still lived in Texas and their latest address was reasonably current. This process resulted in a list of adoptive families whom we would contact initially by mail. (See Appendix A for a copy of this letter.)

In 1979 we described the next steps as follows:

Starting with this list, our sampling procedure began by having an agency employee find the mailing address of the parents who adopted the children of these tested unwed mothers. The next step was to contact the adoptive parents by mail and ask if they would allow one of our field representatives to visit their home and explain the study. These field representatives were a former director and former social worker for the agency, both of whom had been involved with the placement of most of the adoptive children with their adoptive parents. In order to reduce the logistical problems in subsequent testing we concentrated on contacting adoptive parents residing in or near the larger population centers of the state. Some residents of smaller towns were also contacted and visited if the travel plans of our field representatives permitted. If the parents agreed to have their entire family tested, the names and phone numbers were given to a licensed psychologist in their area for scheduling of the tests. All contact with the adoptive families was through adoption agency employees or the psychologists....A total of 416 families were interviewed and agreed to be tested, but available funds restricted actual testing to 300 families. (Horn, et al., 1979, p. 179f.)

4. Some Characteristics of the Sample

The Three Hundred Adoptive Families

The adoptive families each had at least one child adopted from the Methodist Mission Home. Some of them also had other adopted children from the Methodist Mission Home or elsewhere. Quite a number of them also had biological children of their own, born before or after the adoption that brought the family into the sample.

Table 1.1 classifies the families into those having one adopted child, those having two or more children, all adopted, and those having both adopted and biological children.

As you can see, just under half of the families (144/300, or 48 percent) had biological children of their own as well as adopted children, and the majority of those with just adopted children had more than one (122/156, or 78 percent). As mentioned earlier, we made extra effort during recruiting to obtain larger and mixed families, as these provide more information relative to genetic and environmental effects.

Also shown in Table 1.1 are averages on two socioeconomic indicators for the three types of families. The SES measure is an index reflecting mother's and father's education and father's occupation. The income is the estimated annual income of the family, expressed in thousands of

Table 1.1
Three Types of Families

Family Type	Number	SES	Income
One adopted child	34	161.6	12.6
Two or more children, all adopted	122	165.5	14.4
Both adopted and biological children	144	165.6	15.7
Total	300		

Note: SES = socioeconomic status, an arbitrarily scaled, equally weighted composite of mother's and father's education and father's occupational level; Income = annual family income in thousands of 1973 dollars.

dollars in 1973, the year in which the families were interviewed. In either case, the variation is wide within each group, and the average differences between family types are not large enough to be statistically dependable; however, what differences there are suggest that favorable economic factors may have sometimes played a role in adopting multiple children or in combining adopted with birth children.

In any case, the adopted families in the TAP tended to be above average in socioeconomic status, as are adoptive families in general (Stoolmiller, 1999). As an example, Table 1.2 gives educational levels for the TAP fathers, compared to 1970 Census data for Texas men aged 30 to 49 years.

Clearly, the fathers in our sample are better educated than Texas men in general. Some 60 percent had completed college, as against around 17 percent for Texas men in a comparable age group.

The Children in the Texas Adoption Project

Of the 695 children in the study, 368 were boys and 327 were girls, with a tendency toward opposite-sex pairs in families of two or more children. This is because parents adopting two children tended to prefer to adopt a boy and a girl, or if they already had a child, to adopt one of the opposite sex. At the start of the study, the adopted children varied in age from 3 to 19 years, with the average age a little under 8 years. The biological children averaged a couple of years older.

Table 1.3 summarizes, by sex and adoptive status, the number of TAP children assessed in the various phases of the project. These included 635 children originally in the 300 families, and 60 additional siblings added at one or another of the later measurements.

Table 1.2
Education of TAP Fathers

Educational Level	Number	TAP %	Texas %
More than 4 years of college	93	31.6	8.2
4 years of college	88	29.9	9.1
1 to 3 years of college	51	17.3	13.3
4 years of high school	50	17.0	26.6
1 to 3 years of high school	8	2.7	19.8
Elementary school	4	1.3	22.8
Total	294	100.0	100.0

Note: Texas data from 1970 US Census, for men aged 30 to 49. From Horn, Loehlin & Willerman, 1982.

Table 1.3
Children Included in Various Phases of the Main TAP Study

| Study phase | Adopted | | Biological | | |
	Boys	Girls	Boys	Girls	Total
Original study	250	218	88	79	635
10-year follow-up	137	121	52	93	353
Covered in parent interview	141	122	55	61	379
Covered by mail questionnaire	176	151	79	65	471
Total sample	262	231	106	96	695

As is evident from Table 1.3, not all children were measured at every phase. However, the majority of those tested originally were followed up on at least one subsequent occasion—altogether, this group included 528 children, or 83 percent of the initial sample.

5. Studies in the Texas Adoption Project—Chronological Sequence

The Initial Testing

The members of the three hundred families were given a battery of IQ tests and personality questionnaires. Because the families were scattered across the state of Texas, we recruited local psychologists in a number of major Texas cities and arranged to have the families travel to the nearest one to be tested. In addition, we arranged to have the clinical psychologist associated with the Methodist Mission Home travel to test families who lived in regions that were remote from a major urban center. Besides the formal testing of the parents and the children, one parent, usually the mother, filled out a rating scale to describe the personalities of the children (it is included in Appendix B).

A Mail Study of Earlier Adoptive Families

After completion of the initial phase of the study of 300 families, and before the ten-year follow-up described below, we undertook a study by mail of 220 families who had adopted children from the MMH before 1966, the year in which psychological tests began routinely to be given to the residents of the Home. Because of this, comparisons involving the birth mothers were not available for this group. Since the study was done by mail, IQ testing was not practical, and the study was confined to personality traits. However, this group of earlier adoptions had the advantage that the children in the families were old enough to take the same personality questionnaires as their parents, so that within-family comparisons became more straightforward. As it turned out, there was a small overlap between the samples of the two studies—26 families were included in both. For example, a family that adopted children from MMH both before and after 1966 could have been in both studies. This permitted some limited crosschecking between the two.

Two general-purpose personality inventories were selected for use in the mail study: The California Psychological Inventory (CPI) and the Thurstone Temperament Schedule (TTS). These were sent to members of 293 families who had initially agreed to participate in this study; 73 of these failed to complete the study for one reason or another, leaving the final sample of 220 families. These families included 299 adopted and 62 biological children, ranging in age from 14 to 45, with a typical (median) age of 17 for the adopted and 19 for the biological children; the median ages of the adoptive mothers and fathers were 48 and 50, respectively.

The Ten-Year Follow-Up

Our idea about the TAP was always to continue gathering data until the children had fully matured; that is, until their education was completed and they were fully involved with their careers. A final assessment at this time could include evidence of marital adjustment, vocational success, and late-developing behavioral problems. Since such information can only be gathered after decades have passed, these are variables that are only rarely included in adoption studies—but are all the more valuable for this reason.

We realized that in order to extend our study across decades we would need to maintain contact with the adoptive families. If we waited too long after the initial round of testing many families might be lost. After ten years had passed, it was decided that we would make a major effort to renew our acquaintance with these families.

Several other concerns led us to attempt to contact all of the original study participants for retesting. Some of the children in the first round of testing were very young and the number of tests appropriate for this group was limited. Follow-up testing after a lapse of ten years would permit us to gather test data from this younger group that would then be comparable to the data we gathered initially from the older group of children and the adoptive parents. Another opportunity for testing would also give us a second chance to assess the family members who, for one reason or another, were unavailable the first time. Finally, any new additions to the families could be included.

Because we had tested the parents in the original study, and did not anticipate radical changes in their abilities and personalities over a ten-year span, we decided to concentrate at this stage on retesting the child generation, in whom we did expect to see changes. Thus, the main consideration in the ten-year follow-up was to obtain data at an intermediate point in the lives of the children, now mainly adolescents. We gave them, for the most part, the same tests for which we had data available from the birth mothers and the adoptive parents, and again asked a parent to fill out the same questionnaire rating the personalities of the children as was filled out in the original study.

Again, we made use of cooperating psychologists in the major Texas cities to do the bulk of the testing.

Home Interviews with Adoptive Parents

In 1997 we initiated a series of interviews in the homes of the TAP adoptive parents. Our goal was to gather information regarding the life outcomes of the adoptive children. The first series of interviews also aimed at demonstrating to funding agencies that we could be successful in renewing contact and securing the cooperation of the adoptive parents even though it had been over twenty-five years since the start of the TAP. We eventually visited with 167 families in their homes. All but three granted permission to tape the interview.

The interviews were open ended but the following pieces of information were sought in all cases.

1. How old was the child when you brought him home?
2. Was the child a good sleeper?
3. Were there any serious childhood illnesses?
4. How did the child do in school? (elementary and high school)
5. Favorite school subjects and activities?
6. Was the child ever in trouble at school?
7. Was the child ever in trouble with the law?
8. How far did they go with their education?
9. Are they married/divorced?
10. Do they have children?
11. What is their occupation?
12. How many jobs have they had?

13.   Is their marriage a good one?
14.   Are there any current difficulties in their lives?

In some cases, it was not necessary to ask the latter questions directly because by the sixth or seventh question elaborations volunteered by the parents gave clear indications of the future outcomes.

The tapes and notes taken during the interview became the material for the interviewer ratings that were made following the interviews. This interviewer questionnaire covered topics similar to those contained in the outcomes questionnaires that were completed by the parents and the grown children themselves about five years following the interview (as described in the next section). Copies of both questionnaires may be found in Appendix B. The similarity in content allowed us to compare our interviewer judgments to those of the parents and their adopted and biological children. The results from these comparisons are covered in Chapter 4. Later, an index of problem behavior at various age periods was also derived from the interview notes, with results also covered in Chapter 4.

The Outcomes Mail Questionnaire

The parent interviews had provided us with the parents' perspectives on their children's lives and current statuses, but they had done this for only something over half of the sample. We believed that a mail questionnaire might enable us to reach a larger proportion of the participants, as well as providing us with the children's own perspectives on their lives. We wanted to make it short—one page—which we hoped would minimize the chance that the recipient would set the questionnaire aside to fill out on some auspicious future occasion that somehow never arrived. After all, these were busy young adults. We wanted the questionnaire to tell us something about outcomes in such practical spheres as education, occupation, and marriage. We wanted a little history—childhood closeness to parents and adjustment in high school. We wanted at least to sample personal problems: anxiety, drugs and alcohol, trouble with the law. We wanted something on friends and social activity. We wanted a sketch of present personality characteristics.

The questionnaire we developed is shown in Appendix B. Initially, we sent it out to every child in the sample whose address we could obtain. We had asked in the parent interviews for current addresses for their children. We expanded the list by searching the State of Texas' driver's license records. Sometimes we were able to get addresses for other siblings when we located one. We mailed questionnaires to these addresses, with various alerting and follow-up post cards. Often we got filled-out questionnaires back. Sometimes we got post-office notifications of "moved, no forwarding address." Only four persons explicitly declined. In quite a few cases, we simply got no reply, even after follow-up mailings. We don't know in what proportion of these cases the questionnaire failed to reach its intended target, in what proportion it went directly into a wastebasket, and in what proportion it was put off until a more favorable time that never came.

Because there is an advantage in having multiple viewpoints on an individual, we sent the same questionnaire to parents and (with mutual consent) to siblings, with instructions to describe the person in question. We also sent additional copies of the questionnaire to the parents and asked them to describe their own lives. Table 1.4 summarizes the responses to the mail questionnaire.

Table 1.4
Responses to the Outcomes Mail Questionnaire

Mailing	Total Mailed	Post Office Returned	Declined	No Response	Completed	%
Offspring	544	47	4	124	349	64%
Parents	568	100	10	132	266	47%
Siblings	176	0	0	43	133	76%

Altogether, 466 individuals in the offspring generation (about 67 percent) were rated by at least one rater; the average was about 2.5 ratings. In only about 12 percent of cases did we have nothing except a self-rating for an individual. For most purposes, we combined ratings by averaging all the ratings a person received, including his or her self-rating, and assigned that average as the individual's score for that item; for some purposes we considered ratings by self and others separately.

The Criminal Records Search

In Texas, criminal records (beyond minor traffic citations and such) are a matter of public record, searchable by anyone for a small fee. We took advantage of this by carrying out a search of the records for each of the children in the adoptive families. Not surprisingly, most were absent from this list, but we found a few. This permitted us to do a couple of things: first, to check on the accuracy of self- and parental reports about trouble with the law, and second, to check on bias in our follow-ups. Were the people that we were unable to reach substantially different from the ones we did reach, in terms of their criminal records? The answers to these questions will also be given in Chapter 4.

6. Summary and Look Ahead

In this chapter, we have provided a brief history of a study of three hundred adoptive families, the Texas Adoption Project. In the next three chapters of the book, we will summarize the study's findings, and in the final chapter, we will say something about the implications of these findings. Some of these implications relate fairly directly to adoption: What outcomes do parents who adopt a child have reason to expect? Many of the results of the study also have broader implications for our understanding of the role that genes and family environments play in producing differences among individuals and in human development in general.

Our review of the study's findings will (like Caesar's Gaul) be divided into three parts. Each will get a chapter. The next chapter, Chapter 2, will present results on intellectual abilities, an important focus of the TAP. We will mostly look at findings related to general mental ability (e.g., IQ), but will also concern ourselves with more specialized abilities, as exemplified by the subtests of the IQ tests. The chapter following, Chapter 3, will address a second major focus of the study, the roles of genes and environment in personality development and change. The third, Chapter 4, will consider several areas of life outcomes: education, occupation, psychopathology/problem behavior, personal relationships, and happiness.

Our philosophy in presenting the findings will be to be specific: there will be many tables with numbers in them. But we will try to keep these tables simple—for complex details, the curious reader will need to go to the appendices in this book or to the original publications in the technical journals. Or the *really* curious reader (assuming that his or her curiosity is of a scholarly kind) can consult the de-identified data files themselves, to be placed in a permanent archive, the Dataverse Network of the Institute for Quantitative Social Science at Harvard University.

In any case, we wish you Bon Voyage for the journey ahead and hope you find it almost as interesting as we did.

2

Intellectual Abilities in the
Texas Adoption Project

As noted in the preceding chapter, a major motivation for carrying out a study based on adoptive families is that it permits comparisons of family members who are and are not genetically related. Thus, an adoption study can provide evidence of the relative contribution of shared genes and shared environments in producing familial resemblance on a trait. Both genes and environments are necessary for the development of any human trait, and some psychologists are happy to leave matters at that. However, those who are interested in why individuals differ from one another have often asked whether such differences primarily reflect differences in the genes of these individuals, differences in the family environments in which the individuals were reared, or other differences—for example, in their individual experiences outside the family.

In the present chapter, we will be asking questions like these about general intelligence, and, to a lesser extent, about more specialized cognitive skills. After an introduction to the main statistics we will be reporting and the kind of tables we will be reporting them in, we get down to our main business, assessing genetic and shared family environmental effects on intellectual skills. We report the results of applying two approaches to assessing such effects: one approach based on group averages (means) and one based on resemblances among individuals (correlations). In the first approach, we compare the averages of different groups, for example, adopted and biological children or adopted children of higher- or lower-IQ birth mothers. The

---

Note: This chapter is based in part on several earlier publications in specialized journals: Horn, Loehlin, & Willerman, 1979, 1982; Loehlin, Horn, & Willerman, 1989, 1994, 1997; Willerman, Loehlin, & Horn, 1979; these may be consulted for additional details.

second correlational approach is applied first to different kinds of pairings: genetically related and unrelated parent-child pairs and genetically related and unrelated sibling pairs. Then these two are combined with other relevant information to get best overall estimates of genetic and environmental effects in this population. This is done via a procedure called structural equation modeling, or path modeling, the typical method used by contemporary behavior geneticists to summarize genetic and environmental contributions to individual differences on a trait. We then take a brief look at the feasibility of estimating the IQs of the biological fathers of the adopted children from background information, such as educational and occupational data. Next, we extend structural equation modeling to examining the changes in IQ between the original and the ten-year follow-up studies. Finally, we look at specialized aspects of intellectual ability, in a study of the relation between intelligence and problem-solving speed, and in the modeling of genetic and environmental effects on more specialized measures of cognitive skills—the subscales of the IQ tests.

1. About the Presentation of Results in this Book

First, a brief introduction to the ways we will be reporting our results. Most of the tables in the book contain comparisons involving one or more of three statistics: means, standard deviations, and correlation coefficients.

Means and Standard Deviations

The *mean* is already familiar to you—it is the ordinary average: one adds up all the scores of the members of a group and divides by the number of scores to get the average score of a member of the group. Accompanying a mean will often be a *standard deviation*, a measure of

Table 2.1
Means and Standard Deviations of IQs on the Revised Beta Test in Three Groups

Group	Mean	SD	N
Adoptive fathers	104.8	7.5	296
Adoptive mothers	102.1	7.6	292
Birth mothers	100.3	8.9	357

how widely spread out the scores are around the mean. Typically, around two-thirds of cases lie within one standard deviation of a mean. Table 2.1 is an example of a table containing means and standard deviations.

Each row of the table represents one of the three groups of individuals. At the left, the group is identified. The first column in the body of the table contains the average IQ for the members of the group, followed by the standard deviation and the number of cases in the group. As you can see from the last column, IQs on this test were available for both fathers and mothers in most of the three hundred families in the study. (In a few cases, one spouse was missing due to death or divorce, or for one reason or another was not tested.) The number of birth mothers is somewhat larger than three hundred because a number of families had adopted more than one child. Because IQ tests are standardized so that the population mean IQ is 100, you can see from the means that the three groups are of average IQ or slightly above. The adoptive fathers averaged some 2 IQ points above the adoptive mothers, and they in turn some 2 points above the birth mothers.

The standard deviations suggest that there was considerable variation in scores within each group, and overlap between the groups. About two-thirds of the fathers would be expected to fall within one standard deviation (7.5 IQ points) of their mean, i.e., between IQs of 97.3 and 112.3. At the other extreme, about two-thirds of the birth mothers' IQs would be expected to fall between 91.5 and 109.1. Note that this implies that although there was a 4 point IQ difference between the averages for fathers and birth mothers, there was considerable overlap: there would be a number of birth mothers with IQs well above the adoptive father average of 104.8, and a number of adoptive fathers with IQs well below the birth mother average of 100.3. Another implication of these figures, if one knows that the IQ test was constructed to have a standard deviation of 15 in the population, is that the IQs vary much less in these three groups than in the population as a whole. We will have more to say about this point later.

Correlation Coefficients

A third statistic that we will frequently be reporting in our tables is the *correlation coefficient*. This describes how closely two sets of scores go together, in the sense that individuals who are high on one are also high on the other. This closeness is conventionally expressed on a scale of .00 to 1.00. A correlation coefficient of .00 represents no association between scores in the two sets: knowing a person's score on one tells you nothing about whether he will be high, low, or medium on the other. A correlation of 1.00 represents perfect prediction—knowing one of the two scores lets you predict the other exactly. Most of the correlations we will be reporting lie somewhere in between .00 and 1.00. A low value of .10, for example, represents a very slight association between the two sets of scores—they have a little bit in common, but not very much; we can do just slightly better than chance in predicting the one from the other. A value of .50 tells us that there is a substantial association between the two sets of scores; a value of .90 tells us that the association is nearly, but not quite perfect. A minus sign can be attached to a correlation coefficient to indicate that high scores on the one measure go with low scores on the other, but the numerical value of the correlation still tells us the extent to which this is the case. Table 2.2 is an example of a table reporting correlations:

This table asks about the degree to which birth mothers having high IQs have their children placed with adoptive parents with higher IQs and better education. The *r* heading the first column of the table is the symbol for a correlation coefficient. The *N* in this case refers to the number of pairs of scores on which the correlation is based. (Again, the number exceeds three hundred, because some of the adoptive parents are matched with more than one birth mother.) The table suggests that the birth mothers' IQs (which the agency knew about) got matched to a modest degree with the adoptive parents' education (which the agency also knew about), and this resulted in a slight degree of association between birth mothers' and adoptive parents' IQs (the latter were not known at the time of the adoption, but were later measured in our study). Notice that in the first two rows the association is between two sets of IQs, and in the second two rows it is between two different measures—the birth

Table 2.2
Correlations between Birth Mothers' IQs and the IQs and Education of the Parents Who Adopted Her Child

Birth mother IQ with	r	N
Adoptive father IQ	.12	353
Adoptive mother IQ	.12	348
Adoptive father education	.31	356
Adoptive mother education	.25	356

mother's IQ and the highest level of education completed by an adoptive parent. In either case, the correlation coefficient tells us the same thing: the degree to which one set of scores goes with another set, high scores with high scores and low scores with low, and thus the extent to which individual scores in one set can be used to predict individual scores in the other.

A few other statistics will be mentioned in the book, but these three are the main ones. The others will be described as necessary when they are introduced.

"Statistical Significance"

One matter that requires a word here for those not familiar with it is the term *statistical significance*. This refers to a low probability (usually taken as .05, that is, 1 time out of 20) that a given outcome could have been obtained purely by chance in drawing random samples of the size in question. A given difference between two means, for example, may happen by chance when samples are small and standard deviations are large—because, under these conditions, one would expect a good deal of chance variation of means from sample to sample. Similarly, correlation coefficients based on small samples will be expected to vary more by chance than correlation coefficients based on large ones. To say that a given correlation coefficient is "statistically significant" is to say that a correlation of that size or larger is expected to occur less than 5 percent of the time if random samples of that size were drawn from a population in which the actual correlation was zero. All four of the correlations in Table 2.2, for example, are significantly different from zero, as are the differences between means in Table 2.1. With fairly large samples, even quite modest correlations, or mean differences of a couple of IQ points, are unlikely to occur purely by chance, although they may imply only weak prediction.

The probability of obtaining a given result by chance (symbolized by p) can be obtained from various statistical tests that go by such names as t-tests, the Analysis of Variance, and χ^2, and are appropriate for different kinds of comparisons.

The calculations leading to statements about statistical significance depend on assumptions only approximately met by data in real life, so such statements should always be taken as only approximate. Nevertheless, they can provide useful guidelines in sorting statistical wheat from statistical chaff.

2. Intelligence and Intelligence Tests

One major focus of the Texas Adoption Project was on intellectual abilities. Tests of general intelligence ("IQ tests") were administered to all available members of the adoptive families in the initial study (and had been given to most of the birth mothers during their residence in the Methodist Mission Home). Most of these tests consist of a number of relatively homogeneous subtests measuring somewhat different skills, such as vocabulary, spatial analysis, arithmetic, perceptual speed, and so on. Thus, it was also possible to look beyond a single overall index of intellectual competence ("IQ") to more specific perceptual and cognitive skills.

Our primary emphasis will be on the overall score, IQ. The overwhelming empirical fact about specific intellectual skills is that they tend to be substantially correlated with one another in the general population. People who are high on one cognitive skill tend to be above average on others. Likewise, low goes with low. If someone has a high score on vocabulary, and you are asked to predict his or her performance on arithmetic or spatial puzzles or the rapid detection of clerical errors, you should predict an above-average performance. You will sometimes be wrong—not everyone is consistent. But the odds will be in your favor. In other words, different intellectual skills seem to have a good deal in common, a common core (although theorists are by no means in agreement as to exactly what this consists of and why it is there).

Because this common core seems to play a dominant role in accounting for individual differences in educational and occupational outcomes (see, for example, Jensen, 1998) and because psychologists have developed fairly dependable ways of measuring it (IQ tests), it will be our main focus. But because we also believe that many interesting and important questions about intellectual ability are better addressed at a finer level of detail than overall level of competence, we will pursue our questions beyond IQ as our data permit, via the subtests of the IQ tests used in the study.

IQ Tests Used in the TAP

Ideally, we would have liked to give everyone in the TAP the same IQ test. This was rendered infeasible at the outset by the fact that not all the birth mothers had been given the same test while in the Home (and privacy agreements ruled out our attempting to track them down and test them with something else). Furthermore, the IQ test that had been given to the largest number of them, *The Revised Beta Examination*, was not designed or normed for children, who were of central interest to the study.

What we ended up doing was administering an age-appropriate individual IQ test to each member of the adoptive families, and the Revised Beta as well to the parents. For most, the individual IQ test was a test from the Wechsler series—the Wechsler Adult Intelligence Scale (WAIS) for individuals 16 and older, and the Wechsler Intelligence Scale for Children (WISC) for those from 5 to 15. Children too young for the WISC (3 and 4) were given the Stanford-Binet. Although the Wechsler Preschool and Primary Scale of Intelligence (WPPSI) had recently been introduced at the time the study was being planned, it would have been unfamiliar to a number of our testers, and was in any case targeted for the four to six-and-a-half year age range, missing the three-year-olds. A few exceptions to the above age classifications were made at marginal ages based on the judgment of the testers—for example, that a particular child's skills might be better measured by a harder (or an easier) test.

At the time of the retesting in the ten-year follow-up, revised versions of the WISC and WAIS, the WISC-R, and the WAIS-R, had been introduced, and we faced a dilemma: whether to stick with the original versions or go with the revised ones. We decided in favor of the latter, on the grounds that these constituted the best contemporary measures, and would be the ones with which our testers would be most familiar. Also, the sameness of the "same" test ten years later is a bit of a fiction anyway; some of its items will have changed meaning with changing times, and some are no longer in the appropriate difficulty range for the now-older child and so would not even be administered. At this point, the issue of the Stanford-Binet versus the WPPSI had gone away—all members of the child generation were in the appropriate age range for either the WISC-R or the WAIS-R.

Because most of the children were now at ages for which the Revised Beta appropriate, they were given this test as well—so that now Beta IQs were available for all groups: for most of the birth mothers, for nearly all the adoptive parents, and for the adopted and biological children in the follow-up sample.

Table 2.3 shows the number of individuals in various groups tested with each test and the date at which the test was standardized.

One consequence of having used different tests for different groups at different times is that if we want to make comparisons among the IQs, certain adjustments for the aging of the test norms (sometimes called

Table 2.3
Numbers of Persons with Different IQ Tests

IQ Test	Adoptive Fathers	Adoptive Mothers	Adopted Children	Biological Children	Birth Mothers	Norm Date[a]
Revised Beta	296	292	251	89	357	1940
WAIS	292	289	5	22	42	1953.5
WISC	-	-	405	123	8	1947.5
WAIS-R	-	-	142	70	-	1978
WISC-R	-	-	115	24	-	1972
Wechsler-Bellevue	-	-	-	-	3	1936.5
Stanford-Binet	-	-	59	19	-	1932
No. with IQs[b]	296	292	486	183	380	

Note: [a]From Flynn (1984), except for Revised Beta. [b]Differs from column totals, because most individuals had more than one IQ test.

"Flynn corrections") must be made. Many readers may wish to take the details of these adjustments on faith, but for those who want to know more, we provide a fuller explanation of the adjustment procedures in Appendix C. Appendix C also contains additional information about the measurement properties of the tests themselves, such as their reliabilities, the agreement among different tests, and so on.

IQs for Different Groups

Table 2.4 gives the means, standard deviations, and an index of the shape of the IQ distribution, skewness, for a number of the groups and tests in the study. (Scores are adjusted for age of norms, as described in Appendix C.)

Several facts are immediately evident from this table. First, the average IQs on the Wechsler tests are all 100 or above, but not hugely so. We are dealing with a slightly above-average population, but not one highly selected for intelligence. Second, the standard deviations on the Wechsler tests are somewhat reduced, and those on the Beta greatly reduced—the latter are about half the population SD of 15. In general, reduced variability tends to reduce correlations, a fact that we will return to later.

Third, the distributions of IQs often depart appreciably from symmetry, which would be represented by 0 skewness. Skewness indicates a tendency for scores to pile up at one end and stretch out at the other—negative skewness, as predominantly seen here, means a piling up of cases at the high end of the distribution and a spreading out toward the low end.

Table 2.4
IQs for Various Groups and Tests

Group & Test	Mean	SD	Skewness	N
Adoptive fathers, WAIS	107.0	11.8	-.23	292
Adoptive mothers, WAIS	104.5	11.0	-.41*	289
Birth mothers, WAIS	101.3	13.1	-.56	42
Boys, WISC	104.0	11.7	-.08	282
Girls, WISC	103.0	11.1	.03	244
Children, Stanford-Binet	112.6	12.1	-.50	78
Boys, WAIS-R[a]	107.1	14.5	.06	115
Girls, WAIS-R[a]	103.7	13.7	.34	98
Boys, WISC-R[a]	104.9	14.5	-.55*	89
Girls, WISC-R[a]	104.4	12.4	-.04	84
Adoptive fathers, Beta	104.8	7.5	-.53*	296
Adoptive mothers, Beta	102.1	7.6	-.88*	292
Birth mothers, Beta	100.3	8.9	-.89*	357
Boys, Beta[a]	97.6	8.9	-.88*	187
Girls, Beta[a]	96.9	7.6	-.40*	160

Note: [a]In 10-year follow-up study. *Statistically significant skewness, given the sample size.

One source of negative skewness is ceiling effects, that is, a too-easy test for the group in question, so that scores pile up near the top end of the range. There is evidence that this is a factor on the Beta. Table 2.5 gives, on the left, the distribution of scores for one of the Beta subtests, Digit Symbol, which involves the rapid matching of numbers and simple abstract figures. Clearly this test is not difficult enough to spread out performances at the high end. In most cases, the maximum possible score is received by more persons than any other score. The result is a sharply negative skew. Matters are worse for the females, who tend to do better on this test.

On the right-hand side of the table, for comparison, are scores from the Wechsler versions of this test—called Digit Symbol on the WAIS and Coding on the WISC.

Here the typical scores pile up in the middle of the range, and the distribution extends symmetrically out to both extremes. The contrast may be seen in the proportions of the cases receiving the maximum possible score. Only about 1 percent of the total sample receives the maximum score on the Wechsler subtest; 22 percent do on the Beta version—in fact, among the girls, it rises to 40 percent. This particular subtest is fairly extreme, but all six Beta subtests show negative skew for all groups.

Table 2.5

Number of Individuals Receiving Each Score on a Beta Subscale and on a Similar Wechsler Subscale, Showing Ceiling Effects on the Former

	Beta: Digit Symbol				Wechsler: Digit Symbol or Coding				
Score	Fath.	Moth.	Sons	Dau.	Score	Fath.	Moth.	Sons	Dau.
30	40	67	36	67	**19**	2	3	1	9
29	16	33	12	13	**18**	3	3	2	6
28	25	26	22	18	**17**	1	11	6	11
27	24	34	16	11	**16**	5	12	10	20
26	28	27	20	19	**15**	9	25	15	36
25	40	22	21	5	**14**	10	18	26	25
24	17	19	19	8	**13**	13	21	23	24
23	27	22	15	7	**12**	40	53	39	47
22	19	17	9	4	**11**	43	38	44	30
21	25	9	8	2	**10**	66	47	50	16
20	12	5	1	3	**9**	45	29	24	13
19	9	4	3	2	**8**	36	19	26	8
18	7	4	0	1	**7**	13	7	20	5
17	3	1	1	0	**6**	4	3	8	3
16	0	0	2	1	**5**	2	0	2	0
15	1	0	1	0	**4**	0	1	1	1
14	3	2	1	0	**3**	0	0	0	0
N	296	292	187	161		292	290	297	258
%max	13.5	22.9	19.3	41.6		0.7	1.0	0.3	3.5
Skewness	-.8*	-1.0*	-1.3*	-1.3*		.8*	.4*	.2	.1

Note: Fath. = adoptive fathers; Moth. = adoptive mothers; Sons = adopted and biological sons; Dau = adopted and biological daughters. Beta are raw scores, Wechsler are scores scaled on a 1-19 scale; subtests: Digit Symbol on the WAIS, Coding on the WISC. %max = percent of individuals receiving maximum possible score. *Statistically significant skewness

By contrast, the Wechsler results are moderate and mixed: the parents show a little skewness, but it is positive, not negative. The children's score distributions are quite close to normal. The difficulty range of the Wechsler scale permits all levels of performance to be expressed; the too-easy Beta scale fails to distinguish among individuals in the top part of the ability distribution.

Despite these limitations of the Beta test, we will report results from it as well as from the Wechsler tests, because the Beta is the test most often available for a key group in the study, the birth mothers of the adopted children. For practical purposes, the Beta IQs agree reasonably well overall with the Wechsler IQs—for individuals receiving both, the correlation between the tests range from .83 to .92 after allowing for unreliabilities of measurement (see Appendix C for details). Most of the discrepancy of the Beta from the Wechsler test, aside from its lower ceiling, appears to be because it is a nonverbal test. Agreement with an IQ based just on the nonverbal scales of the Wechsler is excellent (Appendix C).

3. Evidence about Heredity and Environment from Comparisons of Means

Tables 2.6 and 2.7 contain the means and standard deviations of IQs on the individually administered IQ tests for various groups in the original and follow-up studies (values for the Revised Beta IQ test were given in Table 2.4). As noted earlier, the members of the adoptive families average slightly above the population mean for IQ—the mean IQs in the various groups range from about 100 to 107, depending on the group and test involved. Because these are Flynn-adjusted scores, they can legitimately be compared to a population mean IQ of 100. The birth mothers of the adopted children are 2 to 6 IQ points, on average, below the adoptive parents, but remain just above the population mean in average IQ. This makes them an unusual group for adoption studies, in which there is often a substantial IQ gap between birth mothers and adoptive parents. This can be considered a weakness of the present data (from a purely scientific standpoint) in that stronger conclusions might have been drawn from the means had the average IQ gap between birth mothers and adoptive parents been greater.

As they stand, the results from the initial study (Table 2.6) are about what one would expect if there is little average genetic difference among the groups, but family environments are playing some role. The mean IQs of the adopted and biological children in the families are similar, and both are like those of the parents in the adoptive families—about equal to the mothers and a point or two below the fathers. In this comparison, we are considering just the adopted children who have birth mothers with IQs. A number of those whose mothers are missing IQs were adopted through agencies other than the Methodist Mission Home; their somewhat lower IQs suggest that some of them may be at a biological disadvantage.

A comparison of the bottom rows of Table 2.6 with those of Table 2.7, which shows testing at the ten-year follow-up, suggests that the average intellectual level of the children remained about the same between the two testings (or, put differently, that the adjustments are working as they

Table 2.6
Mean and Standard Deviation of IQs for Various Groups on Individually Administered IQ Tests; Original Testing

Group	Mean	SD	N
Adoptive fathers	107.0	11.8	292
Adoptive mothers	104.5	11.0	289
Birth mothers	100.6	12.3	53
Adopted children			
With birth mother IQ	105.2	11.9	365
No birth mother IQ	102.8	11.3	102
Biological children	104.7	11.8	164

Note: All IQs Flynn-adjusted. Individual IQ test: Adoptive mothers and fathers = WAIS; birth mothers = WAIS, WISC, or Wechsler-Bellevue; children = WAIS, WISC, or Stanford-Binet.

should be—there would have been an apparent downward shift of about 4 IQ points, had we used unadjusted IQs). The Beta IQs for the children, on the right in Table 2.7, are a few points on the low side, but they would have been much too high—some 13 IQ points higher—had they not been adjusted. (The Beta IQs for the parents and birth mothers—see Table 2.4—appear less out of line.)

Higher- and Lower-IQ Birth Mothers

The lack of obvious evidence for genetic factors in the means of Tables 2.6 and 2.7 should not be taken as implying that there is no such evidence in the study. If we select groups of birth mothers of higher and lower IQ, the means of their children do differ. Tables 2.8 and 2.9 provide examples, based on the data of the follow-up study.

Table 2.7
Means and Standard Deviations of IQs for Children in 10-Year Follow-Up

Group	Individual IQ Test			Revised Beta IQ		
	Mean	SD	N	Mean	SD	N
Adopted children						
With birth mother IQ	105.2	14.4	218	96.9	8.5	206
No birth mother IQ	103.8	12.5	56	98.5	7.1	48
Biological children	105.7	13.5	112	97.4	8.7	93

Note: All IQs Flynn-adjusted. Individual IQ test: WAIS-R or WISC-R

Table 2.8
Mean Beta IQs of Adopted Children of Lower- and Higher-IQ Birth Mothers, by Adoptive Family Socioeconomic Status

	Lower-IQ Birth Mothers		Higher-IQ Birth Mothers	
	IQ	N	IQ	N
Lower-SES adoptive families	94.0	56	98.6	43
Higher-SES adoptive families	95.6	44	99.7	55

Note: Birth mother IQ and adoptive family SES divided at respective medians (middle scores). Difference between columns statistically significant (by Analysis of Variance, *p* < .001); differences between rows and interactions not.

Table 2.9
Mean Beta IQs of Adopted Children of Lower- and Higher-IQ Birth Mothers, by Adoptive Mother's Beta IQ

	Lower-IQ Birth Mothers		Higher-IQ Birth Mothers	
	IQ	N	IQ	N
Lower-IQ adoptive mothers	94.4	32	100.2	41
Higher-IQ adoptive mothers	95.0	52	97.8	70

Note: Birth mother IQ and adoptive mother IQ divided at respective medians (middle scores). Difference between columns statistically significant (by Analysis of Variance, *p* < .001); differences between rows and interactions not.

The Beta IQs of the adopted children have been divided by whether their birth mother was above or below average in IQ, for two groups—in Table 2.8 for adoptive families below or above average in socioeconomic status and in Table 2.9 for adoptive mothers below or above average in IQ. (The SES measure was an index based on adoptive father's and mother's education and father's occupational status.) The result was that having a birth mother of below or above average IQ (left-right comparison) made a difference, on average, of 3 to 5 IQ points in the adopted child's IQ, for either higher or lower SES families or higher or lower adoptive mother's IQ. Having adoptive parents of more education and higher occupational status (top-bottom comparison in Table 2.8) made a 1 or 2 IQ point difference, not statistically significant with these sample sizes, and having an adoptive mother with higher IQ (top-bottom comparison in Table 2.9) had no consistent effect at all.

Evidence based on correlations will be presented later in the chapter.

Selection in the Ten-Year Follow-Up?

Table 2.10 compares data from the first study for families and individuals who did and did not participate in the Ten-year follow-up study. It addresses the question of whether the individuals who continued to participate were a select group in terms of IQ. The answer seems on the whole to be "Yes, somewhat." The birth mothers' Beta IQs weren't different, and the biological children went a trifle the opposite way, but mostly the members of participating families averaged some 2 to 5 IQ points higher. Also included in the table are the adoptive parents' age, education, and occupation. Education is on a six-category scale from low

Table 2.10
Comparison in First Study of Families in and Not in 10-Year Follow-Up

Group & Test	In First Study Only			In 10-Year Follow-Up		
	Mean	SD	N	Mean	SD	N
Adoptive fathers						
WAIS	105.3	13.3	114	108.2	10.7	178
Beta	103.4	8.3	115	105.7	6.9	181
Adoptive mother						
WAIS	101.7	11.6	114	106.3	10.2	175
Beta	100.2	8.2	116	103.3	7.0	176
Birth mother						
Beta	100.4	9.0	145	100.5	8.4	199
Adopted children						
With birth mother IQ	103.8	11.3	160	106.2	12.3	205
No birth mother IQ	100.1	12.4	50	105.4	9.6	52
Biological children	105.0	11.7	71	104.4	12.0	93
Father's age	41.2	5.1	114	39.7	5.0	182
Mother's age	38.0	4.6	115	37.0	5.1	181
Father's education	5.8	1.7	117	6.1	1.4	181
Mother's education	5.0	1.3	117	5.5	1.1	181
Father's occupation	2.6	1.6	117	2.3	1.3	181

Note: All IQs Flynn-adjusted. IQ tests, children: WAIS, WISC, or Stanford-Binet, depending on age. Beta = Revised Beta Examination. Fathers and mothers included if families had at least one child in follow-up; birth mothers and children based on individual children in or not in follow-up. Education: 1 = lowest, 8 = highest; occupation, 1 = highest, 7 = lowest.

to high (1 = elementary school, 6 = more than four years college), and occupational level on a seven-category modified Warner scale, which runs from high to low (1 = high, 7 = low). The parents in participating families tended to be younger (by about a year) and higher in educational and occupational status.

None of these differences is especially surprising. In younger families, more of the children were still at home and available for testing. And one would expect more intelligent and educated parents to place a greater value on the abstract notion of contributing to knowledge via research. Still, the consequence, at least for the parents, is more elevated means and further reduction in variation. Trends are less consistent for the birth mothers and for the children, suggesting that the selection occurred primarily via the parents.

Different Kinds of Families?

Another factor that could, in principle, complicate the interpretation of the data would be differences among the different types of adoptive families. Some families adopted only one child, for example, others two or three. Some families have only adopted children, others have both adopted children and their own biological children. (There are no all-biological-child families in this study, because the families were selected based on their having adopted a child.)

Table 2.11
Three Kinds of Families

	Adopted—1	Adopted—2+	Mixed	p
Father's age	39.3	41.2	39.8	.05
Mother's age	36.6	37.9	37.4	.35
Father's education	5.7	6.1	6.1	.37
Mother's education	5.2	5.4	5.3	.76
Father's occupation	2.8	2.4	2.3	.16
Father's WAIS IQ	100.5	108.5	107.6	< .001
Father's Beta IQ	100.5	105.2	105.7	< .001
Mother's WAIS IQ	102.0	104.9	104.8	.29
Mother's Beta IQ	100.0	102.3	102.5	.15
Number of families	40-41	120-127	126-130	
Child's IQ (original study)	108.3	104.3	104.5	.12
Number of children	41	254	336	

Note: All IQs Flynn-adjusted. p = probability of this large a difference among groups occurring by chance (based on an Analysis of Variance).

Table 2.11 shows several parental variables—father's and mother's education, father's occupation, father's and mother's ages, and father's and mother's IQs—and one child variable, IQ, for the three groups mentioned above: families with one adopted child; families with two or more children, all adopted; and families with both adopted and biological children.

On the whole, these types of families are not very different, except on father's IQ, which averages a few points lower in the families that adopted only a single child. These fathers tend also to be a little younger. On other parental variables—father's and mother's education, mother's age or IQ, father's occupation—the average differences among these three groups of families are not statistically significant. What small differences there are in father's education and occupation go along with father's IQ—less education and a lower-status job for the fathers of the single adopted child. However, the lower IQ of the father appears not to have handicapped the child any—if anything, the single adopted children averaged higher on the IQ test, although this could be a chance difference because the number of these families is fairly small.

4. Evidence about Heredity and Environment from Family Correlations

Evidence from Correlations between Parents and Offspring

It has sometimes been said, including by us, that means and correlations can give different information about the influence of heredity and environment on a trait, such as IQ. This is true, but only in a limited sense. Turkheimer (1991) has argued persuasively against what he calls this "two realms" hypothesis: development is a single process, he insists; it occurs in individuals; it has consequences for both means and correlations; it results in both individual and group differences. It is sometimes the case that differences in group means will provide a better window on this single process than will the individual differences reflected in correlations; in other instances correlations can be more informative. But this is a matter of how variables vary between and within the groups studied, not about fundamental differences in how things happen in the development of the trait.

In the case of the Texas Adoption Project, as we have seen, the overall group means do not tell us much about heredity and environment, because the birth mothers appear not to be very different in their genetic potential from the adoptive parents. However, when the birth mothers are divided into those of higher and lower IQ, as was done in Tables 2.8 and 2.9, we can see the effect of this difference in the mean IQs of their children. An additional step in this direction can be taken by calculating correlations, which relate the IQs of individual parents and children, as well as the IQs of genetically related and unrelated children growing up together in the same families.

Table 2.12 shows correlations for parents and offspring, for various combinations of families. On the left-hand side of the table are shown correlations based on genetically unrelated parent-child pairs, whose resemblance must chiefly reflect environmental factors (plus the results of any selective placement of children by the adoption agency, a point we will consider later). For example, higher-IQ parents might provide environments conducive to intellectual achievement—might place more emphasis on intellectual activities for their children, have more books around the house, and so on. On the right-hand side of the table are genetically related parent-child pairs. The parent also contributes to the child's environment in the first two of these columns, but not in the third (except possibly prenatally—discussed later).

Table 2.12
Correlations between Revised Beta IQs of Parents and Individual IQs of Children in Original and Follow-Up Study

	Genetically Unrelated		Genetically Related		
Group	F-Ad	M-Ad	F-Bio	M-Bio	B-Ad
Families participating in first study only					
Raw	.14	.19	.41	.24	.36
Reliability-adjusted	.18	.24	.53	.31	.48
Families participating in both studies, child at original testing					
Raw	.07	.05	.02	.17	.22
Reliability-adjusted	.10	.07	.03	.23	.31
Families participating in both studies, child at 10-year follow-up					
Raw	.07	-.02	.25	.19	.26
Reliability-adjusted	.10	-.03	.33	.24	.36
Number of pairs	203-257	205-248	70-95	70-92	145-200

Note: F, M = father and mother in adoptive family; Ad, Bio = adopted, biological child in adoptive family; B = birth mother of adopted child. Number of pairs = number of children, because a parent may be paired with more than one child. Individual IQ tests: WAIS/WISC/Binet in original study, WAIS-R/WISC-R in follow-up.

Low correlations based on Ns of these sizes show a fair amount of sampling variation, and these do. Nevertheless, it is clear that the correlations on the right-hand side of the table, which reflect genetic resemblance, tend on the whole to be larger than those on the left-hand side, which do not. In each case, both raw correlations and correlations adjusted for the unreliability of the IQ tests are shown.

In the first section of the table, which represents families tested in the original study who did not participate in the follow-up, the correlations appear to run higher than those in the families that participated in both studies. Among the families participating in both studies, the correlations at the time of the follow-up involving adoptive mothers appear to be a little lower than the corresponding correlations involving fathers or birth mothers. This is unexpected on a simple environmentalist hypothesis, because it is the mothers who have had the most interactions with the children—the fathers have presumably had less, and the birth mothers of the adopted children none at all—at least none postnatally. But prenatal effects are unlikely to be important in accounting for resemblances here—if they were, we would expect the IQ correlations of the adoptive mothers with their biological children to be higher than those of the fathers, and they are not.

Could restriction of range explain some of this? The adoptive parents are a selected group in terms of their initial entry into the study, and were further selected by their willingness to cooperate in the follow-up. Restriction of range lowers test reliability—the ability to make discriminations among individuals—which in turn lowers correlations. Therefore, reliability-corrected versions of the raw correlations are also provided in the table. In general, the relationships in the raw correlations persist in the adjusted ones. For example, the lower correlations involving the adoptive mothers appear not to be solely a function of a greater restriction of range in this group; adjusted for unreliability, they remain lower. It remains the case that the correlations on the left of the table, reflecting environmental relationships, tend to be lower than those on the right, which include genetic resemblance.

If we take seriously the differences between the correlations involving the birth mothers and the adoptive mothers on the right-hand side of the table, we would have to argue that environmental relationships between parents and their children, far from creating IQ resemblances between them, tend to *diminish* IQ resemblance. The birth mothers have had no interaction with their children, and the adoptive mothers have had a great deal with theirs. Yet the sizes of the IQ correlations tend to go in the opposite direction.

One alternative possible explanation for low adoptive mothers' correlations is selection—that mothers in families who found the greatest differences between themselves and their children were more motivated to participate in the follow-up study. We will return to this issue after considering the sibling data.

Evidence from Correlations between Siblings

In addition to correlations between children and their parents—the parents who give birth to them or who rear them or both—adoption studies provide information about individuals who are brought up together as siblings, but who may or may not share genes.

Table 2.13 provides some data on IQ correlations between genetically related and unrelated siblings in adoptive families. These are calculated by a double-entry procedure; i.e., each pairing in the relevant category is entered twice, once in each direction, and the correlation calculated over all such pairs. The number of pairs given in the table is one-half the *N* used for the calculations, that is, a pair entered both ways is counted only once.

Several points of interest emerge from this table. First, as was true in the case of the parent-child correlations in Table 2.12, the correlations tend to be higher for the genetically related pairs on the right than for

Table 2.13
IQ Correlations between Genetically Related and Unrelated
Individuals Reared as Siblings

	Genetically Unrelated		Genetically Related
IQ Tests	Ad-Ad	Ad-Bio	Bio-Bio
Families participating in first study only			
Wechsler	.30	.36	.46
Families participating in both studies, at original testing			
Wechsler	.14	.10	.27
Families participating in both studies, at 10-year follow-up			
Wechsler	-.04	.06	.22
Beta	.04	-.05	.32
Numbers of pairs	67-96	82-119	16-37

Note: Ad, Bio = adopted, biological child in adoptive family. Tests: Beta = Revised Beta Examination; Wechsler = WAIS/WISC/Binet in original study, WAIS-R/WISC-R in follow-up.

the genetically unrelated pairs on the left. Second, the correlations at the first testing were generally higher in the families that did not choose to participate in the follow-up than in the families that did. Third, the correlations in the latter group between genetically unrelated pairs dropped from low positive at the time of the first study (.14, .10) to essentially zero at the time of the follow-up.

The numbers of pairs are not so large as to put these conclusions beyond all question. This is particularly true in the case of the biological siblings—there were not a large number of families who had two or more offspring of their own in addition to adopting the child that brought them into the study. There were, in fact, 49 such families out of the total 300. (An additional 82 families had one biological child plus adoptees; they could contribute to the genetic parent-offspring pairings in Table 2.12, and to the biological-adopted sibling pairs here, but not to the biological sib pairs.) Our present interest, however, is mainly descriptive. We will undertake some statistical testing in connection with model fitting later in the chapter.

The apparently lower sibling correlations in the families participating in the follow-up are reminiscent of the parent-child results. The parents in these families were on average slightly younger and better educated than those in the non-participating families, but the differences were not dramatic (Table 2.10). Was there something about the children? One obvious possibility to consider in the case of lowered correlations is restriction in range, but Table 2.10 tends to rule this hypothesis out. On the whole, the standard deviations of children's IQs in the follow-up families were not less than those in the families who did not elect to participate further. In the two larger of the groups, they were, if anything, greater. Alternatively, as we speculated might be the case for differences between mothers and children, it is possible that mothers whose children were more different from each other might be more curious about the reasons why than mothers whose children were less different. We have one piece of indirect evidence that may support such a hypothesis. Parents with only one child, who would presumably not be subject to this motivation, were less likely to participate in the follow-up than those with multiple-child families (44 versus 66 percent).

Spouse Resemblance

Also important for the IQ modeling we are about to undertake is the correlation between spouses and why it occurs. Table 2.14 provides some relevant information.

Table 2.14
Correlations between Spouses for IQ and Education

Group	Wechsler IQ	Beta IQ	Education	Pairs
Families in first study only	.34	.26	.54	125-131
Families in both studies	.26	.18	.48	155-165
All families	.31	.24	.52	280-296
With education statistically controlled	.09	.17		

The correlations in the table suggest that moderate correlations between spouses exist for IQ and will need to be allowed for in the modeling. As in some of the other tables, they are slightly lower for the families who participated in both the original study and the ten-year follow-up. The fact that the correlations for educational level are somewhat higher than those for IQ suggests that a factor in spouses' originally getting together may well be their joint presence in the same educational institutions or occupational settings. There remains some correlation, especially for Beta IQ, after statistically controlling for the effects of education. This may suggest a stronger relationship between the verbal aspects of intelligence and education than the nonverbal aspects.

Path Models of IQ in Families

A great deal of interesting information may be gleaned from looking at relationships piecemeal in familial data, as we have done so far. However, the method of choice for most contemporary researchers is to fit path models to the data for all of the relationships. By fitting a path model simultaneously to data on parents and children one can obtain single best estimates of the strengths of the underlying genetic and environmental influences, as well as statistical evaluations of the overall fit of models, and tests of whether models that are more elaborate are required or if simpler ones will do.

We cannot give a full treatment here of the methodology of path analysis, or structural equation modeling, as it is often called nowadays. Readers interested in a general introduction may wish to consult Loehlin (2004), or, for specific applications to behavior-genetic modeling, Neale and Cardon (1992).

Model Fitting to Parent, Sibling, and Spouse Correlations

An important feature of structural equation or path models, as we will be using them, is the distinction between observed variables and latent variables. The observed variables, in the present case, are the measured IQs. The latent variables are the true variables lying behind the observed variables, plus the genetic and environmental factors that lie a step further back. In the conventions of path modeling, latent variables are represented by circles, observed variables by squares. A second important feature of such models is the set of connections among the various observed and latent variables. These connections take two forms: causal, where one variable is assumed to have a causal influence on the other, or correlational, where two variables may be correlated, but no assumption is made as to why. A causal relationship is represented by an arrow from the causing to the caused variable. A correlational relationship is represented by a two-headed arrow connecting the two variables in question.

The various latent variables and their interrelationships are hypothesized to account for the correlations among the observed variables. The test of a given model is how well it can do this. The following example illustrates how this is accomplished.

An elementary path diagram of a family is shown in Figure 2.1. Two observed variables are shown in squares at the bottom of the figure: IQ_1 and IQ_2, the measured IQs of the two children in the family. Two corresponding latent variables, I, are shown in circles just above them; they represent the actual intelligences of the children, which the measured IQs approximate with some degree of error (symbolized by the short vertical arrows below the squares, representing factors other than the child's true intelligence that influence a particular IQ test score. These might include mood of the child, distractions and accidents of testing, appropriateness of the test, skill of the tester, etc.). Two latent variables are shown in circles at the top of the figure: I_F, father's intelligence, and I_M, mother's intelligence. Mothers' and fathers' intelligences are allowed to be correlated, as shown by the two-headed arrow s between I_F and I_M. They are also assumed to have causal effects on the children's intelligences, as shown by the directional arrows x and y leading downward from them to the circles representing the latter. These arrows would include any genetic or direct environmental effects parents might have on the intelligences of their children. Father's intelligence is also assumed to affect (but not to be identical with) his score on an IQ test, as shown by the arrow leading downward to the left, and mother's intelligence to affect her measured IQ,

Figure 2.1
An Elementary Path Model of a Family

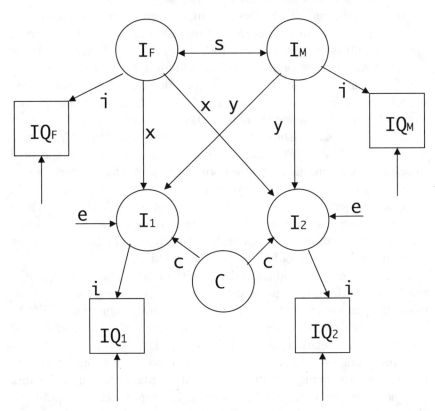

Note: Observed variables (squares): IQs of father (F), mother (M), and two children (1, 2). *Latent variables* (circles): intelligences (I) of M, F, 1, and 2; common environment of siblings (C). *Paths* (directional arrows): x, y = effect of father's, mother's intelligence on child's intelligence; c = effect of common environment on child's intelligence; e = other influences on child's intelligence; i, j square roots of test reliabilities; unlabeled vertical arrows = errors of measurement. *Correlation* (bi-directional arrow): s = correlation of spouses' intelligence.

as shown by the arrow leading downward to the right. The connections between observed and true scores can be estimated by the square roots of the test reliabilities. These paths are labeled j and i in the adult and child generations—for simplicity assumed to be the same within each generation, but one could differentiate the reliabilities for fathers and mothers, or first and second children, if desired. Finally, the diagram includes one more latent variable, C, common family environment, which represents any environmental factors independent of parental intelligence that may affect both children's intelligence via the paths labeled c.

Now, given a model like this and any specified set of values for its paths, one can calculate the implied correlations among its observed variables, and ask the simple question: "Does this set of values yield the observed correlations, or not?" (This calculation can be done by hand in small diagrams; in general, one lets a computer do it.) The goal in such modeling is to seek a set of values for the paths that will come as close as possible to reproducing the observed correlations. If a set of values is located that does a reasonable job, one can then ask further questions, like: Will it still work if the paths from fathers and mothers are specified to be equal? Can one eliminate the correlation between the parents' intelligences and still get a good fit? What if one omits the direct parent-child paths altogether? Or the family environmental ones? And so on. There is a test involving a statistic called chi square (χ^2) that can be used to see if a simplified version yields a significantly worse fit to the data than the original one did and should, therefore, be ruled out.

Given a set of correlations among the observed variables IQ_F, IQ_M, IQ_1, and IQ_2 (and information about test reliabilities), can we solve for the values of the paths in the path diagram? After inserting values into the paths i and j, we have five unknown paths to solve for—x, y, s, c, and e—and six observed correlations among F, M, I_1, and I_2 to do it with, so there is hope for a solution. Alas, however, there remains a causal ambiguity. The path c is environmental, but the paths x and y contain some unknown mix of genetic and environmental influences. To properly answer questions about the influences of heredity and environment, what we would like is a design in which some children have genetic connections to the parents and some do not—such as an adoption study.

Figure 2.2 is a generalized path diagram for an adoption study like the present one. It is in the spirit of Fig. 2.1, but considerably more complicated, now including two sets of parents and two kinds of children, and splitting apart genetic and environmental paths. However, it is solvable for the values of its paths under reasonable assumptions.

In Figure 2.2, we now have four children at the bottom of the diagram. Two, N_1 and N_2, are natural biological children of the parents, and two, A_1 and A_2, are adopted. The parents are still F and M at the top, but the biological parents of the adopted children now enter the picture: the birth mothers, B_1 and B_2, and the biological fathers, X_1 and X_2. There are no IQ tests for X_1 and X_2, but for the others there is a measured IQ in the square corresponding to his or her actual intelligence in the circle.

Figure 2.2
Path Diagram for an Adoptive Family

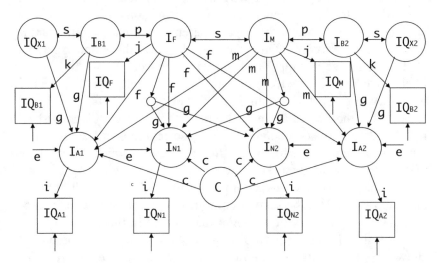

Note: Circles represent latent variables (e.g., intelligence), squares represent observed variables (e.g., IQ). F, M = father, mother in adoptive family; A_1, A_2 = two children separately adopted into the family; N_1, N_2 = two natural biological children of F and M; B_1, B_2 = birth mothers of A_1 and A_2; X_1, X_2 = biological fathers of A_1 and A_2; C = shared environmental variables (other than parental intelligence) that may influence children's IQ. g = genetic parent-child path; f, m = environmental parent-child paths; s = spouse correlation; p = correlation due to selective placement; i, j, k = square roots of respective reliabilities. Small, unlabeled circles represent "phantom variables" (see text).

The shared family environment, C, at the bottom remains the same as before, except that it now applies to all four children. However, the paths between generations are now split into a genetic path *g* and the environmental effects of the parents' intelligence, labeled *f* or *m*. Together *g* and *f* play the role that *x* did in Figure 2.1, and so do *g* and *m* with respect to *y*. The little unlabeled circles below I_F and I_M are known as "phantom variables." They are merely a technical device for keeping the genetic and environmental paths separate in the diagram.

At the top of the diagram, two parental correlations are shown: *s*, the correlation between spouses as before, and *p*, a possible correlation between the birth mothers and adoptive parents' intelligence introduced by selective placement of children by the adoption agency. To avoid undue clutter, only a few correlations among parental variables are shown—the path model actually used included all possible correlations among the six parental intelligences, derived from such assumptions as that the spouse correlation and the placement correlation were independent of one another, that selective placement occurred only via the birth mothers but equally with respect to both adoptive parents, and that the birth parents' intelligences were correlated to the same degree as the adoptive parents'. Had any of these assumptions been wildly inaccurate, we would most likely have had a model that did not fit the data, and it would have been necessary to go back and rethink the model.

We gave the Figure 2.2 model and the familial correlations shown in Table 2.15 to the computer. These are correlations of Beta IQs in the families of the ten-year follow-up, the families for which the child generation received the Beta. The model fit the data quite well.

The solution for the unknown path values is shown in the first column of Table 2.16. The second column of the table shows a reduced model consisting only of the significant paths in the initial solution. The initial full model provides a quite satisfactory fit to the data, as shown by the nonsignificant value of χ^2. The "degrees of freedom," df, for the χ^2 test represent the difference between the number of paths solved for, 6, and the number of correlations fitted, 14. From the χ^2 and df, one can get an estimate of the probability that a discrepancy of this size would occur merely by chance in sampling. A difference of the size observed provides no reason to reject the model, as there is a high probability that a discrepancy this large could result merely from chance ($p > .90$).

The column labeled "Reduced Model" indicates how well a simplified model containing only two sets of paths—the genetic paths g and the spouse correlations s—will do in reproducing the observed correlations. There are four more degrees of freedom because the paths f, m, c, and p are fixed to zero values and no longer solved for, but the discrepancies are still well within the range likely from chance ($p > .80$). Also shown in the table are the results of tests on individual paths, which are done by setting each to zero and seeing if this results in a significant worsening of the fit of the model (as tested by a χ^2 with 1 df). The g and s paths are statistically significant in each model, but none of the others are. In short, a model containing only two assumptions, that parents resemble each other (to some degree) in intelligence and that they transmit their intelligence (to some degree) to their biological offspring via their genes, can account quite well for the fourteen correlations observed in the data.

Table 2.15
Observed Correlations on the Revised Beta IQ Test for Families
in the 10-Year Follow-Up

Correlation Between	Correlation	Pairs
Adoptive parents (M & F)	.164	175
Adoptive mother and birth mother (M & B)	.028	193
Adoptive father and birth mother (F & B)	.093	199
Birth mothers of two adopted children (B$_1$ & B$_2$)	-.030	38
Adoptive mother and biological child (M & N)	.205	87
Adoptive father and biological child (F & N)	.205	90
Adoptive mother and adopted child (M & A)	-.019	244
Adoptive father and adopted child (F & A)	.082	252
Birth mother and her adopted-away child (B$_1$ & A$_1$)	.333	198
Birth mother and other adopted child (B$_1$ & A$_2$)	.021	109
Birth mother and biological child in family (B & N)	.045	92
Adopted and biological child (A & N)	-.031	107
Two adopted children (A$_1$ & A$_2$)	-.017	75
Two biological children (N$_1$ & N$_2$)	.328	27

Table 2.16
Path Estimates from Model Fitting

Path	Full Model	Reduced Model
g	.371*	.355*
f	.041	.000
m	-.093	.000
c	.000	.000
s	.221*	.225*
p	.099	.000
χ^2	3.469	6.486
df	8	12
p	> .90	> .80

Note: * $p < .05$, 1 df, for increase in χ^2 when path deleted

Model Fitting to Changes in IQ over Time

The model fitting reported in the preceding section was to Beta IQs in both generations. However, for the child generation, we have individual IQ tests administered on two occasions approximately ten years apart. What can we say about the stability or change of IQs across the ten years? Do the relative roles of genes and environment in accounting for individual differences remain about the same, or change? For example, one hypothesis might be that stability is due to the persisting effect of genes on the processes underlying performance on IQ tests, and change is due to changing environmental influences. But genes are not necessarily constant in their effects over the course of development, and family environments provide a degree of stability—parents may change to some extent, but mostly remain fairly constant; drastic shifts in socioeconomic status can take place, but do not often, and so forth. So both stability and change might occur for either genetic or environmental reasons.

What happens when one fits a path model to the two-occasion IQ data? We won't attempt to lead you through all the details of the path model (it is shown in an appendix in Loehlin, Horn, & Willerman, 1989, if you are curious). You can think of it as something like Figure 2.2 with the child generation represented twice. We looked at three different assumptions about persistence of intelligence over time: first, that it is mostly a matter of the same genes continuing to act; second, that it represents the enduring effects of the common family environment; and third, that persistence occurs primarily at the level of the trait itself, irrespective of its causation.

Besides using IQs from individually administered tests for the adoptive family members, there were some other differences in the modeling. C was specified to be the socioeconomic status of the adoptive family, estimated from the parents' education and occupation. The participants' genotypes relevant to intelligence were included as additional latent variables, so it was not necessary to include "phantom variables" in the diagram to keep genetic and environmental paths apart. The model was considerably more complicated, involving thirty-six observed correlations and ten unknown paths. The assumptions under which it was fit were similar to those used in the model fitting described earlier in this chapter, and equally good fits were obtained.

The results can be summarized briefly. Both genetic and shared environmental effects were statistically significant at the time of the initial testing. Between the time of the first and second testing, the genetic contribution increased, but the effect of shared environment did not. A model for trait persistence that solely involved the genes or the shared environment was less satisfactory than one that assumed that persistence occurred chiefly at the level of the trait itself.

Thus, the best-fitting model had both genes and environments contributing to individual differences in IQ at the original testing (with the genes explaining more). Then, over the ten years between the original study and the follow-up, new genetic effects entered the picture, but new shared environmental effects did not; indeed, the relevant path at the latter time was slightly (though non-significantly) negative. By the time of the follow-up, when the members of the child generation were mostly adolescents and young adults, the results were in general agreement with the findings from the Beta IQs (which were for those ages). Perhaps the most noteworthy difference was that the selective placement correlation, p, was significant in the IQ-change modeling but not for the Beta IQ modeling. This might conceivably reflect the greater importance of verbal factors in the Wechsler IQs. The spouse correlation, s, was significant in both.

Estimating the IQs of Birth Fathers

In the model fitting, the birth fathers' IQs were represented as unknowns, with various assumptions made about their relationships with other variables in the model. Although the adoption agency did not have IQ test results for the birth fathers, they often had a fair amount of information about them: what level of education they had had achieved, what educational institutions they had attended, what jobs they had worked at, and so on. Of course, sometimes only very limited information was available in the files concerning the birth father; indeed, in a number of cases the identification of an individual as the biological father was uncertain or suspect.

Nevertheless, it seemed to us worthwhile to look at cases in which paternity seemed relatively certain, and in which there was sufficient data to make some sort of estimate of the birth father's IQ. This would allow us to evaluate the feasibility of the method, and to check on some of the assumptions we had made in the model fitting.

One of us (JMH) and a graduate student, Richard Arnold, went through the agency files and judged, first, the likelihood that the individual named was indeed the father of the child in question and, second, estimated his IQ from any available data. Sometimes the files contained statements of doubt regarding paternity from the birth mothers, her parents, and/or agency interviewers. If both raters did not agree that the man was very probably the birth father, the case was dropped from further consideration. If they did agree, each made an independent estimate of his IQ, using a baseline figure adjusted up or down for various kinds of available information. Because the great majority of the fathers were white males from Texas, the baseline IQ was taken as 99. This was then adjusted up or down based on available information about the IQs of individuals in various categories such as level of education, ethnicity, and region of origin (see Table 2.17). For those who had pursued an occupation, adjustments were made based on a table of average IQs for sixty-three occupations given in Willerman (1979b, p. 162f). For those who had attended college, further adjustments were made based on the selectivity of the college and the major field, if known. Because the information available varied from case to case, the raters were permitted a certain amount of individual judgment in arriving at a final IQ estimate.

Two examples of estimates may serve to give a sense of the outcomes: (a) White, born in Texas, age 21, student at Rice University majoring in Engineering—estimated IQ = 124; (b) White, Texas, age 25, left school in 10th grade, laborer and garage mechanic—estimated IQ = 87.

There were 139 cases in which the raters were in agreement that an individual was most likely the father of an adopted child in the study and sufficient information was present in the files to make some sort of estimate of his IQ. The two independent estimates proved to be in excellent agreement, as evidenced by a correlation of .95 between them. The average of the two was taken as a final estimate of the birth father's IQ.

Although the estimates were not used in the model fitting described earlier, they provide at least a provisional check on two of the assumptions made there. First, was the correlation between birth father and child similar to that between birth mother and child? It was. The correlation

Table 2.17
Adjustments to Base IQ to Reflect Ancestry, Region of Origin, and Education

Category	IQ Adjustment
Ancestry or region of origin	
Jewish	+5.0
Hispanic	-7.0
Northeast US	+3.5
North Central US	+1.0
Western US	+3.5
Education completed	
0-7 years	-15.5
8 years	-7.2
9-11 years	-1.6
High school graduate	+2.0
13-15 years	+9.3
College graduate	+17.2

between birth father's estimated IQ and the Beta IQ of the child at the ten-year follow-up was .31 (N = 130). The corresponding correlation for birth mothers—restricted to cases with birth father estimates—was .29 (N = 127; a few cases were missing because not all the birth mothers received the Beta). The correlation between the birth mother's Beta IQ and the estimated IQ of the birth father was .15. That for the measured Beta IQs of spouses in the adoptive families was .18. Thus, the assumption used in the model fitting, that the same spouse correlation applied in the two cases, was unlikely to have introduced any substantial distortion.

5. More Specialized Aspects of Intelligence

A Study of Problem-Solving Speed

Intelligence is usually conceptualized and measured in terms of the difficulties of the problems that an individual can solve, but intelligence can also be thought of as measured in a different way: in terms of how rapidly a person can solve problems as a given level of difficulty. Some IQ tests, for example, have timed subtests, so the speed at which an individual performs the required tasks enters into his or her score.

The WAIS IQ tests taken by the adoptive parents included a subtest, Block Design, in which the person being tested has to copy a series of increasingly difficult designs with colored blocks. Some, although not all, of the examiners recorded the time taken to complete each item, in addition to whether the examinee got it right or not. We developed a measure of problem-solving speed by adding together the times required to solve items 3-6 on the Block Design subtest, restricting ourselves to individuals who got all four of these items right. Most did: these were all fairly easy items for this group. Items 1 and 2, in which the examiner demonstrated the solution, were eliminated, along with the later items, which were sufficiently difficult that quite a number of examinees were unable to solve them within the allotted time limits. About 63 percent of all protocols had times recorded for all the relevant designs. Only about 2 percent of parents were excluded for missing any of items 3-6, the ones we were using for the speed score. An estimate of reliability was obtained from the intercorrelation of time scores among the four items. This proved to be .61. This represents a moderate degree of reliability for assessing a true underlying trait despite the chance factors involved on any given trial. For example, the blocks were scattered randomly by the examiner at the start of each problem; from some configurations the solution would be easier than from others.

The time scores were markedly skewed; to reduce this skewness we used their logarithms. We also reversed the direction of scoring so that numerically higher scores meant faster performance.

We then asked, first, "Is the Block Design problem-solving speed score of an individual a measure of his or her intelligence, in the sense of correlating with traditional measures of IQ?" The answer was, "Yes, to some degree." The correlation of the speed score with overall WAIS IQ was .45 for the adoptive fathers and .39 for the adoptive mothers. Correcting for the unreliability of the speed and IQ measures suggests true-score correlations of about .62 and .54, respectively. Problem-solving speed and IQ are not measuring exactly the same thing, but they clearly overlap considerably. Note that this correlation is not simply an artifact, as the four Block Design items from which the speed score was derived were items that everyone in the selected sample got right, so that these items did not contribute to differences in overall IQ.

A second question was whether the parents' speed scores were related to their children's IQs, and whether this differed by whether or not the child was genetically related to the parent. It would have been interesting to derive a speed score for the children as well, but this proved impractical, as a substantial number of children missed one or more of the early Block Design items.

The results for IQ (measured at the time of the original study) were a statistically significant correlation of .37 of the adoptive father's problem-solving speed with a biological child's IQ, but a nonsignificant correlation of .10 with an adoptive child. Adoptive mothers, however, showed nonsignificant correlations with both, .15 and .10, respectively. Stronger correlations of fathers than mothers with their children's cognitive skills have been a recurring motif in this chapter. We do not know why, unless it means that mothers interact with their children in a different way than fathers do. If so, it appears not to be in a way that increases the intellectual resemblance between mother and child.

Beyond General Ability: The IQ Subtests

Each of the IQ tests in the study, except for the Stanford-Binet used for the three- and four-year-olds in the initial testing, is composed of a group of relatively homogeneous subscales. Some of these are mainly verbal in character, such as Vocabulary (defining words) or Similarities (saying how two things are alike). Some involve numerical reasoning, such as Arithmetic (simple word-problems). Some require visual or spatial skills, such as Block Design (copying patterns using colored blocks). Some emphasize immediate memory, such as Digit Span (repeating back a series of digits presented by the examiner). Some stress perceptual speed, such as Digit Symbol (matching numbers and symbols). Since the subscales are substantially correlated with one another, they all appear to be measuring something in common, which we have been referring to as general intelligence or IQ. But since they are less than perfectly inter-correlated, each may be measuring something distinctive as well. In the next few sections of the chapter, we will consider the IQ tests at the level of their subscales.

Subscale Correlations: Wechsler and Beta Tests

We begin with adoptive and biological parent-child correlations for the Wechsler Verbal and Performance subscales, and for the Revised Beta. We have combined data from the WISC and WAIS, which have similar subscales, although administered in a somewhat different order. (Subjects who received the Stanford-Binet or an earlier Wechsler test, the Wechsler-Bellevue, are omitted.)

Table 2.18 contains these correlations. On the left of the table are correlations based on pairs of individuals who were biologically unrelated, i.e., adoptive mothers and fathers and their adopted children. On the right are correlations between individuals who were biologically related (to the extent of sharing half their genes), the adoptive parents and their biological children, and the birth mothers and their adopted-away child.

The correlations vary appreciably across subscales, due partly, no doubt, to sampling error. This applies particularly to those for the birth mothers on the WAIS/WISC subscales, which are based on the small sample of 21 birth mothers who had been given these tests. Nevertheless, for the table as a whole the correlations for the biologically related pairs on the right tend to be higher than those for the biologically unrelated pairs on the left. This regularity is particularly evident in the summary groupings, the verbal and performance IQs on the Wechsler scales and the Beta IQ.

Distinctive Aspects of Specific Abilities

The various correlations for the subscales given in Table 2.18 reflect what these tests share as well as what is distinctive to each. How best

Table 2.18
**Correlations on IQ Test Subscales between Parents Tested in Original Study and
Children Tested at the Time of the 10-Year Follow-Up**

| | Genetically Unrelated | | Genetically Related | | |
Subscale	F-Ad	M-Ad	F-Bio	M-Bio	B-Ad
WAIS/WISC verbal subscales					
Information	.02	.08	.36	.28	.12
Comprehension	-.02	-.03	.28	.21	.45
Arithmetic	.02	.10	.30	.04	.47
Similarities	.10	.01	.16	.23	.51
Digit Span	-.02	.04	.17	.06	.12
Vocabulary	.10	.11	.40	.33	--
Verbal IQ	.06	.03	.32	.21	.44
WAIS/WISC performance subscales					
Digit Symbol/Coding	.09	.09	.21	.27	.36
Picture Completion	-.05	-.04	.29	-.01	-.13
Block Design	.13	.07	.27	.16	.54
Picture Arrangement	-.06	-.03	.16	-.05	.16
Object Assembly	.02	-.13	.30	.05	.31
Performance IQ	.09	.06	.41	.12	.27
Revised Beta subscales					
Maze	.17	.12	.05	.21	.18
Digit symbol	-.00	-.03	.11	.00	.25
Error recognition	-.09	.03	.11	.19	.24
Formboard	.06	.06	.23	.15	.40
Picture completion	.12	.11	.09	-.07	.08
Identities	.01	-.10	.14	-.04	.05
Beta IQ	.08	-.02	.20	.20	.34
Number of pairs	239-254	234-249	88-94	86-92	21 for Wechsler 198-199 for Beta

Note: F, M = father, mother in adoptive family; Ad, Bio = adopted, biological child in adoptive family; B = birth mother of adopted child. Tests: in original study, Wechsler Adult Intelligence Scale (WAIS), or Wechsler Intelligence Scale for Children (WISC), depending on age; in follow-up = WAIS-R or WISC-R, depending on age. Vocabulary subscale was not administered to birth mothers.

to separate these? Previous behavior genetic studies involving multiple measures have employed different tactics to deal with this problem. For its simplicity, we adopt here a strategy originally proposed by Robert Nichols (1965), who estimated the heritability of each of the five subtests of the National Merit Scholarship Qualifying Test after statistically removing the effects of the total NMSQT score. We carried out the procedure with the data from the Revised Beta, which was the test available for the largest number of individuals at the least disparate ages.

We followed a variant of Nichols' strategy described above, in order to examine the specific effects in isolation from the common effects. First, residual scores were obtained via a statistical procedure called multiple regression. This procedure was used to predict the score of an individual on each subtest from his or her scores on the other five subtests. Then these predicted scores were subtracted from the observed scores, leaving an unpredicted residual. This yields six uncorrelated sets of residual scores, each based on the unique aspects of one test after removing what it has in common with the others. Family correlations were then obtained for these residual scores; they are shown in Table 2.19.

For convenient comparison with the original Beta subscale scores reported in Table 2.18, we have rearranged the rows from this table involving the residualized parent-child correlations; they are presented in Table 2.20.

On the left-hand, environmental side of the table, these correlations are much like the corresponding correlations for the full Beta subscales—too low to suggest much, if any, parent-child resemblance in the specific aspects of these skills that may have arisen from imitation, deliberate

Table 2.19
Family Correlations for Residualized Beta Subtests, Used in Model Fitting

Correlation	Maze	Digit Symbol	Error Recogn.	Form-board	Picture Compl.	Ident-ities	Number of Pairs
r_{MF}	.09	.13	.01	.05	-.05	-.04	175
r_{MB}	.05	.04	-.05	.02	.05	.10	193
r_{FB}	-.02	-.03	-.12	.15	.06	-.12	199
r_{BB}	.19	.04	.16	.04	-.22	.15	38
r_{MN}	.16	-.03	.07	.09	-.07	-.06	87
r_{FN}	.02	.06	.07	-.01	.03	.04	90
r_{MA}	.15	-.01	.06	.05	.15	-.04	244
r_{FA}	.14	.04	-.12	.04	.07	.06	252
r_{B1A1}	.08	.17	.16	.31	.03	-.03	198
r_{B1A2}	-.04	.02	.19	-.19	-.01	.05	109
r_{BN}	-.03	-.03	-.13	-.05	-.09	.09	92
r_{AN}	-.01	-.01	.06	-.06	.11	.04	107
r_{AA}	.17	-.04	.04	-.08	.17	.02	75
r_{NN}	-.08	.20	.24	-.09	.14	-.04	27

Note: See Table 2.15 for full descriptions of the familial correlations.

Table 2.20
Parent-Child Correlations of Residualized Beta Subscale Scores

Subscale	Genetically Unrelated		Genetically Related		
	F-Ad	M-Ad	F-Na	M-Na	B-Ad
Maze	.14	.15	.02	.16	.08
Digit symbol	.04	-.01	.06	-.03	.17
Error recognition	-.12	.06	.07	.07	.16
Formboard	.04	.05	-.01	.09	.31
Picture completion	.07	.15	.03	-.07	.03
Identities	.06	-.04	.04	-.06	-.03
Number of pairs	252	244	90	87	198

instruction, or shared experiences. For the adoptive parents and their biological offspring, again factors such as these do not seem to be producing notable parent-child resemblance for the specific abilities—and the genes do not seem to be doing much of it either: such resemblance as was observed in the earlier table apparently depended largely on the general factor common to the subscales. Also, it should be kept in mind that what is left after taking out the common factor contains a substantial proportion representing errors of measurement. Interestingly, some specific resemblance seems to remain between the birth mothers and their adopted-away children on some of the Beta subscales, most notably the spatial abilities tapped by Formboard.

Path Modeling: Specific Skills

Are these residual subscale scores, representing the skills specific to each subtest, themselves influenced by the genes? Are they influenced by family environment? How do they compare to the general factor, represented by IQ, in these respects? One can pursue such questions by fitting an appropriate path model to the sets of correlations in the columns of Table 2.19. The model used was the same one employed earlier for Beta IQ. As a reminder, the model involved six paths: g, the genetic path from a parent to a child; m and f, the environmental paths from the adoptive mother and father to a child; c, the effect of the shared environment of siblings (over and above the effect of the parents); s, the correlation between spouses (assumed to be the same for birth and adoptive parents); and p, the correlation between the birth mother and the adoptive parents produced by any selective placement of the child by the adoption agency.

One preliminary problem had to be addressed. The solution of the model requires values for the paths from true to measured abilities. In the earlier model fitting, these were obtained as the square roots of the reliabilities of IQ measurement in the various groups. What values should be used for the present model fitting? Presumably, the original subscales are lower in reliability than the IQs and the residualized subscales still lower. The following very rough approximation was used. It was assumed that individual scales would have reliabilities averaging about .10 lower than the Beta IQ itself—this rule of thumb was derived by comparing WAIS-R Performance subtests with Performance IQ for the WAIS-R standardization sample (comparable information was not available for the Beta itself). Then, for each of four groups in the present sample—adoptive mothers, adoptive fathers, birth mothers, and children—the shared variance (from the multiple regressions) was subtracted from the average subscale reliability estimated by the rule of thumb. The resulting values were quite similar in the four groups, so the square root of their mean was used throughout for the analysis (a value of .60). Obviously, this provides only a very rough estimate, but it seemed preferable to assuming that the residualized subscales were as reliable as the full IQs, or, worse yet, that they were perfectly reliable.

Table 2.21
Model Fitting to Residualized Beta Subscale Scores of Table 2.19

Path	Maze	Digit Symbol	Error Recogn.	Form-board	Picture Compl.	Ident-ities	Beta IQ
g	-.02	.23*	.36*	.51*	-.19	-.09	.37*
f	.22[a]	.10	-.23	-.20	.29[a]	.16	.04
m	.35[a]	-.15	.13	-.12	.36[a] *	-.09	-.09
c	.00[a]	.00	.40	.00	.52[a]	.17	.00
s	.25	.36	.00	.18	-.16	-.11	.22*
p	.06	.02	-.29*	.24	.13	-.03	.10
χ^2	6.27	3.59	6.81	15.17	5.42	6.67	3.47
df	8	8	8	8	8	8	8
p	> .50	> .80	> .50	> .05	> .70	> .50	> .90

Note: [a] Environmental paths cannot jointly be set to 0. *p < .05, based on chi square difference test as described in connection with Table 2.16.

The results of the model fitting are shown in Table 2.21, with the results for the overall Beta IQ from Table 2.16 included at the right for comparison. The model fit acceptably in all six data sets, although for one, Formboard, the fit was somewhat marginal. Three of the subscales had significant specific genetic variance: Formboard, Error Recognition, and Digit Symbol. The Formboard test requires the subject to show how figures could be fit together to form a square. In Error Recognition, the task is to discover which of several objects is anomalous, e.g., a coat missing a sleeve. In Digit Symbol, the testee must rapidly match numbers with geometric symbols. Each of these tasks apparently requires different specific gene-based abilities in addition to general intelligence. For the three remaining subscales, the genetic contribution is apparently largely confined to the general factor.

Two of the residualized scales, Maze and Picture Completion, showed an appreciable specific contribution of family environment, in the sense that if the paths f, m, and c are simultaneously set to zero, there is a significant increase in chi square. The Maze subtest requires the testee to trace a simple path through a maze; Picture Completion requires him or her to draw in the missing parts of objects (e.g., a hand missing a finger).

The sixth test, Identities, in which the subject has to determine rapidly whether two drawings or numbers are or are not identical, did not show significant specific variance associated either with the genes or with shared family environment. The one other path in Table 2.21 that achieves a conventional level of statistical significance, the negative selective placement correlation for Error Recognition, makes no obvious sense. We hope that it is the one finding that would be expected to occur by chance when making thirty-six significance tests.

How do these results compare with those for Beta IQ as a whole? The fit of the same model to the original IQ correlations is shown in the rightmost column of Table 2.21. That model fit very well ($p > .90$), with two significant paths, the genetic path and the spouse correlation. Thus, there was no substantial overall effect of family environment on IQ, although some of the subtests showed specific effects. For the genes, there was a substantial effect for overall IQ, as well as specific effects on three of the subtests. The only significant effect for spouse resemblance occurred for the general measure.

What about the intriguing, although nonsignificant, negative environmental path from mothers to offspring seen for overall IQ? The evidence is mixed at the level of specifics. There are similar nonsignificant negative estimates for three of the residual factors, but the only two large ones are both positive.

The general result that specific abilities may show some degree of genetic influence independent of general intelligence is consistent with a number of previous reports (e.g., Martin & Eaves, 1977; LaBuda, De-Fries, & Fulker, 1987; Tambs, Sundet, & Magnus, 1988; Cardon, Fulker, DeFries, & Plomin, 1992). Detailed comparisons across studies are difficult, because of differences in measures and populations. However, an independent genetic component in spatial ability measures has been a fairly frequent finding. The results for the Formboard subtest in our study are consistent with this. In addition, Cardon and his colleagues failed to find a genetic perceptual speed factor independent of the general factor, as did we, taking Identities as a measure of perceptual speed.

Contributions of shared environment to specific abilities have usually not been found, although Martin and Eaves (1977), in an analysis based on twin data, reported them for spatial and reasoning abilities. Maze, which has a spatial component, showed such an effect in our study, but another spatial measure, Formboard, did not. Picture Completion, which showed a shared environmental effect, involves reasoning, but then so does Error Recognition, which did not. Clearly, questions remain that only more data will answer.

Specific versus General Intellectual Abilities—Summary

On the whole, biologically related family members show higher correlations on IQ test subscales than do biologically unrelated individuals who share family environments via adoption. Among the subscales showing this pattern most clearly were measures involving spatial abilities—Block Design on the Wechsler tests and Formboard on the Beta.

Using residual scores from the Beta subtests, we were able to investigate the sources of familial resemblance in the distinctive aspects of different intellectual performances, separately from the shared aspects that contribute to the overall IQ. We found three subscales with unique genetic contributions, two with unique family environmental contributions, and one with neither.

The details of these findings should be considered provisional until they are confirmed or refuted in other research. Nevertheless, on the whole our study lies on the side of those that hold that there is indeed something genetic beyond general intelligence. In particular, spatial ability looks like a candidate; there may be others as well. We found a place for family environmental effects on a couple of the specific factors, although not on general intelligence—in fact, for general intelligence, and perhaps for spatial ability, there were hints of an environmental effect making for family *dis*similarity. This result, however, must be considered tentative until replicated.

3

Personality in the Texas Adoption Project

Intellectual abilities were discussed in the preceding chapter. A second major interest of the Texas Adoption Project has been in personality. To what extent are the personality differences we observe in those about us a result of differences among their genes? To what extent are they a consequence of differences among the families in which these individuals grew up? To what extent are they attributable to other systematic factors, such as unique combinations of genes and environments, the interplay among family members, the differences in experience that members of the same families may have? Or are many of the differences just due to chance—to accidental events of one kind or another affecting development before or after birth?

An adoption study will not enable us to answer all such questions, but it can help us address some of them. Are there family resemblances in personality? If so, are they as great among genetically unrelated individuals growing up together as they are among genetically related individuals? Do birth mothers resemble their adopted-away children in personality? Do the mothers and fathers in adoptive families show an equal degree of resemblance to their children, and if so, is this the same for both biological and adopted children?

1. Personality Measures Used in the TAP

What we can say about personality based on an adoption study depends on how well we can measure it. In considering which assessments to use,

---

Note: This chapter is based in part on several earlier publications in specialized journals: Loehlin, Horn & Willerman, 1981, 1990; Loehlin, Willerman & Horn, 1982, 1985, 1987; Loehlin 1985, 1986; these may be consulted for additional details.

we began with the test that had been given to most of the birth mothers while residing at the home for unwed mothers. It was the Minnesota Multiphasic Personality Inventory, the MMPI (Hathaway & McKinley, 1967). A shortened 373-item version of the test had been used with the birth mothers. This covers all the items that are scored on the regular scales of the test, but not necessarily all those included in the many additional experimental scales that have been developed from the MMPI items over the years. We gave this same shortened version to the mothers and fathers in the adoptive families. The MMPI is not suitable for young children, but by the time of the follow-up study most were old enough for it. We gave them the full 566-item MMPI.

Although the MMPI is sometimes used for assessing personality variation among normal persons, its chief focus is on psychopathological traits. We wanted to use some measures focused on normal personality as well, at least in the adoptive families. The Cattell series of questionnaires was intended to measure at several ages a number of the sixteen personality factors described by Raymond B. Cattell (see, e.g., Cattell, et al., 1970): these tests include the 16PF for adults (over 18), the High School Personality Questionnaire (HSPQ) for ages 13 to 18, and the Children's Personality Questionnaire (CPQ) for ages 8 to 12. That still left half the children unmeasured. Therefore, in addition to the questionnaires, we asked a parent (which was usually the mother) to rate all the children in the family on a series of twenty-four bipolar trait scales. These were originally chosen to give coverage to the Cattellian factors, but an initial factor analysis of them suggested that they could be used to tap three broad dimensions of personality, which we will call Extraversion, Good Socialization, and Emotional Stability. In the currently popular Big-Five factor scheme, these correspond roughly to Extraversion, Conscientiousness, and Neuroticism (reversed). Usually, in dealing with the ratings, we will use these three summary dimensions rather than the twenty-four individual rating scales.

Recall that a separate mail study was carried out based on earlier adoptions from the same agency. Birth mother measures were not available for this group, but the children were old enough to be given the same inventory as their parents. Two different questionnaires were used: the California Psychological Inventory (Gough, 1957) and the Thurstone Temperament Schedule (Thurstone, 1953).

Table 3.1 gives the number of individuals scored on each of the personality measures.

Table 3.1
Numbers of Persons Taking Different Personality Tests

Test	Adoptive Fathers	Adoptive Mothers	Adopted Children	Biological Children	Birth Mothers
Trait ratings (original)	-	-	454	140	-
Trait ratings (follow-up)	-	-	270	110	
Trait ratings (interviews)	-	-	141	71	-
MMPI	285	285	184	82	337
Cattell scale (original)	282	283	219	101	-
16PF (follow-up)	-	-	187	84	-
CPI (mail study)	196	202	266	59	-
TTS (mail study)	206	243	283	60	-

Note: MMPI = Minnesota Multiphasic Personality Inventory, children tested at follow-up, 373-item shortened version used for adults in original study; Cattell scale = 16PF for ages over 18, HSPQ for ages 13-18, CPQ for ages 8-12; CPI = California Psychological Inventory; TTS = Thurstone Temperament Schedule. Interviews = trait ratings filled out by parents in interviewed families. Mail study = separate sample from earlier MMH adoptions.

2. The Rating Composites

Table 3.2 gives the ratings from the parent rating scale that were scored for each of the three factors.

The parent doing the ratings was given a questionnaire with twenty-four 9-point graphic rating scales, each consisting of a horizontal line marked at nine points, with the digits 1 through 9 beneath them. (The questionnaire is reproduced in Appendix B.) A set of the Table 3.2 adjectives labeled each end of the scale. (To minimize response sets, the scales for the various factors were intermixed in the questionnaire and the end labels occasionally reversed—for details, see Loehlin, Horn, & Willerman, 1981.) The parent was instructed to place a number on the line for each of her children, indicating how that child compared to the average child of that age on the trait in question. Ratings of 1 and 9 represented the extremes, a rating of 5 meant average. In scoring the scales, items were reversed and combined appropriately. A parent sometimes failed to rate each child on each dimension. Missing ratings were treated as follows: if missing two or fewer items, the score was the mean of completed items; if missing three or more items, the scale was scored as missing.

Table 3.2
Bipolar Ratings Scored on the Three Parent-Rating Dimensions

Positive Pole	Negative Pole
Extraversion	
Warm-hearted, outgoing	Reserved, detached
Talkative	Reserved
Full of zest	Restrained
Happy-go-lucky, enthusiastic	Serious, sober
Socially bold, adventurous	Shy, timid
Easygoing, participates	Critical, aloof
Good Socialization	
Controlled, self-disciplined	Uncontrolled, follows own urges
Conscientious, moralistic	Disregards rules, expedient
Earnest	Frivolous
Compulsive in following social rules	Careless of social rules
Sensitive to threats	Unresponsive to threats
Mature, faces reality	Affected by feelings, changeable
Emotional Stability	
Emotionally stable, calm	Emotionally less stable, easily upset
Unfrustrated, composed	Frustrated, fretful
Complacent, untroubled	Worries, guilt prone
Relaxed	Tense
Self-assured, secure	Apprehensive, insecure

Note: Scales scored for a given factor have loadings $\geq .50$; within each group, scales are listed in order from higher to lower loadings.

Reliability and Consistency over Time

Table 3.3 gives the internal consistency reliabilities of the three composite scales and their correlations across the ten to twelve year intervals between ratings. It can be seen that the three composites have reasonably high internal consistencies (.76-.85) considering the fairly small number of items on which each is based. The cross-time correlations are lower, as they reflect actual changes in individuals as well as any inconsistency of measurement across the two occasions. Individuals appeared to maintain their relative standing on Extraversion somewhat better than on Good socialization or Emotional stability from the first to the second occasion of rating, although from the second to the third, Good socialization was equally high. Reliabilities were fairly similar at the three rating occasions. The apparent slight increasing trend in reliability, if real, might be due to practice effects, to an increasing clarity of personality with age, to selection of the families continuing in the study, or in the case of

Table 3.3
Reliabilities for Three Rating Composites and Correlation across Time

Composite	No. of Items	Reliabilities			Cross-Time Correlations	
		Original Study	10-year Follow-up	Parent Interviews	r_{12}	r_{23}
Extraversion	6	.83	.85	.81	.49	.50
Good socialization	6	.76	.82	.84	.32	.54
Emotional stability	5	.78	.79	.84	.35	.37
No. of children		575	354	195	331	147-9

Note: Reliabilities are based on internal consistency (Cronbach alphas). r_{12} = correlation from original to follow-up; r_{23} = correlation from follow-up to parent interviews.

the third occasion of rating, to the fact that it was based on two parents' judgments, rather than one.

Means for Subgroups and Occasions

Table 3.4 gives means and standard deviations on the three rating occasions for children subdivided by sex and whether an adopted or biological child.

The first thing to notice about the table is that all the averages, both for the adopted and the biological children, are above the scale midpoints of 5.0—that is, the parents on the whole judged their children as more outgoing, better behaved, and better adjusted than the average child of their ages. This is not to say that no children were judged by their parents to be introverted, poorly socialized, or emotionally unstable. The standard deviations suggest that the scores varied widely enough around their means so that a substantial number of children were rated below 5.0.

A closer scrutiny of the table suggests some other trends. Tests of significance (based on a statistical procedure called repeated measures Analysis of Variance), which were made for the group of 125 children who were rated on all three occasions, suggested that the means differed systematically in several ways. Table 3.5 summarizes some of these. Because there were no significant differences involving the two sexes, these are combined in this table.

For these individuals, the ratings varied significantly over the three traits and the three occasions of testing, and there were differences in

Table 3.4
Means and Standard Deviations of Rating Composites in Original Study, Ten-Year Follow-up, and Parent Interviews, for Adopted and Biological Children of Both Sexes

Group & Study	Extraversion Mean	SD	Socialization Mean	SD	Stability Mean	SD	N
			Males				
Adopted							
Original	6.32	1.41	5.41	1.19	5.54	1.31	243
Follow-up	5.85	1.50	5.23	1.43	5.47	1.37	142
Interview	5.81	1.28	5.44	1.42	5.62	1.25	77
Biological							
Original	5.97	1.35	5.39	1.00	5.66	1.26	78
Follow-up	5.79	1.23	5.40	1.04	5.54	1.34	61
Interview	5.98	1.26	5.51	1.04	6.21	1.13	31
			Females				
Adopted							
Original	6.59	1.24	5.48	1.03	5.76	1.15	209
Follow-up	5.83	1.36	5.28	1.33	5.28	1.22	127
Interview	5.96	1.24	5.52	1.44	5.58	1.44	31
Biological							
Original	5.96	1.19	5.38	1.00	5.48	1.14	58
Follow-up	5.83	1.45	5.64	1.10	5.57	1.24	47
Interview	5.75	1.11	6.21	1.06	5.55	1.09	33

Note: Some Ns vary slightly across traits as a result of missing data. Figures given in the table are the minimum Ns.

Table 3.5
Means for Three Rating Composites for Three Occasions, Based on 125 Individuals Rated on All Three Occasions

Group & Study	Extraversion	Socialization	Stability	Mean	N
Adopted					92
Original	6.36	5.55	5.63	5.84	
Follow-up	5.66	5.09	5.27	5.34	
Interview	5.89	5.49	5.58	5.64	
Biological					32
Original	6.06	5.07	5.50	5.54	
Follow-up	5.90	5.60	5.83	5.78	
Interview	6.09	6.03	5.97	6.03	
Combined					124
Original	6.28	5.43	5.60	5.77	
Follow-up	5.72	5.22	5.41	5.45	
Interview	5.94	5.63	5.68	5.74	
Overall mean	5.98	5.43	5.56	5.66	125

Note: Interview = ratings by interviewed parents (one parent or average of both). Some Ns vary slightly across traits as a result of missing data. Figures given in the table are the minimum Ns.

the latter depending on whether the children were adopted or biological. Across the three traits, as seen in the means at the bottom of the table, the ratings were somewhat higher on the Extraversion dimension than the other two. Across the three occasions, as seen in the vertical group of three means toward the lower right of the table, the ratings were lower at the time of the follow-up, when the child generation were mostly adolescents, than they were in the original study, when they were mostly children, or at the time of the parent interviews, when they were mostly adults. Within this overall pattern, there were differences depending on whether the children were adopted or biological, as seen in the six means above these in the column. At the time of the original testing the adopted children were rated higher than the biological children, but by the time of the ten-year follow-up this difference had reversed, and the adopted children were rated lower—and continued to be as adults. Thus, if the adopted children wound up with somewhat less favorable ratings, it was not because the parents started out with a bias against them, but rather that the children's behavior led to a change in the parents' views.

The preceding analysis was based on families that participated on all three rating occasions, so we are comparing the same set of individuals throughout. However, we still may wonder whether selection based on the children's personality is taking place in general in the study. Do the children involved in the later studies differ systematically from those who were in the first study only? The answer, shown in Table 3.6, is mostly "No."

The only statistically significant difference for any of the three individual traits in the table is that the adopted children were, on average, more extraverted than the biological children. This difference is present in both the families that did and did not participate in follow-up studies, so that it is not somehow an artifact of selection for participation. None of the differences between those who did and did not participate in the later studies is statistically significant or substantial, so we need not be very concerned about selective biases of this kind for these traits.

Table 3.7 makes the comparison between different types of families that was made in the case of IQ—between families with a single adopted child, families with more than one child, all adopted, and families with both adopted and biological children.

For Extraversion and Stability, there was a significant difference across family types: parents with just a single adopted child tended to rate that child higher. In both cases, it seems to be an only-child phenomenon, as parents with two or more children tended to give fairly similar ratings

Table 3.6
Means and Standard Deviations in the Original Study, for Children Only in that Study, and for Children Who Also Participated in the Later Studies

Group	Extraversion Mean	SD	Socialization Mean	SD	Stability Mean	SD	N
	Males						
Adopted							
Original only	6.33	1.38	5.32	1.19	5.51	1.29	66
Original and follow-up	6.32	1.49	5.52	1.14	5.56	1.31	132
Original and interview	6.25	1.41	5.41	1.28	5.47	1.32	130
Biological							
Original only	6.01	1.28	5.04	1.00	5.52	1.20	21
Original and follow-up	6.02	1.42	5.54	1.00	5.73	1.36	51
Original and interview	6.10	1.54	5.51	.95	5.83	1.26	35
	Females						
Adopted							
Original only	6.78	1.23	5.51	.94	6.00	1.29	58
Original and follow-up	6.57	1.20	5.50	1.06	5.80	1.04	118
Original and interview	6.43	1.26	5.50	1.10	5.58	1.09	110
Biological							
Original only	6.09	.93	5.36	.64	5.32	1.36	13
Original and follow-up	5.84	1.22	5.21	1.01	5.36	.95	33
Original and interview	5.90	1.31	5.42	1.11	5.52	1.22	41

Note: Some *N*s vary slightly across traits as a result of missing data. Figures given in the table are minimums.

Table 3.7
Means of Children on Parent Rating Composites in Three Kinds of Families, Original Study

Composite	1 Child, Adopted Mean	SD	2+ Children, All Adopted Mean	SD	Both Kinds of Children Mean	SD
Extraversion	7.31	1.01	6.27	1.34	6.28	1.33
Socialization	5.75	1.02	5.49	1.15	5.35	1.05
Stability	6.33	.88	5.60	1.21	5.57	1.26
N	34		228		326	

Note: Some *N*s vary slightly across traits as a result of missing data. Figures given in the table are minimums.

in all-adoptive or mixed families. The difference across family types for Socialization is similar to the other two, but less marked and only of borderline statistical significance ($p = .07$).

One can speculate about the reasons for the higher parental ratings of only children. Perhaps parents with more than one child are more conscious of differences between children both within and outside the family, and less likely to automatically assign favorable ratings. Perhaps parents with only one child have greater emotional investment in the child's turning out well. It would be instructive to compare ratings in one-biological-child families to those in one-adopted-child families, but the sample does not include any of the former, because entry into the study required having at least one adopted child.

The Other Two Dimensions of the Big Five

As noted earlier, the rating composites discussed in the preceding sections correspond roughly to three of the so-called Big Five factors that have been found to characterize trait-descriptive terms in several languages and to be reflected in various personality inventories and rating scales. When we were preparing the rating scales to be filled out by the parents following the parent interviews, we decided to add some items to get at the other two of the Big Five, Agreeableness and Openness. We added these at the end, so that the questionnaire for the first twenty-four items would be identical with those filled out in the original and ten-year follow-up studies. We added twelve items, six targeted at each of the two added dimensions.

Table 3.8 lists the twelve items and their loadings on the two factors that emerged in a factor analysis of the ratings on these items (including separately the ratings by the fathers and the mothers). Because the two factors were specified in the analysis as uncorrelated with each other, the factor loadings can be interpreted as the correlations of the item with the factors.

In each case, five of the six items load predominantly on a single factor, Factor I for the Agreeableness items, and Factor II, for Openness. One item in each case was split between the two factors and excluded from the final five-item scale. Scales were scored as previously: items with negative loadings were reversed, and scoring was based on the mean of completed items if missing two or fewer items, otherwise the scale was scored as missing.

The two new composites had internal consistency reliabilities of .88 and .63. The .88 for Agreeableness is quite comparable to those for the original three scales (see Table 3.3); the .63 for Openness is somewhat lower, although it still represents substantial consistency.

Table 3.9 shows means by sex and adoptive or biological status for all five dimensions. It is based on all children who were rated in this adult phase—the average of the two parents' ratings was assigned if both rated.

Table 3.8
Factor Loadings of 12 New Items, for Fathers and Mothers

Item	Factor I		Factor II	
	Fathers	Mothers	Fathers	Mothers
Items targeted for Agreeableness				
*Unselfish vs. Selfish	.72	.69	.03	.05
*Wary vs. Trusting (-)	-.55	-.38	-.17	-.13
*Helpful vs. Indifferent to others	.68	.66	-.09	-.03
Shows off vs. Modest	-.31	-.49	.24	.30
*Agreeable vs. Disagreeable	.73	.79	-.01	.00
*Quarrelsome vs. Good natured (-)	-.75	.78	-.01	.09
Items targeted for Openness				
*Likes variety vs. Likes routine	.12	.07	.51	.42
*Enjoys ideas vs. Thinks concretely	.23	.29	.52	.58
Narrow interests vs. Wide interests	-.47	-.38	-.43	-.30
*Practical vs. Imaginative (-)	.06	.00	-.52	-.63
*Poetic vs. Down-to-earth	-.20	-.16	.48	.46
*Conventional vs. Original (-)	.01	-.11	-.42	-.56

Note: Principal factor analysis with varimax rotation. *Included in final scale; (-) indicates item scored in reverse direction.

Table 3.9
Means and Standard Deviations of the Big Five Rating Scales in Interviewed Families

Scale	Adopted				Biological			
	Males		Females		Males		Females	
	Mean	SD	Mean	SD	Mean	SD	Mean	SD
Extraversion	5.81	1.28	5.96	1.23	5.98	1.26	5.76	1.09
Socialization	5.44	1.42	5.52	1.44	5.51	1.04	6.19	1.05
Emotional stability	5.62	1.25	5.58	1.44	6.21	1.13	5.56	1.08
Agreeableness	6.06	1.41	6.16	1.55	6.71	1.02	6.61	1.18
Openness	5.01	1.77	5.00	1.17	5.08	1.19	4.95	.85
N	77		31		62		34	

Note: Some *N*s vary slightly across traits as a result of missing data. Figures given in the table are minimum *N*s.

Extraversion and Openness showed no significant differences across the rows of the table. Socialization did not either, although the differences in favor of females and biological offspring approached significance (p values of .06). Emotional stability ratings differed by sex, with males being judged more stable (the difference was mostly due to the biological offspring). And finally, Agreeableness differed by adoptive status, with the biological offspring rated as significantly more agreeable.

The ratings from the interviewed families permitted an analysis not available from the single-parent ratings of the original and follow-up studies, the comparison of fathers' and mothers' ratings of their children.

Table 3.10 shows these ratings. It is based on ratings by fathers and by mothers on the five traits for the four groups of children. For fathers, there was one statistically significant difference between adopted and biological children: fathers rated their biological children higher on the scales defining the Agreeable dimension. Mothers showed a similar difference, that did not quite reach the .05 criterion (p was .054). The differences between mothers and fathers were statistically evaluated on the subset of 149 cases rated by both. None was significant.

Table 3.11 shows the level of agreement between mothers and fathers on their ratings in another way, by the correlations between them.

There is substantial, although not perfect, agreement between the two spouses' ratings. We would not expect them to agree perfectly, since there is measurement error in both. Shown to the right, for comparison, are the internal consistency reliabilities for these scales in this sample, as presented earlier. It is evident that spouse agreement is higher or lower dependent on the measurement quality of the scales—Openness, for example, is lowest on both and Agreeableness, highest, and the rank order agreement is perfect.

3. The Cattell Scales

The Cattell scales turned out to present some problems, at least for the children in the initial testing. As previously noted, only about half of the children were old enough to be given any questionnaire at all. Two-thirds of those who were old enough took the child's version, the CPQ, whose norms and equivalence to the other versions of the questionnaire are in some doubt. We remarked in our initial reporting of these data: "The results for 8- to 12-year olds measured by the CPQ seem some-

Table 3.10
Mean Ratings by Fathers and Mothers in Interviewed Families

	Adopted		Biological	
Scale	Boys	Girls	Boys	Girls
Extraversion				
By father	5.86	5.80	5.86	5.75
By mother	5.81	6.03	6.12	5.66
Socialization				
By father	5.36	5.58	5.55	6.17
By mother	5.53	5.48	5.46	6.03
Emotional stability				
By father	5.62	5.66	6.19	5.59
By mother	5.68	5.45	6.20	5.22
Agreeableness				
By father	6.19	6.05	6.63	6.51
By mother	6.03	6.23	6.79	6.45
Openness				
By father	4.91	4.93	4.97	4.91
By mother	5.11	5.09	5.22	4.91
No. of fathers	62	53	29	31
No. of mothers	69	53	28	25

Note: Some *N*s vary slightly for different traits as a result of missing data. Figures given in the table are minimum *N*s.

Table 3.11
Correlation between Mothers and Fathers Rating the Same Children

Composite	Correlation	N	Internal-Consistency Reliabilities
Extraversion	.68	149	.81
Socialization	.70	149	.84
Emotional stability	.70	149	.84
Agreeableness	.73	145	.88
Openness	.57	145	.63

what peculiar, with departures from the population mean in unexpected directions on several scales and standard deviations departing more from the norms than in the other three groups. Since the ratings of these same children do not show analogous differences . . . we are inclined to suspect that the CPQ norms may be at fault" (Loehlin, et al., 1981, p. 315). And later: "The extraversion and socialization scales and rating factors show essentially no agreement at all for the CPQ" (ibid, p. 322).

Because of these problems, we will concentrate here on the results from the follow-up sample in which the children were old enough to take the adult Cattell questionnaire, the 16PF, the one which was taken by their parents at the time of the initial testing.

Table 3.12 shows mean scores in four groups on fifteen of the 16PF factors. The scores are on a standardized scale, called "stens," on which the mean is 5.5 in the general population on which the test was normed, and the standard deviation is 2. Thus, a score of 6.5 is half a standard deviation above the mean—this implies that about 3 persons in 10 in the reference population would score above that level. Each scale is identified by a Cattellian letter label, plus an adjective roughly characterizing its content. The omitted scale is B, intelligence, which is not like the others, but is measured by a handful of verbal analogy items and tends to be of relatively low reliability (Cattell, et al., 1970). The scores on this scale are negatively skewed in the present sample, suggesting that it was too easy for this population; in any case we have assessed intelligence extensively in other ways (see Chapter 2).

Most of the means in Table 3.12 fall in the range 4.5 to 6.5, that is, close to the population mean, but there is a significant tendency for higher scores for the adopted children on the scales E and F, Dominant and Enthusiastic. This is also true of scale Q_1, radical attitudes. Scale F,

Table 3.12
Means on 16PF Scales for Child Generation in Follow-up Sample

Scale		Adopted		Biological	
		Boys	Girls	Boys	Girls
A.	Warmhearted	5.93	6.15	5.54	5.82
C.	Stable	6.26	6.31	6.29	6.13
E.	Dominant	6.72	6.81	6.54	5.76
F.	Enthusiastic	6.80	6.68	6.65	5.61
G.	Conscientious	5.29	5.17	5.40	5.05
H.	Venturesome	6.41	6.63	5.94	6.24
I.	Sensitive	5.11	5.52	4.98	5.24
L.	Suspicious	5.61	5.47	5.77	5.13
M.	Imaginative	4.81	5.00	5.17	4.29
N.	Shrewd	5.25	5.00	5.48	5.66
O.	Guilt prone	4.62	4.70	5.13	5.13
Q_1	Radical	5.53	5.43	4.96	5.03
Q_2	Self-sufficient	5.71	5.72	5.88	6.03
Q_3	Controlled	5.75	5.69	5.85	5.47
Q_4	Tense	5.32	5.61	5.52	5.61
	N	104	96	48	38

Enthusiastic, shows a significant sex difference as well, with the boys in this sample higher than the girls, relative to their norms. And one scale, M, Imaginative, shows a complex pattern involving both sex and adoptive status, with the adopted boys and the biological girls low compared to the other two groups.

Table 3.13 shows adoptive and biological pairings on the fifteen personality scales of the 16PF, which the parents filled out at the time of the original study and the children at the ten-year follow-up. In general, the correlations are quite modest, but those in the left-hand two columns, where there is an absence of genetic relationship, average close to zero (.04 and .01), while those in the right-hand two columns, where a genetic relationship is present, are higher (averaging .11 and .12). Evidently, being members of the same family does not make parents and children very much alike in personality; what modest resemblance there is mostly occurs only when genes are shared.

Table 3.14 gives intra-class correlations for three kinds of sibling pairings on the 16PF scales: pairs of siblings, both adopted; pairs consisting of an adopted and a biological child; and pairs of biological children. The adopted-biological and the adopted-adopted pairs are alike in not sharing genes, but they differ slightly in how selective placement affects them—in theory, it should have more effect in the former case than in the latter. Since there is little reason to suppose that selective placement for personality traits is a major factor in this case, the two columns for practical purposes may be regarded as equivalent, and the differences between them taken to provide an indication of the effect of sample size on low correlations in fairly small samples such as these. Sampling fluctuation is even more of an issue with the small number of pairings of biological children, a scarcity resulting from the fact that not very many parents had two or more biological children of their own in addition to the adopted child that brought them into the study.

Unlike the parent-child relationships, there is not much evidence in Table 3.14 that siblings who share genes are more alike than siblings who do not. The average in column 3 is a *little* higher than the average of columns 1 and 2, but with these sample sizes, the differences could easily just reflect chance factors. A couple of traits—Sensitive and Controlled—show a pattern that might suggest a genetic component, but of these only Sensitive shows much of a genetic pattern in the parent-offspring correlations of Table 3.13.

One reason for relatively low sibling correlations might be the effects of contrast between siblings. In comparison with a highly extraverted

Table 3.13
Adoptive and Biological Parent-Child Correlations on 16PF Scales

| | Adoptive | | Biological | |
Scale	Father-Child	Mother-Child	Father-Child	Mother-Child
A. Warmhearted	.07	-.12	.16	-.24
C. Stable	.09	.07	.05	.24
E. Dominant	.04	-.08	.18	.26
F. Enthusiastic	.06	.07	.16	.10
G. Conscientious	-.01	.04	-.01	-.13
H. Venturesome	.03	.02	.11	.16
I. Sensitive	.07	.07	.14	.25
L. Suspicious	-.04	.03	-.19	.12
M. Imaginative	.04	.06	.29	.18
N. Shrewd	.02	-.01	-.04	.24
O. Guilt prone	.02	-.03	.07	.05
Q_1 Radical	.07	.09	.11	-.03
Q_2 Self-sufficient	-.04	-.08	.18	.31
Q_3 Controlled	.02	.05	.04	.23
Q_4 Tense	.01	.08	-.04	.14
Mean	.04	.01	.11	.12
Pairings	180	178	81	81

Table 3.14
Sibling Intra-class Correlations on 16PF Scales

Scale	Adopted-Adopted	Adopted-Biological	Biological-Biological
A. Warmhearted	-.37	.04	.27
C. Stable	.03	-.02	-.10
E. Dominant	.22	.08	-.21
F. Enthusiastic	-.27	-.03	-.18
G. Conscientious	-.09	-.09	-.16
H. Venturesome	-.22	.23	.04
I. Sensitive	-.04	.09	.25
L. Suspicious	-.01	-.05	-.01
M. Imaginative	-.05	.17	.17
N. Shrewd	.14	.09	-.15
O. Guilt prone	.00	.21	-.01
Q_1 Radical	.07	.06	.12
Q_2 Self-sufficent	-.09	-.11	.04
Q_3 Controlled	.10	-.16	.45
Q_4 Tense	.10	.09	.17
Mean	-.03	.04	.05
df within families	46	72	22

Note: df within families = number of individuals in category minus number of families.

brother, a sibling may come to see himself and be seen by others as something of an introvert, even though, in comparison with children in general, he may be above average in extraversion. Or he might in fact come to behave in more introverted ways than would have been the case in the absence of the extraverted brother. Another factor that might contribute to low correlations involving adoptive siblings is that they tend to be of opposite sexes. Adoptive parents tended to adopt a girl as a second child if they had adopted a boy first, or vice versa, or to adopt a child of the opposite sex to an existing biological child. This could lead pairs to be less alike than they would have been if paired at random.

In the absence of more extensive data, there is no entirely satisfactory way of making genetic inferences under these circumstances, but Table 3.15 presents one approach based on the parent-offspring 16PF data. This makes use of a statistic used by geneticists called a midparent-midoffspring regression. It essentially describes the prediction of the average offspring score on a trait from the average score of the two parents. Table 3.15 shows this separately for adopted and biological offspring.

It is evident that the average of the adopted children on a trait shows little, if any, predictability from the average of the parents. All but three of the coefficients fall within the range -.10 to +.10 and none of the exceptions—Stable, Sensitive, and Radical—is high enough to provide compel-

Table 3.15
Midparent-Midoffspring Regressions for 16PF Scales

Scale		Adoptive Offspring	Biological Offspring
A.	Warmhearted	-.01	-.18
C.	Stable	.23	.41
E.	Dominant	-.08	.41
F.	Enthusiastic	.06	.44
G.	Conscientious	-.02	-.20
H.	Venturesome	.00	.26
I.	Sensitive	.12	.28
L.	Suspicious	-.01	.00
M.	Imaginative	.06	.39
N.	Shrewd	.06	.26
O.	Guilt prone	.01	.21
Q_1	Radical	.16	.01
Q_2	Self-sufficient	-.10	.56
Q_3	Controlled	.01	.21
Q_4	Tense	.02	.14
	Mean	.03	.21
	Families	134	60

ling evidence to the contrary. The average coefficient across the 15 scales is .03. On the other hand, the coefficients for the biological offspring tend to be more substantial. More than half of them (eight of fifteen) are higher than the highest coefficient for the adoptive relationships. The average coefficient is .21. One straightforward interpretation of this table is that about one-sixth (.21 minus .03) of the individual variation measured by the scales of this inventory is due to the genes, and nearly all the rest reflects factors unique to individuals (plus fallibility of the measurement of the traits). This conclusion discounts the sibling resemblance data, on the grounds of more limited sample sizes and the possible complicating presence of sex differences and contrast between siblings.

4. The CPI and the TTS in the Separate Mail Study

Recall that in a study based on a different sample of 220 families from the same adoption agency, two personality questionnaires, the California Psychological Inventory (CPI) and the Thurstone Temperament Schedule (TTS), were administered by mail to parents and children. These families were from adoptions that had taken place at an earlier period, so the children were old enough to take the same questionnaires as their parents.

Several checks were made on the quality of the data obtained. The CPI contains a twenty-eight-item scale, called Communality, containing items nearly always answered in the same way by members of normal populations. Low scores on this scale may be indicative of invalid responding—getting lost on the answer sheet, answering at random, carelessness or facetiousness, and so on. The CPI manual suggests that scores of 20 or less on Communality be regarded with suspicion, so respondents getting such scores were excluded from further analysis. It is of some interest that adopted sons were disproportionately represented among the seventeen excluded cases, which included three fathers, no mothers, eleven adopted sons, no biological sons, one biological daughter, and two adopted daughters.

The present sample overlapped slightly with the main TAP sample—26 families participated in both. The CPI contains 116 items in common with the MMPI, so it was possible to examine the consistency of response on these items for those parents who had taken the MMPI as part of the TAP some five or six years earlier. The typical item-by-item agreement was 84 percent for both mothers and fathers. This can be compared to a study done at the University of Oregon, in which students took both the MMPI and the CPI (Goldberg & Rorer, 1964). The 84 percent consistency of the parents in the present study across an interval of five or six years was nearly as high as the 86 percent consistency for male and 88 percent for female college students over an interval of two weeks.

Finally, a consistency score was obtainable from twelve items on the CPI that are repeated within the questionnaire itself. These consistencies were (after exclusion of the low-communality cases): 88 percent for fathers, 92 percent for mothers, 89 percent for adopted sons, 88 percent for biological sons, 90 percent for biological daughters, and 91 percent for adopted daughters. In the Oregon study of college students mentioned earlier, the consistencies on these items were comparable—89 percent for males and 90 percent for females. Thus, we can have reasonable confidence in the dependability of our results.

Tables 3.16 and 3.17 present parent-child correlations for the scales of the CPI and TTS, separately for fathers and mothers with their biological and adoptive children. The correlations were calculated after statistically adjusting for age and sex differences in response to the scales.

Looking together at the two tables, 3.16 and 3.17, we see that the majority of correlations of parents with adopted children are low and positive. The means are .07, .04, .03, and .01, in the two tables. Sixty-two percent (31 of 50) of the correlations lie in the range .00 to 10, with only 14 percent above that level. The biological correlations are not very large, but they tend to be a little larger, with means of .07, .15, .17, and .09. Only 28 percent of the correlations are in the .00 to .10 range, with 54 percent above. This suggests that environment, or environmentally-based factors such as imitation or identification, are causing very little parent-child resemblance. The genes add something for the biologically related pairs, but still the vast majority of variation is due to factors unique to individuals (and measurement error).

The sibling correlations in Tables 3.18 and 3.19 tell much the same story, although the group of biological-biological pairs is very small. The genetically unrelated pairs show average correlations of .06, .02, -.04, and -.03; i.e., close to 0, overall. The correlations for the biologically-related pairs fluctuate considerably, as would be expected from the small sample sizes, but they center at .15 and .16 for the two questionnaires. Only 24 percent of the correlations for unrelated siblings lie above +.10; 56 percent do for biological siblings.

With samples of these sizes we cannot have great confidence in trait-to-trait differences, but we can at least ask for which scales biologically-related correlations tend to exceed adoptive ones consistently across par-

Table 3.16
Adoptive and Biological Parent-Child Correlations on CPI Scales

Scale	Adoptive		Biological	
	Father-Child	Mother-Child	Father-Child	Mother-Child
Dominance	.04	-.04	.13	.25
Capacity for status	.20	.09	.18	.18
Sociability	.08	.01	.20	.15
Social presence	.18	.06	.42	.26
Self-acceptance	.04	.07	.20	.42
Sense of well-being	.13	.00	-.16	.02
Responsibility	.06	.05	.12	.15
Socialization	-.03	-.02	.16	.06
Self-control	.08	.03	.00	-.07
Tolerance	-.01	.06	-.03	.27
Good impression	.06	-.01	-.01	.17
Communality	.10	.13	.21	.04
Achievement via conformance	.03	-.07	-.23	-.01
Achievement via independence	.10	.07	.22	.27
Intellectual efficiency	.14	.07	.09	.12
Psychological-mindedness	.06	-.03	-.27	.08
Flexibility	.12	.11	.10	.30
Femininity	-.07	.07	.01	.05
Mean	.07	.04	.07	.15
Pairings	24	25	52	53

Note: Correlations computed after statistically removing the effects of age and sex on scores.

Table 3.17
Adoptive and Biological Parent-Child Correlations on TTS Scales

Scale	Adoptive		Biological	
	Father-Child	Mother-Child	Father-Child	Mother-Child
Active	.03	.02	.33	-.02
Vigorous	.00	.11	.36	.29
Impulsive	.07	.01	.13	.05
Dominant	.04	-.04	.09	.14
Stable	.06	.02	.06	.01
Sociable	.07	-.03	.22	.13
Reflective	-.04	.01	.00	.03
Mean	.03	.01	.17	.09
Pairings	257	271	56	54

Note: Correlations computed after statistically removing the effects of age and sex on scores.

Table 3.18
Sibling Intraclass Correlations on CPI Scales in Adoptive Families

Scale	Adopted-Adopted	Adopted-Biological	Biological-Biological
Dominance	.03	.05	-.18
Capacity for status	.12	.01	.60
Sociability	.13	-.06	.22
Social presence	-.05	-.12	.70
Self-acceptance	-.01	.05	-.13
Sense of well-being	.14	.12	-.03
Responsibility	.00	.33	.61
Socialization	.03	.10	-.01
Self-control	-.06	.03	.34
Tolerance	.07	.04	.09
Good impression	.02	.26	.21
Communality	.07	-.13	-.19
Achievement via conformance	.11	.11	-.47
Achievement via independence	.07	-.16	.23
Intellectual efficiency	.12	-.09	.50
Psychological-mindedness	-.04	.04	.32
Flexibility	.14	.04	.28
Femininity	.22	-.24	-.21
Mean	.06	.02	.16
df within families	80	48	14

Note: Correlations computed after statistically removing the effects of age and sex on scores. *df* within families = number of individuals in category minus number of families.

Table 3.19
Sibling Intraclass Correlations on TTS Scales in Adoptive Families

Scale	Adopted-Adopted	Adopted-Biological	Biological-Biological
Active	.03	-.28	.06
Vigorous	.10	.27	.42
Impulsive	-.27	-.10	.23
Dominant	.08	-.05	-.42
Stable	-.01	-.02	.27
Sociable	-.21	-.05	.38
Reflective	-.02	.04	.08
Mean	-.04	-.03	.15
df within families	80	48	14

Note: Correlations computed after statistically removing the effects of age and sex on scores. *df* within families = number of individuals in category minus number of families.

ent-offspring and sibling correlations. Four CPI scales meet this criterion: Sociability, Social presence, Responsibility, and Achievement via independence. Two TTS scales do: Vigorous and Sociable. Three of these scales fall generally in the extraversion domain: Sociability and Social presence on the CPI and Sociable on the TTS. Two may be related to personal maturity: Responsibility and Achievement via independence. The items on the sixth scale, Vigorous on the TTS, are primarily related to traditionally masculine interests and activities—outdoors, sports, mechanical, and the like.

Model Fitting to Twins and Adoptees on the CPI

One of the motivations for selecting the CPI and the TTS for the mail study was the availability of data on these questionnaires from twins and other genetically relevant groups, permitting some joint model fitting.

The first of these projects involved fitting heredity-environment models to data from the CPI from two twin samples in addition to the present adoption study. One of the twin samples consisted of 99 adult male identical twin pairs (designated MZ for monozygotic) and 99 male fraternal twin pairs (DZ, for dizygotic). These were twin brothers who were veterans of the Vietnam War (Horn, Plomin, & Rosenman, 1976). The other twin sample consisted of same-sex twin pairs among high school juniors who took the National Merit Scholarship Qualifying Test in 1962 (Loehlin & Nichols, 1976). They included 202 male MZ pairs, 288 female MZ pairs, 124 male DZ pairs, and 193 female DZ pairs. Altogether, in the combined twin and adoption data, there were 1737 pairings in seventeen subgroups subdivided by sex, generation, and adoptive status. Biological sibling pairs from the adoption sample were excluded from the modeling because of tiny sample sizes when subdivided by sex and because the DZ twins amply represent the biological sibling category. Biological parent-child pairings from the adoption study were retained, along with the various adoptive pairings. Table 3.20 presents the additional correlations from the twin samples.

A look at the correlations in Table 3.20 suggests at least two things. First, the MZ correlations, averaging .43, .50, and .48, are decidedly higher than the DZ correlations, at .18, .25, and .32. We would expect MZ correlations twice as high as DZ correlations if the resemblance is due to shared genes, because the MZ twins share all their genes and the DZ twins share only half of theirs. Twice as high, roughly, is what we get, although this varies across scales and samples.

Second, the DZ correlations, averaging in the neighborhood of .25, run somewhat higher than the biological sibling correlations in Table 3.18,

Table 3.20
Correlations of MZ and DZ Twins on CPI Scales

Scale	MZm-V	DZm-V	MZm-N	MZf-N	DZm-N	DZf-N
Dominance	.52	.27	.57	.50	.13	.36
Capacity for status	.53	.22	.54	.60	.36	.54
Sociability	.48	.17	.52	.54	.24	.33
Social presence	.50	.19	.51	.55	.14	.31
Self-acceptance	.47	.22	.42	.55	.14	.37
Sense of well-being	.42	.12	.54	.45	.33	.27
Responsibility	.44	.32	.57	.43	.29	.40
Socialization	.43	.24	.52	.55	.16	.48
Self-control	.45	.12	.56	.57	.27	.36
Tolerance	.46	.17	.59	.48	.30	.39
Good impression	.41	.14	.49	.46	.32	.28
Communality	.20	.05	.31	.42	.25	.12
Achievement via conformance	.41	.00	.48	.44	.06	.25
Achievement via independence	.48	.23	.57	.52	.40	.42
Intellectual efficiency	.48	.28	.57	.47	.29	.38
Psychological-mindedness	.34	.18	.47	.37	.28	.19
Flexibility	.47	.11	.43	.51	.25	.18
Femininity	.23	.15	.41	.30	.26	.14
Mean	.43	.18	.50	.48	.25	.32
Pairs	99	99	202	288	124	193

Note: MZ = monozygotic pairs, DZ = dizygotic pairs, m = male, f = female, V = Vietnam veterans sample, N = National Merit sample.

which averaged .16. One reason for this might be that the individuals in the DZ pairs are the same sex and age, whereas those in the biological sibling sample are not.

In order to look at all the CPI data simultaneously, also allowing for differences in sample sizes and scale reliabilities, we fit heredity-environment models to the twin correlations and the relevant correlations from the adoption study. The details of the model fitting are too complex to present here (they may be found in Loehlin, 1985). The main results may, however, be summarized as follows:

1.   Overall, a moderate contribution of the genes to individual differences on the personality scales, estimated at about 40 percent of the total; little systematic contribution from family environments, 5 percent or less; a substantial portion attributable to unreliability of measurement,

about 30 percent. The remaining 25 percent or so is a residual category reflecting individual differences in experience, gene-environment interactions, and so forth.

2.   Models that allowed for differences among the scales tended to fit significantly better than models assuming all scales to be the same.

3.   Models that separated the genetic influence into additive and non-additive effects of the genes fit significantly better than models that did not. (Additive genetic effects are the effects of individual genes, transmissible from parent to child; non-additive genetic effects are those due to configurations of genes. Gene configurations are shared by identical twins, but are broken apart in the recombination of parental genes between generations, and hence are likely not to be shared by other siblings.)

4.   Generation differences (adults versus adolescents) tended to carry more weight than gender differences in explaining the correlations.

Model Fitting to Twins, Families and Adoptees on the TTS

The TTS also provided model-fitting opportunities. The data were available for somewhat different groups. In addition to the adoptive sample, these included two twin samples—102 MZ and 119 DZ pairs from the Vietnam veterans twin sample mentioned previously and 45 MZ and 34 DZ pairs from a Michigan adolescent twin sample (Vandenberg, 1962). In addition, data were available from an unpublished study of twins and their offspring based on a different group of Vietnam veteran twins. This last allowed interesting comparisons, such as the correlation of an MZ twin with his twin's children as compared to his own—two groups of children to whom he is equally similar genetically because his twin's genes are the same as his own, but who differ with respect to the family in which they were reared. Another interesting comparison involves correlations between one of his children and one of his twin's. They are first cousins socially, but half-siblings genetically (different mothers but genetically identical fathers). Table 3.21 shows correlations on the TTS scales for the various additional groups.

Again, the MZ groups show substantially higher correlations than the others: on average, .46, .46, and .38, in comparison with DZ, sib, and parent-offspring correlations in the range .06 to .14. The correlations for the DZ groups are not, in this case, higher than those for ordinary siblings. The resemblance of an MZ twin to his twin's children (average correlation of .13) is as high as his resemblance to his own (average correlation of .12), suggesting minimal effects of family environment. Against this, the

Table 3.21
Correlations of Twins and Twin-Family Groups on TTS Scales

Scale	MZ Mich	Vet	DZ Mich	Vet	Twin-Family MZ	PC	PTC	Sib	HSib
Active	.59	.49	-.01	-.05	.36	.15	.21	.27	.14
Vigorous	.67	.44	.37	.23	.62	.06	-.02	.32	.17
Impulsive	.39	.52	-.11	.02	.35	.09	.18	.07	.06
Dominant	.56	.58	.27	.03	.37	.22	.24	.21	.35
Stable	.19	.19	-.02	-.04	.51	.10	.02	.01	-.02
Sociable	.47	.45	.00	.08	.30	.22	.30	.17	.12
Reflective	.35	.52	.27	.15	.18	.00	.00	-.10	.01
Mean	.46	.46	.11	.06	.38	.12	.13	.14	.12
Pairs	45	102	34	119	44	149	121	102	84

Note: MZ = monozygotic pairs, DZ = dizygotic pairs; Mich = Michigan twin sample, Vet = Vietnam veterans twin sample; PC = parent-child, i.e., MZ twin and own child, PTC = parent and twin's child; Sib = genetic siblings, HSib = genetic half-siblings, i.e., cousins via MZ pair.

average correlation of genetic half-sibs reared in different families (.12) is almost as high as that of genetic full sibs reared in the same family (various DZ and sib groups), which suggests the possibility that some environmental factor acting against similarity, such as contrast, is operating in the latter. In any event, the various familial correlations involving shared genes tend to run somewhat higher than the purely adoptive correlations in Tables 3.17 and 3.19 that did not.

Again, one can assess all these correlations simultaneously by fitting heredity-environment models. Because the CPI modeling had suggested little effect of gender on the correlations, the sexes were combined for this analysis. The biological sibling pairings from the adoption study were again excluded on the grounds of small sample size and the availability of several other biological sibling groups.

The results were similar in general to those from the CPI. A model estimating a single genetic value for each scale suggested that on average about half the individual variation on these scales (48 percent) might be attributable to the genes and that significant scale-to-scale variation was present. A model also allowing for shared family environments did not yield a significant improvement of fit over this one. Allowing for part of the genetic variation to be non-additive yielded a better fit than a purely additive model.

5. The MMPI

As noted earlier, many of the birth mothers of the adopted children had been given the MMPI during their stay at the Methodist Mission Home, and so we gave the MMPI to the adoptive parents and, at the time of the ten-year follow-up, to those children who were then old enough to take this test, which was most of them. The MMPI is a questionnaire that is mainly focused on dimensions of psychopathology—it has scales labeled schizophrenia, depression, hysteria, paranoia, and so on. However, it has been given to many normal populations, and although individuals in these populations seldom achieve extreme scores on the psychopathology scales, they do tend to vary along these dimensions, and different degrees of suspiciousness, anxiety, eccentricity, and so on, may be considered as descriptors of differences among the personalities of ordinary people. (In a later chapter, we will report some results based on extreme scorers on one of the MMPI scales, Psychopathic deviate.)

Table 3.22 lists the eight basic MMPI scales we have used (we excluded one scale, Masculinity-femininity, *Mf*, on the grounds that it would likely have different relationships in the two sexes). Along with each scale name is a brief description of the characteristics it might be expected to reflect as they occur at the pathological extremes or vary within the normal population.

Means and Family Correlations on the MMPI Scales

Table 3.23 contains means and standard deviations of these MMPI scales for five groups: adoptive fathers, adoptive mothers, biological

Table 3.22
MMPI Scales

Scale Name	Abbreviation	Characteristics
Hypochondriasis	Hs	concern with bodily functions; imagined illnesses
Depression	D	feelings of despondency and worthlessness
Hysteria	Hy	physical symptoms replacing emotional problems
Psychopathic deviate	Pd	disregards social rules and others' feelings; often in trouble
Paranoia	Pa	suspiciousness; feelings of persecution
Psychasthenia	Pt	fears, obsessions, compulsions
Schizophrenia	Sc	withdrawn; strange thoughts and actions
Hypomania	Ma	overactivity, overexcitement, scattering of attention

Table 3.23
Means and SDs on MMPI Scales in Five Groups

Scale	Adoptive Fathers		Adoptive Mothers		Biological Children		Adoptive Children		Birth Mothers	
	M	SD	M	SD	M	SD	M	SD	M	SD
Hs	52.5	7.8	50.4	7.2	49.7	9.4	49.8	9.2	53.4	8.7
D	51.5	8.6	50.6	9.0	51.3	12.1	49.9	11.2	56.8	10.1
Hy	57.2	7.5	55.7	6.9	54.4	9.3	53.2	7.9	57.8	8.6
Pd	55.1	8.1	52.7	8.3	58.2	10.9	59.8	11.6	66.0	11.6
Pa	53.7	7.5	54.9	7.8	56.9	8.9	56.9	10.2	59.9	10.6
Pt	53.1	8.1	52.1	8.0	55.3	11.8	55.5	11.4	58.8	8.9
Sc	52.5	7.9	51.2	7.4	57.5	12.2	59.4	14.9	60.6	11.2
Ma	55.5	9.9	51.3	9.9	62.4	12.3	64.8	12.5	59.1	11.2
Mean	53.9	8.2	52.4	8.1	55.7	10.9	56.2	11.1	59.1	10.1
N	385		385		82		197		352	

Note: T-scores (mean = 50, SD = 10).

children, adopted children, and the birth mothers of the adopted children.

The scores on these scales are expressed as "T-scores"; that is, they were scaled so that they have means of 50 and SDs of 10 in the normal population on which the test was standardized. The means of the adoptive parents show them to be a fairly average group in terms of these norms: most of the means are within half a standard deviation (5 points) of the normative population means, and no mean is elevated as much as three-fourths of a standard deviation. The means of the two groups of children are somewhat higher, averaging slightly over half a standard deviation above the general adult mean. This is presumably a function of the youth of these groups—teenagers tend to have elevated scores on scales like Pd and Ma relative to adults (see, e.g., Colligan & Offord, 1992). Highest of all on the MMPI scales are the birth mothers, who average nearly a full SD above the women in the norm group. Part of this is likely due to their relative youth (average age when tested, 19.5). The moderate elevation on the first three scales, Hs, D, and Hy, is probably a result of their pregnancy—married women who are pregnant tend to show a similar elevation on these scales (Horn, et al., 1975). But pregnancy would not be expected to affect the last five scales and, in particular, the average of over 1.5 SDs above the mean on Pd suggests that there must have been a fair number of seriously troublesome individuals in this group. (We return to this issue in the next chapter.)

The SDs in Table 3.23 suggest that the adoptive parents were somewhat restricted in range on the MMPI scales, but that the children and the birth mothers were not. The parent SDs center at just over 8 as compared to the normative 10. It is plausible that, as a group of prospective adoptive parents, they were both self-selected and screened by the adoption agency against extreme psychopathological tendencies. The two child groups and the birth mothers show a normal degree of internal variation (SDs of about 10). Reduced SDs tend to reduce correlations, so we would expect that correlations involving adoptive parents' MMPI scores might be somewhat affected, but correlations involving the other three groups should not be.

Parent-offspring correlations on the MMPI scales are given in Table 3.24.

The correlations of the adoptive parents with their adopted children hover around 0—as many of the correlations are positive as negative, and the overall means of .01 and .02 again suggest that similarity-producing factors, like children imitating their parents, do not play much of a role in shaping personality for these traits. The correlations with the biological children are low, averaging .06 and .08, but at least they are all positive. The correlations between the birth mothers and their biological children (the adopted children in the TAP families) tend to be appreciably higher. This may partly reflect the restriction of range in the adoptive parents, but it may also suggest the presence of similarity-reducing environmental factors, such as contrast, in families.

Table 3.24
Parent-Child Correlations on MMPI Scales

Scale	Father-Adopted	Mother-Adopted	Father-Biological	Mother-Biological	Birth mother-Adopted
Hs	.11	-.01	.01	.01	.18
D	-.05	.09	.02	.12	.22
Hy	.06	-.02	.15	.06	.14
Pd	.13	.05	.12	.06	.24
Pa	-.10	-.02	.08	.10	.03
Pt	-.04	.03	.03	.04	.16
Sc	-.03	.00	.04	.08	.22
Ma	.08	-.02	.06	.08	.12
Mean	.01	.02	.06	.08	.16
N	193	190	81	81	142

Table 3.25 provides correlations for other pairings. The first three columns give the resemblances between siblings. The two sets of correlations involving genetically unrelated pairs—adopted-adopted or adopted-biological pairings—are both fairly low. Those involving biological-biological pairs are not much higher. This suggests that if the genes are playing much of a role in shaping personality there must be offsetting environmental effects in operation, such as competition or contrast. The last three columns of the table provide other correlations, between the spouses in the TAP families, and for their resemblance to the birth mothers of the children they adopted (this would reflect, for example, any selective placement of children by the adoption agency). Both of these correlations tend to be low enough to suggest that other correlations involving these traits should not be much affected by them.

Table 3.26 presents midparent-midoffspring regressions for the MMPI scales. (Table 3.15 gave corresponding results for the 16PF.) This indicates the extent to which the departure from the mean of the parents predicts that of their children. If that were 0 for adopted children, the regression for the biological children would provide an estimate of heritability, the extent to which individual differences on the scales reflect the genes. The regressions for the adopted children are not quite 0, so one might interpret the excess for the biological over the adopted children in this way. This would suggest an overall heritability for these scores of about 23 percent, or somewhat more if we adjust for restriction of range of the

Table 3.25
Sibling, Spouse, and Selective Placement Correlations on MMPI Scales

Scale	Adopted-Adopted	Adopted-Biological	Biological-Biological	Husband-Wife	Father-Birth Mother	Mother-Birth Mother
Hs	.07	.14	.13	.06	.11	.01
D	.09	.16	.19	.00	.01	.11
Hy	-.15	-.10	.06	.10	.01	-.04
Pd	.02	.06	-.06	.06	.05	.01
Pa	.30	-.18	.26	.12	-.04	.00
Pt	.10	.17	.23	-.01	.15	.04
Sc	.08	.09	.17	.14	.03	.00
Ma	.20	-.16	-.20	.03	-.02	.02
Mean	.09	.02	.10	.04	.04	.02
N	44	69	20	281	339	338

Note: For siblings, intraclass or interclass correlations, and N is degrees of freedom within families.

Table 3.26
Midparent-Midoffspring Regressions on MMPI Scales

Scale	Adoptive Offspring	Biological Offspring
Hs	.20	.09
D	.21	.24
Hy	-.00	.40
Pd	.17	.16
Pa	-.14	.21
Pt	.06	.53
Sc	-.02	.47
Ma	-.03	.25
Mean	.06	.29
Families	135	61

parents. Another estimate of heritability can be obtained by doubling the correlation between birth mother and adopted child from Table 3.24. This would suggest a figure of about 32 percent, although this could be a little high if the birth mothers and fathers are correlated for pathological traits. In any case, these estimates suggest that the genes may be contributing something like 25 percent to individual differences in these traits. (The 16PF regressions of .03 and .21 would suggest around 18 percent for those.)

Another limitation is that the genetic effects estimated in this way are just the so-called "additive" ones, and non-additive, or configurational, genetic effects may play a significant role in personality—if so, the 25 percent figure mentioned above underestimates the total effect of genes on the traits measured by the MMPI.

Finally, the estimates apply to the traits as measured, the scores on the MMPI scales. We would expect them to be higher for the underlying traits themselves, assuming that random errors of measurement are tending to attenuate the regressions (that is, to weaken the parent-child predictions).

Can we say whether some traits are more influenced by the genes than others? Not with much confidence, for several reasons. First, with small samples, correlations may vary considerably, and with undependable estimates for both traits involved, differences between them are pretty unreliable. Second, the MMPI scales are not independent, in part because the same items may be scored on more than one scale. This tends to produce an artifactual inflation of the correlation between the scales in question. Third, there is the possibility of substantial non-additive genetic influences being involved, as mentioned earlier, further complicating matters. Nevertheless, we can at least look for scales that show the signs of substantial genetic influence: biological parent-offspring regressions well in excess of adoptive ones (Table 3.26), relatively large correlations between birth mother and adopted child (Table 3.24), and relatively large biological sibling correlations (Table 3.25). The MMPI scales best meeting these criteria would seem to be *Pt* and *Sc* (two scales that share a number of items, and thus are substantially correlated). It is at least conceivable that the weakened contact with the realities of the social and physical worlds that is embodied in these traits would have a biological underpinning, but it is not obvious why others—*Pa*, for example—would not share this. (*Pa* qualifies on two of the three criteria, but the exception, birth mother and adopted child, is based on the largest sample.)

Resemblances to Birth Mothers in Families with Two Adopted Children

We also looked at genetic parent-child resemblance via a different approach, one controlling for a large number of possibly distorting variables. There were sixty-four of the original TAP families in which there were at least two adopted children with MMPIs for both birth mothers. Now we can ask questions of the form: Did the more extraverted child have the birth mother that was better adjusted? Was this true of the better-socialized child? Of the more emotionally stable child? (We used the parent ratings from the original study to maximize the number of available families.) The answers are given in Table 3.27, and some of them are surprising.

Table 3.27
Correlations between Child Differences on Rating Scale Dimensions and Birth Mother Differences on MMPI Scales, for Families with Two Adopted Children with Birth Mother MMPIs

MMPI Scale	Extraversion	Good Socialization	Emotional Stability
Hs	-.15	.19	.38
D	-.26	.17	.30
Hy	-.05	.27	.37
Pd	.10	-.04	.25
Pa	-.16	.29	.33
Pt	-.19	.14	.12
Sc	-.13	.05	.23
Ma	.19	-.26	.00
Mean	-.08	.10	.25

Note: N = 64 families, children's ratings from original study (average age 7 years). Effect of children's ages removed statistically.

For extraversion, they are not surprising: the majority of negative signs indicate that most of the correlations are in the direction of the more extraverted child's mother scoring lower (i.e., as better adjusted) on the MMPI scales. The two exceptions, *Pd* and *Ma*, represent psychological disturbances having an extraverted flavor, making it plausible that common genes might be involved.

For good socialization, however, the majority of the MMPI scales are correlated in the opposite direction, with more maladjustment of the mother predicting better behavior on the part of the child. Again, the two exceptions are *Pd* and *Ma*, and it is at least possible that these extraverted forms of maladjustment of the mother would be associated with more resistance to socialization on the part of a child who shares her genes; whereas anxiety proneness might lead to readier conformity.

However, emotional stability presents a more serious paradox. The better-adjusted child tended not to be the one with the better-adjusted birth mother, but the one with the *worse*-adjusted birth mother; this is consistently so across the MMPI scales; and many of the correlations are not tiny.

In order to look more closely at these differences, we did an analysis of the MMPI items to sort out the ones that the birth mother of the more extraverted child was most likely to have said "Yes" to, and so on for the other groups. (We actually did this with a subsample of fifty-two of the sixty-four families, a group for which we also had birth mother IQ scores, to see if this was a contributing factor—it turned out not to be.)

We used an arbitrary criterion of a difference of 25 percent between the two sets of mothers' agreement with the item. For example, take the MMPI item reporting loneliness. Of the fifty-two mothers of the more extraverted child, only ten marked it "True." For the fifty-two mothers of the more introverted child, twenty-seven did. The difference, 19 versus 52 percent, i.e., 33 percent, exceeds 25 percent, so it goes into Table 3.28 as endorsed more frequently by the birth mother of the more introverted child. As can be seen, there was one other item in this category, reporting shyness. No items qualified for the mother of the more extraverted child. Such as they are, these two items are consistent with a genetic mother-child resemblance for introversion: the mother saying "True" to these items had a child who was more likely to be introverted than another child in the same adoptive family whose birth mother had said "False" to them.

We carried out this same analysis with the other two rating dimensions, Socialization and Emotional stability. In both we found a larger

Table 3.28

MMPI Items Differentially Endorsed by the Birth Mothers of Two Adopted Children in a Family

---

Birth mother of more extraverted child
    (none)
Birth mother of more introverted child
    2 items: shy, lonely.
Birth mother of better socialized child
    9 items: shy, reacts emotionally, worries, lacks self-confidence, takes things hard.
Birth mother of less socialized child
    6 items: doesn't blame those who take advantage, sex life is satisfactory, few fears.
Birth mother of more emotionally stable child
    7 items: difficult relationships with family, feels intensely, would like to be a
        journalist, often lonely.
Birth mother of less emotionally stable child
    4 items: daily life interesting, sleeps well, few physical symptoms of anxiety.

Note: Items were endorsed at least 25% more often by the birth mother in question. Child comparisons based on parent ratings in original study.

number of differentiating items: 15 for socialization and 11 for stability. The items endorsed by the mother of the better-socialized child are a somewhat heterogeneous group, but several have to do with sensitivity and shyness (including the two introversion items from the preceding group). The items endorsed by the mother of the less socialized child, on the other hand, included several that tended to exonerate antisocial behavior, such as not blaming someone who takes advantage of others. Other items were suggestive of a low anxiety level—a satisfactory sex life and few fears.

Thus, for introversion and socialization at this closer level of scrutiny there seemed to be at least some level of continuity between mother and child, a continuity presumably transmitted by the genes (or prenatally) since the birth mother did not rear the child.

Emotional stability was different. The *less* emotionally stable child has a birth mother who seems to be on good terms with her environment. By contrast, the mother of the child who was rated as more emotionally stable has difficulties with her family and others, and feels things intensely. Consistent with the Table 3.27 results, we have a paradox here: The less well adjusted of the two birth mothers, the one with higher MMPI scores who endorses more items indicative of stress, has the child who is rated more emotionally stable.

We do not know for certain what this means. Maybe it is just a statistical fluke, although fifty-two families is not a negligible number. Maybe young women who are aware of the stresses in their worlds are "really," in some sense, better adjusted than those who are not. One possibility, the one we emphasized when originally presenting these results, is that we may be dealing with genotypes that are exceptionally sensitive to the environment in which they develop. In the benign, accepting atmosphere provided by the adoptive parents, they turn out just fine. In the presumably less benign atmosphere in which the birth mothers themselves grew up, they had problems. Technically, this is known as a "genotype-environment interaction," and there is currently a good deal of interest in such phenomena (e.g., Cadoret, et al., 1995; Caspi, et al., 2003; Price & Jaffee, 2008; Turkheimer, et al., 2003). We do, however, urge caution upon the reader. We have no direct evidence for difficult environments in the families of the birth mothers beyond those that may have been produced by their own behavior. (Recall that the birth mothers largely came from middle-class families.) Moreover, the interviews we did suggested less than perfect harmony in some of the adoptive families. Other research using other methods must confirm the robustness of the phenomenon and elucidate its causal structure. This may require relating particular genes to environments. Optimists may derive hope from the tremendous expansion in recent years of our ability to study the relationship of specific genes to behavioral trends.

6. Personality Change

Modeling Personality Change

In an earlier section of this chapter, we presented an analysis of the changing of parental ratings over three occasions of ratings for adopted and biological children (see Table 3.5). That analysis was based on the 125 children rated all three times. We had earlier carried out a model-fitting analysis of personality change based just on the original study and the ten-year follow-up. This analysis could be made using a larger group of 302 children, yielding sample sizes more satisfactory for model-fitting purposes. The details are reported in Loehlin, et al. (1990), but we can summarize the method and results here.

A path model was fit to the three parental ratings on the two occasions, a model with the following features: ratings on the first occasion were assumed to be a function of the age of the child, the child's actual status on the underlying trait, and a random error of measurement. Ratings on the second occasion reflected persistence of the trait from the first occasion, a change over the ten-year interval, and again a random measurement error. Both a linear and a nonlinear effect of age were allowed, as well as correlations among the three ratings. (Stability tended to be positively correlated with both Extraversion and Socialization; the latter to be essentially uncorrelated with each other.) The model was fit separately to the adopted and biological children and the differences between the two groups assessed.

Table 3.29 shows the correlations, means, and SDs to which the path model was fit. Data for the 229 adopted children are shown above the main diagonal and to the right, and data for the 83 biological children are below the diagonal and to the left. Correlations with a linear and a quadratic component of age at initial testing are included (Age1 and Age1^2) to allow for the fact that the children were initially tested at a range of ages and that the biological children were on average older by a couple of years.

The results of the model fitting were: (1) the age effects, the co-variation among the three traits, and the degree of persistence of the traits across time could be equated for the adopted and biological groups; (2) both linear and nonlinear effects of age on the traits were significant; (3) a significant degree of persistence over the ten-year interval was present for all three traits; (4) changes over time for Socialization and Emotional stability were significantly different for the adopted and biological chil-

Table 3.29
Means, SDs, and Correlations for 3 Rating Composites on 2 Occasions, for 229 Adopted Children (above Diagonal) and 83 Biological Children (below Diagonal)

	Ex1	So1	St1	Ex2	So2	St2	Age1	Age1^2	Mean	SD
Ex1	1.00	-.24	.36	.53	-.09	.04	-.28	-.27	6.43	1.38
So1	-.11	1.00	.26	-.14	.35	.18	.25	.21	5.52	1.08
St1	.44	.10	1.00	.19	.12	.33	-.09	-.06	5.64	1.18
Ex2	.44	-.16	.17	1.00	-.08	.31	-.16	-.14	5.86	1.45
So2	.06	.24	.00	.01	1.00	.38	.07	.06	5.27	1.37
St2	.27	.06	.35	.36	.34	1.00	-.04	-.01	5.42	1.29
Age1	-.05	.15	.09	.00	-.02	-.05	1.00	.97	7.40	2.96
Age1^2	-.07	.11	.10	.00	-.03	-.07	.98	1.00	63.30	52.74
Mean	5.95	5.40	5.62	5.73	5.65	5.78	9.50	108.60		
SD	1.36	.98	1.24	1.36	1.00	1.75	4.29	88.81		

Note: Ex = Extraversion; So = Socialization, St = Stability; 1,2 = 1st and 2nd occasion; Age1 = age at first testing; Age1^2 = square of Age1.

dren; (5) at the time of the first testing, the adopted children were rated as slightly—although not significantly—more extraverted, better behaved, and more emotionally stable; (6) by the time of the second testing, the adopted children had changed in the direction of poorer socialization and less emotional stability, substantiating the trends noted in Table 3.5.

This is not to say that the adopted children were rated unfavorably—the means in Table 3.29 still represent points above the midpoints of the scales. They had, however, moved from slightly more favorable ratings than the biological children at Time 1 to appreciably less favorable ratings at Time 2. Given that the birth mothers were on the whole more poorly adjusted than the adoptive parents (see Table 3.23), this might be considered a tendency of both sets of children to develop over time in the direction of their biological parents.

Life Events and Personality Change

At the time of the follow-up, we asked participants to fill out a "Life Events Questionnaire" in which they indicated what important things had happened to them in the interval since the original testing. In Table 3.30 we ask whether the occurrence of such events is related to personal-

Table 3.30
Correlation of Life Events with Personality Change

Life Event	Extraverted	Good	Stable
My family moved from one town to another.	.00	-.09	.03
My family moved from one house or apartment to another in the same town.	.00	-.04	.02
I had a serious illness.	.03	-.03	-.04
A parent was seriously ill.	-.02	-.05	-.04
A parent died.	-.08	-.06	-.03
A grandparent, aunt, or uncle who was close to me died.	.08	.04	.02
I went away from home to attend a school or college.	.04	-.07	.00
I won an individual award in an interscholastic or similar athletic, academic, or artistic competition.	-.03	.10	.07
I worked at a full-time job for a month or more.	.10	-.08	.09
I was elected to office.	.09	.13	.07
I was greatly influenced in my life by someone outside of my immediate family.	-.04	-.06	-.00
I joined a church.	.06	.05	.03
I fell in love (deeply, seriously).	.06	-.05	.03
Total negative events (first six)	.03	-.07	.00
Total positive events (last seven)	.08	.01	.08

Note: Personality change = changes from original study to 10-year follow-up in parent rating factors Extraversion, Good Socialization, Emotional Stability. $N = 309$.

ity changes, which we assessed by differences in the three parent rating factors between the two occasions of testing. The answer appears to be, "little, if at all." Only 1 of the 45 correlations is nominally statistically significant (the .13 between Good socialization and "I was elected to office") and, since this is fewer than the 5 percent expected by chance, it is probably prudent not to take the exception very seriously. Cumulating positive and negative events (bottom of the table) has no notable effect. None of this is to say that life events do not ever affect individuals' personality traits. It may just be that the participants varied so much in their response to particular events that consistent trends did not emerge.

4

Achievement, Adjustment, Outcomes

In this chapter we focus on long-term real-life outcomes for the children in the TAP families, as distinguished from the measurements of current abilities and personality that provided most of the data in Chapters 2 and 3. The distinction is not absolute—we do include some childhood data in this chapter, for example—but there is a difference in emphasis. The chapter begins with two broad topics, academic achievement and psychopathology/problem behavior, and concludes with sections addressing occupational outcomes, personal relationships, and happiness. Much of the evidence in this chapter comes from the outcomes questionnaire.

For the outcomes questionnaire, we will primarily rely on the combined score: the average of all those rating the given individual, including parents, siblings, and him- or herself. Typically, there was considerable agreement among these raters, as evidenced by interrater reliabilities in the range .51 to .97.

A factor analysis of the outcomes questionnaire suggested the presence of five underlying factors, which we labeled Maturity, Successful marriage, Externalizing problems, Closeness to parents, and Academic achievement. For some purposes in this chapter, we will make comparisons in terms of these summary factors, although we will more often deal directly with the individual questionnaire items.

Some, although not all, items on the outcomes questionnaire were also included on the rating sheet filled out by the interviewer following the parent interview. (Both questionnaires are included in Appendix B.) Table 4.1 compares the interviewer ratings with the outcome questionnaire

---

Note: This chapter is based in part on several earlier publications in specialized journals: Willerman, Horn, & Loehlin, 1977; Willerman, Loehlin, & Horn, 1992; Loehlin, Horn, & Ernst, 2007, 2009; these may be consulted for additional details.

Table 4.1
Degree of Agreement of Interviewer's Ratings with Combined
Rating on Outcomes Questionnaire

Interviewer's Rating	Outcome Questionnaire Rating	
	r	N
Highest level of education completed	.94	320
Level of responsibility of job	.49	297
Stability of occupational history	.62	288
Stable and happy marriage	.54	257
Problems of an externalizing type		
vs. drugs and alcohol	.55	317
vs. trouble with the law	.53	317
Problems of an internalizing type		
vs. anxiety and depression	.43	319
Sociability		
vs. many friends in high school	.55	302
vs. current friends and social activity	.42	298
Independent, self-reliant	.43	317
Mature, responsible, helpful		
vs. mature, helpful	.53	320
vs. conscientious, reliable	.60	320

Note: In cases where items from the outcomes questionnaire only roughly correspond with the interviewer item, the relevant outcomes items are indicated by "vs."

rating, for cases in which both were available for the same or comparable items. The first column shows the correlation between the two ratings, the second, the number of pairings on which the correlation is based. It is evident that the interviewer's impression following the interview agrees moderately well with the combined judgment of the parents, siblings, and self on the outcomes questionnaire that was filled out some five years later. This is not altogether surprising, since the parents' perceptions of their children's lives can affect both of these measures. Nevertheless, it provides some additional assurance of the meaningfulness of the outcome questionnaire results.

1. Academic Achievement

The TAP has several kinds of evidence related to academic achievement. First, there is information on the level of education achieved by the adoptive parents, some of the birth fathers, the birth mother and her parents, and the biological and adopted children themselves. Second, for the child generation we have self, sib, and parent ratings from the outcomes questionnaire concerning how good a student the individual was when in high school, as well as ratings on the same scale by the parents about themselves. Finally, for part of the sample we have scores on the Wide Range Achievement Test, a measure of academic achievement with subscales covering reading, spelling, and arithmetic.

Highest Level of Education Achieved

Table 4.2 presents data on the educational level achieved by the adoptive fathers and mothers, their biological and adopted offspring, and the birth mothers of the adopted children.

The data for the adoptive parents were from the time of the original study, that for the offspring are from the outcomes questionnaire, when most had completed their education, and that for the birth mothers from the adoption agency records. This last very likely underestimates the eventual educational achievement of this group, as many of them were in their teens when they became pregnant, and some of them presumably obtained further education after giving up their child for adoption. Indeed, one of the motivations of many of these girls and their families in giving up the child was to allow the girl to continue her education. Yet, even as it stands, the birth mothers were not a seriously backward group educationally—the majority were high school graduates, and 43 percent had had some post-high school education. We return to this point shortly.

Table 4.2
Highest Level of Education Reached by Individuals in the Texas Adoption Project

	Adoptive		Offspring		Birth
Educational Level	Father	Mother	Adopted	Biological	Mother
1. Less than HS grad	11	9	4	1	112
2. HS graduate	49	70	67	17	65
3 Some post-HS	51	86	99	41	124
4. College graduate	88	98	96	60	10
5. Some postgraduate	99	35	61	30	1
Total	298	298	327	149	312
Mean	3.72	3.27	3.44	3.68	2.11

Note: Entries are numbers of individuals for whom this is the highest level reached. HS = High school. The educational levels have been recoded from their original form to put them on comparable scales.

The adoptive parents were on the whole a well-educated group: the majority of the fathers were college graduates, and the majority of the mothers had had at least some post-high school education. Their children also achieved well educationally. The biological children went significantly beyond the adopted children, but even the latter approximated the average level of their adoptive parents.

How much did individuals in the child generation resemble their parents in the level of formal education attained? Did this differ for males and females or by biological or adoptive status? Table 4.3 provides some relevant information, in the form of correlations between children and parents. For the adult generation, the data are from the original study. For the child generation, they are the average of the judgments from the outcomes questionnaire—made by the individual, his or her parents, and any available siblings. As one might expect, these informants were, in general, in excellent agreement. Based on the correlations among their responses, the reliability of the overall average rating is estimated as .97.

We do not have a comparable set of judgments on the parents' educational level, but we do have self-reports from the outcomes questionnaire for a number of the parents. The correlation of these self-reports with the educational data from the original study is .89 for fathers ($N = 134$) and .77 for mothers ($N = 128$). Unlike the estimates for the child generation, these were obtained some thirty years apart, and a less than perfect

Table 4.3
Correlation of the Educational Attainment of the TAP Children with That of Their Biological and Adoptive Parents

Child Group	Correlations With				
	Adoptive Father	Adoptive Mother	Birth Mother	Birth Mother's Father	Birth Mother's Mother
Adopted					
sons	.16* (174)	.22* (174)	.16 (118)	.33* (102)	.32* (111)
daughters	.10 (148)	.13 (148)	.13 (89)	.12 (85)	.20 (84)
Biological					
sons	.40* (71)	.15 (71)	---	---	---
daughters	.24 (56)	.32* (56)	---	---	---

Note: Number of pairings in parentheses. *$p < .05$.

agreement can reflect real changes over time as well as error—changes represented by the completion of work toward a degree, say, or by the addition of some form of postgraduate training. In comparing correlations of children with their mothers and their fathers, it should be kept in mind that the educational attainments of the latter two are correlated, if for no other reason than the fact that spouses often first encounter each other in educational or occupational settings. In the TAP data, the correlation between spouses' educational attainment was .52, based on 298 pairs.

The correlations in Table 4.3 tell a somewhat mixed story. The correlations for the adoptive relationships are all positive, suggesting that non-genetic factors may be making at least some contribution to them—although the correlations are fairly low (in the range .10 to .22). The correlations representing the resemblance of the biological children in the adoptive families to their parents appear to be somewhat higher. Although the limited number of pairings suggests that caution in interpretation is called for, there is an interesting suggestion that the correlations may be higher in the same-sex relationships (fathers with sons and mothers with daughters) than in the cross-sex relationships, complicating interpretation, but perhaps suggesting social factors. The simplest gene-based hypotheses, in which educational resemblance would reflect parents passing along to their offspring genes contributing to intellectual skills or conscientious performance, would predict that the four biological correlations would be equal, and higher than the adoptive ones. Such a hypothesis would also predict the existence of correlations of the adopted children with their birth mothers. These correlations in the table are also positive but low. One limitation on them, as we have noted, is the fact that a number of the birth mothers would not have completed their education when they became pregnant. We attempted to assess such an effect by obtaining the correlation between the adopted child's educational level and that of the birth mother's parents, also available in the adoption agency's files. The assumption was that this might provide a better indication of her ultimate academic achievement than the level she had achieved at the time she became pregnant. These correlations, shown in the right-hand columns of the table, were indeed slightly higher than those with the birth mother herself. Because they are across two generations rather than one, they would not be expected to be as large as the correlations in the last two rows of the table—however, they do not fall far short. There is a different asymmetry here—sons higher than daughters—again suggesting the advisability of some caution in interpretation.

Parental Education Related to Child Measures

How, if at all, are parents' and children's educational levels related to the sorts of personality and ability variables we have discussed in the preceding two chapters? We would not be surprised to find some relationship with IQ, but what about personality? Table 4.4 gives correlations between father's and mother's educational levels and their child's ratings on the three personality dimensions—for children rated more than once, the average was used.

The straightforward answer is that these correlations are all negligible—none departs significantly from zero for any group of children. At least within the limited range of this sample, having a more educated parent appears to have no systematic effect on one's personality.

Is this true for intelligence as well? Table 4.5 provides the answer and, in this case, it is a different one. With one trivial exception, all the correlations in the table are positive, and the majority are statistically significant.

For the girls, the correlations for the biological relationships tend to be higher, suggesting the effects of genes, but this is not the case for the boys, for which the correlations for the adoptees are as high or higher. In any case, unlike with personality traits, there are significant associations between parental educational level and children's IQs. This association may in part reflect environmental factors, since it holds for both adopted and biological children. Note that these correlations are based on the earlier measure of IQ, for which environmental factors appeared to be relatively more important (Chapter 2).

Table 4.4
**Correlations of Adoptive Parent Educational Levels with
Child Personality Ratings**

Child	Adoptive Fathers Educ.			Adoptive Mothers Educ.			Pairs
	Extr.	Good	Stable	Extr.	Good	Stable	
Males							
Adopted	-.02	-.06	-.00	-.09	.04	-.04	256
Biological	-.03	.08	.09	.03	-.02	.01	86
Females							
Adopted	-.02	-.01	.07	.06	-.05	.08	220-221
Biological	.16	-.13	.04	.00	-.10	.01	75-76

Note: Educ. = highest educational level attained. Extr. = Extraversion, Good = Good socialization, Stable = Emotional stability. Average ratings, if rated more than once.

Table 4.5
Correlations of Adoptive Parent Educational Levels with Child IQ

| Child | Adoptive Fathers Educ. | | | Adoptive Mothers Educ. | | | |
	VIQ	PIQ	IQ	VIQ	PIQ	IQ	Pairs
Males							
Adopted	.21*	.18*	.27*	.15*	.09	.17*	221-251
Biological	.20	-.00	.14	.09	.13	.17	74-84
Females							
Adopted	.12	.16*	.18*	.07	.11	.12	183-212
Biological	.31*	.34*	.40*	.32*	.28*	.40*	66-73

Note: Educ. = highest educational level attained; VIQ, PIQ = verbal, performance IQ from WAIS or WISC (1st N); IQ = IQ from WAIS, WISC, or Stanford-Binet (2nd N). *$p < .05$.

What about the relationship of the child's IQ and personality traits to his or her own educational attainment? Table 4.6 provides this information. The combined judgment of educational attainment by self, parents, and siblings on the outcomes questionnaire is correlated with average personality ratings and IQs.

Children's eventual educational attainment is related to their parents' judgment of them as well socialized and emotionally stable and less, if at all, to extraversion/introversion. If anything, the relationships are stronger for adopted than biological children, particularly in the case of females. A child's higher IQ is a predictor of more education, and verbal IQ is a better predictor than performance IQ, although the latter shows some association in the case of male adoptees. Finally, none of these

Table 4.6
Correlations of Child's Own Educational Attainment with Personality and IQ

Child	Extr.	Good	Stable	VIQ	PIQ	IQ	Pairs
Males							
Adopted	-.02	.29*	.20*	.29*	.29*	.30*	154-173
Biological	.12	.24*	.09	.32*	-.01	.26*	56-71
Females							
Adopted	.15	.31*	.21*	.32*	.13	.28*	121-148
Biological	-.00	.08	.16	.36*	-.04	.22	44-57

Note: Educational attainment from outcomes questionnaire. Extr. = Extraversion; Good = Good socialization; Stable = Emotional stability; average ratings, if rated more than once. VIQ, PIQ = verbal, performance IQ from WAIS or WISC; IQ = IQ from WAIS, WISC, or Stanford-Binet. *$p < .05$.

correlations is very high—the eventual level of education that a child achieves is affected by many external circumstances in addition to the child's personality and ability; limitations in measurement presumably play a role as well.

Outcomes Questionnaire—Good Student

One of the outcomes questionnaire items asks the rater to indicate, on a 9-point scale, how good a student the rated individual was in junior high and high school. The agreement among the raters on this point was good, although not quite as good as that on highest level of education achieved—the estimated reliability for the good student rating was .86.

Tables 4.7 and 4.8 give correlations of the overall good student rating with several other variables, for males and females and for adopted and biological offspring. The other variables are Conscientiousness (also an averaged rating from the outcomes questionnaire), IQ measures from the original and follow-up studies, family socioeconomic status, and age. (Age was at the time of the first study, but age differences would be approximately maintained through the subsequent measurements.)

Table 4.7 shows the correlations for males above the diagonal and for females below. The correlations for males and females show a generally similar pattern; the rating of good student is positively related to ratings of conscientiousness and to scores on the two IQ tests and is essentially unrelated to family socioeconomic status within this sample. There is a minor correlation (of about .15) with age, but this is somewhat ambiguous in interpretation—the older participants were at the time of rating further removed from their high school days and the possibility exists that this correlation may simply reflect more inflation in the memory of how good a student they were. It is, of course, plausible that being a good student should in fact be associated both with conscientiousness and with cognitive ability as measured by IQ tests.

A rough test of the equivalence of the male and female correlation matrices was undertaken by fitting a common matrix to both. The test was approximate, because the procedure used assumes that all the correlations in each matrix are based on the same cases, and these are not exactly the same (although most are in common). We used for N in the fitting program (LISREL) the average of the sample sizes. The χ^2 test also makes various assumptions about normal distributions and the like, which the real scores often do not meet very well. Thus, the probabilities given should be taken as only approximate. However, even approximately,

Table 4.7
Average Ratings as Good Student Correlated with Several Other Measures
(Males above, Females below Diagonal)

Score	Gd stu	Consc	IQ1	IQ2	SES	Age
Good student	1.00	.51	.28	.41	-.01	.16
Conscientious	.33	1.00	.11	.08	.03	.08
IQ, original study	.31	-.01	1.00	.69	.25	.10
IQ, follow-up	.39	-.09	.64	1.00	.13	.00
Socioeconomic status	-.02	.04	.27	.09	1.00	.06
Age	.15	-.04	.09	-.01	.08	1.00

Note: Fit of common model to male and female offspring: $\chi^2 = 12.15$, 15 *df*, *p* > .50. *N*s, males = 162-337, mean 238; females = 140-289, mean 201. Labels at top same as measures listed at the left.

it is clear that the differences between the correlations for males and females could easily be explained by chance: a χ^2 statistic smaller than its degrees of freedom represents an excellent fit of a common model to the two sets of correlations.

Table 4.8 provides the same correlations among adopted and biological offspring, for males and females combined. There is general similarity between the two sets of correlations—in particular, being a good student was again correlated with conscientiousness and IQ in both groups. However, the overall difference between the two matrices was statistically significant (*p* < .01). Four correlations had different signs for the adoptive and biological offspring: conscientiousness ratings and IQ at both testings were positively correlated for adopted children and negatively for biological children and, likewise, conscientiousness and age. The op-

Table 4.8
Average Ratings as Good Student Correlated with Several Other Measures
(Adopted above, Biological below Diagonal)

Score	Gd stu	Consc	IQ1	IQ2	SES	Age
Good student	1.00	.48	.27	.39	-.05	.14
Conscientious	.27	1.00	.14	.04	.03	.07
IQ, original study	.37	-.26	1.00	.66	.23	.11
IQ, follow-up	.39	-.13	.70	1.00	.10	-.09
Socioeconomic status	.06	.04	.34	.16	1.00	.09
Age	.08	-.18	.11	.14	.05	1.00

Note: Fit of common model to male and female offspring: $\chi^2 = 47.76$, 15 *df*, p < .01. *N*s, adopted = 213-467, mean 321; biological = 89-159, mean 118. Labels at the top same as measures listed at the left.

posite was the case for the correlation between age and IQ at the second testing. A model that allowed just the IQ-conscientiousness correlations to differ between the groups fit the data acceptably ($\chi^2 = 15.38$, 13 df, $p > .10$). Given that the statistical tests involved are only approximate, one might not want to take these differences overly seriously, but, on the face of it, the suggestion is that for the biological children those of lower IQ tended to compensate with increased conscientiousness but for the adopted children this was not the case.

Is being a good student in high school related to one's parents' highest level of academic achievement or to one's own? Is this different for males and females, or for adopted and biological offspring? Table 4.9 provides some evidence. None of the correlations in the first two rows of the table differs significantly from zero. All of the correlations in the third row do. This indicates that an individual's reputation as a good student in high school is (within this middle-class sample) essentially unrelated to the level of formal education achieved by his or her parents but is a predictor of how much education the individual will obtain. This is true for both males and females, and for adopted and biological offspring.

Table 4.9
Correlations between Rating as a Good Student in Junior High and High School and Highest Level of Education Achieved

Group	Males	Females	Adopted	Biological
Father's education	.00	-.02	-.05	.13
Mother's education	-.03	-.08	-.03	-.11
Own education	.47*	.46*	.47*	.42*
N	244-252	204-213	322-324	126-141

*Note: *$p < .05$

The Wide Range Achievement Test

In thinking about the relationship between intelligence and academic achievement, we realized after we had begun the study that it would be useful to have an explicit measure of academic competence to compare with the IQ test scores. So we added an achievement test to our battery, the Wide Range Achievement Test (WRAT), which measures performance in three traditional academic areas: reading, spelling, and arithmetic. Thus, for a subsample of the TAP children, we have scores on these three measures in addition to a traditional, individually administered IQ test. Are these related? Table 4.10 gives the answer.

Table 4.10
Correlations between Wechsler IQs and WRAT Subscale Scores

Scale	VIQ	PIQ	Reading	Spelling	Arithmetic
Wechsler Verbal IQ	1.00	.59	.69	.66	.59
Wechsler Performance IQ		1.00	.46	.50	.51
WRAT Reading			1.00	.75	.50
WRAT Spelling				1.00	.63
WRAT Arithmetic					1.00

Note: N = 156

Clearly, all the intercorrelations in Table 4.10 are positive and substantial, and it is not obvious that the correlations between the IQ and WRAT subscales are notably less than the correlations within each instrument. We tested this statistically by model fitting. We compared a model having a single latent variable with paths to all five tests to a model with two correlated latent variables, one with paths to the two IQ scales, and the other with paths to the three WRAT scales. The latter model fit significantly better than the former (with a difference in χ^2 of 7.12 for 1 *df*, $p < .01$), although neither fit particularly well. Allowing a (small negative) correlation for specific factors between the WRAT scales of Reading and Arithmetic produced an acceptable fit for the two-latent-variable model. Thus, IQ and general academic performance appeared to be distinct, but they were closely related—the estimated correlation between the two latent variables in the final model was .88.

Can we draw any conclusions about heredity and environment from these data? Because in the present subsample there was further depletion of the already-small number of biological sibling pairs, we had little confidence in correlations among these. However, in seventy-one families with at least two unrelated siblings, we compared the resemblance of genetically unrelated siblings on IQ and the WRAT scales as an index of environmental effects. Table 4.11 shows these correlations.

There is nothing here to suggest that performance on these academically oriented scales is influenced by shared family environments to a greater degree than is performance on a standard IQ test. Indeed, for the Reading and Arithmetic subscales there appears to be little if any correlation between siblings who do not share genes.

Table 4.11
Correlation of Genetically Unrelated Siblings on IQ and WRAT Scales

Scale		Correlation
WRAT		
	Reading	.04
	Spelling	.24
	Arithmetic	.09
IQ		
	WAIS/WISC	.29

Note: Intraclass correlations based on 156 children in 71 families.

2. Psychopathology and Problem Behavior

In the preceding sections of this chapter we have looked at educational achievement. The second major group of studies we describe is addressed to issues of psychopathology and problem behavior, as they occur in the families of the TAP. In Chapter 3, we emphasized normal personality variation. Here we focus on behavioral disturbance. This disturbance is usually not in the form of major psychoses like schizophrenia—expected to be rare in this as in most non-institutionalized populations—but in the more minor deviations from socially-approved behavior that bring concern to parents, spouses, teachers, ministers, and other upholders of social norms.

MMPI Pd

As noted earlier, the Minnesota Multiphasic Personality Inventory, the MMPI, had been administered in the home for unwed mothers to many of the birth mothers of the adopted children. It was also administered in the TAP to the parents in the adoptive families at the time of the original study and to the children in these families at the time of the ten-year follow-up.

The Psychopathic deviate (*Pd*) scale, it will be recalled, is a measure of the extent to which an individual's behavior betrays a lack of concern for social norms and a lack of sensitivity to the feelings of others. Scores on this scale were substantially elevated among the birth mothers as a group. Their mean *T*-score was 66. *T*-scores are based on a normative mean of 50 and SD of 10, so this represents a considerable elevation, and implies the presence of many mothers with scores even higher.

Two analyses were undertaken using this scale: one contrasting adopted children who scored exceptionally high or low on *Pd*, and one comparing the children of adoptive and birth mothers who had above- or below-average *Pd* scores for their group.

The first analysis compared a group of high-*Pd* adoptees (*N*=21, mean *Pd* = 75) with a group of relatively low-*Pd* adoptees (*N*=51, mean *Pd* = 49). The high-*Pd* adoptees also tended to score higher than the low-*Pd* group on the other MMPI scales—although not as much higher as on *Pd*. The high- and low-*Pd* groups did not differ notably in IQ; there were non-significant average differences in favor of the low-*Pd* group of 1.2 IQ points at original testing and 3 IQ points at follow-up. In terms of personality traits, on the 16PF the high *Pd* group scored as significantly more dominant (E), suspicious (L), and non-conforming (Q_1), and less conscientious (G), and controlled (Q_3).

The birth mothers and the adoptive parents of the two groups were also compared. The birth mothers of the high-*Pd* group were significantly higher on six of the eight MMPI clinical scales, and exceptionally so on *Pd*. Nearly half (48 percent) of the birth mothers of the high-*Pd* adoptees themselves had *Pd* scores in the 70+ range, as opposed to only about 20 percent of the mothers of adoptees from the low-*Pd* group. As to the adoptive parents, the adoptive fathers of the high and low groups did not differ significantly in mean *Pd*, but the adoptive mothers of the high-*Pd* group were moderately but significantly elevated on this scale. It seems unlikely that this was an effect rather than a cause of their children's difficult behavior, as the mothers' MMPIs were obtained at the time of the original study, when the adopted children were young and still receiving relatively favorable parental ratings (see Chapter 3). Imitation might be a factor, but if so, why not the fathers? Another possibility, which we are inclined to favor, is that higher-*Pd* adoptive mothers were less likely to act promptly to control their children's tendencies toward misbehavior.

The second approach we took was to divide each set of mothers, birth and adoptive, into relatively higher- and lower-scoring groups on *Pd*, and compare the *Pd* scores of the four resulting combinations: those children with both adoptive and birth mothers high, those with both low, and two groups with one each—one with the birth mother high and the adoptive mother low, and one the other way around. The division into higher- and lower-scoring mothers was done separately in the two groups: "higher" means above average for their group. In absolute terms, the birth mothers had considerably higher *Pd* scores than the adoptive mothers.

Table 4.12

MMPI *Pd* Scores of Adopted Children having Lower- and Higher-*Pd* Birth and Adoptive Mothers

	Adoptive Mother				
Birth Mother	Lower *Pd*		Higher *Pd*		Combined
Higher *Pd*	18.71	(34)	20.33	(30)	19.42	(64)
Lower *Pd*	16.95	(38)	18.17	(36)	17.54	(74)
Combined	17.78	(72)	19.11	(66)	18.41	(138)

Note: Means are for raw *Pd* scores, not *T*-scores, *N*s in parentheses. *SD*s range from 3.85 to 5.14 in the various subgroups.

Table 4.12 provides the results. Having either a higher-*Pd* birth mother or a higher-*Pd* adoptive mother makes a difference: the children of the low-low groups have the lowest mean, 16.95; those of the high-high groups have the highest, 20.23; and the other two are intermediate, 18.71 and 18.17. The average difference of 1.88 points between children of the higher- and lower-*Pd* birth mothers is statistically significant ($p = .02$); the corresponding difference of 1.33 points for the adoptive mothers is marginal ($p = .09$); there is no evidence of an interaction—the effect of having a higher- or lower-*Pd* birth mother is about the same for the children of both groups of adoptive mothers, and similarly for the effect of having a high or low adoptive mother.

Thus, both kinds of analysis indicate that the *Pd* scores of adopted children are more predictable from the *Pd* scores of their birth mothers, who provided genes and prenatal environments, than from the *Pd* scores of the adoptive mothers, who reared the children after birth. There was, however, some degree of association in the latter case (although not with the *Pd*s of the adoptive fathers). As to the children, those selected on the basis of high or low *Pd* scores tended to differ on a range of personality characteristics, but not significantly for IQ. Finally, the effects of the *Pd*s of birth mothers and adoptive mothers were essentially independent. Other adoption studies have had mixed results on this last point. Some have found interactions in the sense of an elevation of antisocial behavior only in the equivalent of our high-high group. Others have found genetic and environmental influences to make relatively independent contributions.

Index of Problem Behaviors from Parent Interviews

As indicated earlier, one phase of the adoption project was a series of interviews with the adoptive parents that took place between 1997 and

2001, when the children in these families were adults, mostly in their thirties. One or both parents in 167 of the original 300 families were personally interviewed (representing about 56 percent of the families). The interviews were carried out in their homes and focused on the life experiences of each of the children in the family. The interview was informal, but the interviewer had a series of probes to insure that various topics were covered.

Based on the notes from the interviews, an Index of Problem Behaviors was developed (IPB; Ernst, 2006). The items scored at each of three ages—childhood, adolescence, adulthood—are listed in Table 4.13. Three independent raters coded the interviews. The coding varied somewhat with the nature of the item, but most typically was on a four-point scale (0 = no indication, 1 = rarely or never, 2 = sometimes, 3 = a lot of the time). Inter-rater reliability estimates for the initial ratings averaged .75 across items for childhood, .82 for adolescence, and .82 for adulthood. Discrepancies were reviewed by the three raters and a consensus rating was arrived at. In the few instances in which a consensus was not reached, the median of the three ratings was used.

In addition to the IPB scores, recall that subsequent to the interview the interviewer filled out a rating sheet for each child, summarizing impressions from the interview. Two of the items referred to problem behaviors: of an externalizing kind (e.g., antisocial behavior, substance abuse), and of an internalizing kind (e.g., anxiety, depression). Table 4.14 shows the relationship of these ratings to the IPBs scored from the interviews.

Evidently, the interviewer's rating of externalizing problems agrees well with the Index of Problem Behavior, especially for adolescence and adulthood. It is also evident that the IPB, although increasingly related to internalizing problems with age, reflects these less than it does externalizing problems.

We were interested in relating the IPB scores of the adopted children to their birth and adoptive mothers' evidence of psychological problems, both general and specific. Two measures based on the MMPI were obtained for each birth and adoptive mother. The first, intended as a broad measure of psychopathology, consisted of the number of scales on which the individual obtained a T-score of 70 or higher. The second, intended as a specific measure, was her MMPI *Pd* score. Table 4.15 gives means and SDs of IPB scores for male and female adoptees in childhood, adolescence, and adulthood.

In adolescence and adulthood, the adopted offspring showed significantly higher means than the biological offspring. The difference was in

Table 4.13
Items Scored for the Index of Problem Behaviors at Three Ages

Childhood	Adolescence	Adulthood
Poor student	Poor student	Physical aggression
Truant	Truant	Verbal aggression
Rule violating	Rule violating	Manipulative
Physically aggressive	Physically aggressive	Tells lies
Tantrums	Verbally aggressive	Destruction of property
Manipulative	Manipulative	Alcohol use
Lied	Lied	Drug use
Bullied others	Snuck out	Gambling
Petty theft	Destruction of property	Theft (major)
Cruelty to children	Alcohol use	Sex assault (perpetrator)
Cruelty to animals	Drug use	Promiscuous
Inappropriate sex behavior	Theft (major)	Arson
Ran away	Sex assault (perpetrator)	Self-mutilation
Diagnosed with disorder	Promiscuous	Child abandonment
	Arson	Child abuse
	Self-mutilation	Adultery
	# at fault car accidents	Check/credit fraud
	# arrests	# divorces
	# convictions	# illegitimate pregnancies
	# tickets/warrants	# at fault car accidents
	# illegitimate pregnancy	# arrests
	# ran away	# convictions
	# suicide attempts	# tickets/warrants
	Diagnosed with disorder	# suicide attempts
		Diagnosed with disorder

Table 4.14
Correlations of IPBs with Interviewer's Ratings

| Interviewer Rating | Index of Problem Behavior | | |
	Childhood	Adolescence	Adulthood
Externalizing problems	.35	.70	.70
Internalizing problems	.07	.20	.39

Note: Ns 359 and 358 for externalizing and internalizing in both childhood and adolescence, 354 in adulthood.

Table 4.15
Index of Problem Behavior Averages for Male and Female Adoptees at Three Ages, Based on Parent Interviews

Age	Adopted				Biological			
	Male		Female		Male		Female	
Childhood	2.64	(2.40)	2.34	(2.85)	2.17	(2.04)	1.89	(2.28)
Adolescence	5.98	(5.52)	6.50	(6.61)	3.57	(3.26)	3.21	(3.11)
Adult	2.37	(3.92)	2.91	(5.41)	1.00	(2.58)	1.07	(2.30)

Note: Means, with standard deviations in parentheses. Raw score scales not directly comparable across ages because of different items and scoring. *N*s: adopted males 134-137, females 118-119; biological males 53-54, females 56-57.

the same direction in childhood, but not statistically significant. Interestingly, among the TAP adoptees after childhood, the usually reported sex difference in problem behaviors in favor of males was not present. In fact, the females tended to show more problem behaviors in adolescence and adulthood than the males, although the differences were not statistically significant. The biological children did differ (not significantly) in the expected direction (males higher) in childhood and adolescence, but showed no sex difference as adults.

As suggested by the large standard deviations relative to the means, the IPB scores tend to be substantially skewed, so the results of these statistical tests should be regarded as at best approximate. (Some analyses based on dichotomizing the IPB variables are described later in the chapter.)

Table 4.16 shows correlations between the IPB and parent rating factors and IQ in childhood and adolescence. These are calculated over all children, both biological and adopted.

Table 4.16
Correlations of Index of Problem Behavior with IQ and Parental Rating Factors at Childhood and Adolescence

Measure	IPB Childhood		IPB Adolescence	
	Boys	Girls	Boys	Girls
Extraversion	.15	-.00	.03	-.04
Good socialization	-.26*	-.27*	-.18	-.49*
Emotional stability	-.15	-.16	-.24*	-.26*
IQ	-.40*	.04	-.29*	-.04

Note: Childhood = ages 4-12; adolescence = ages 13-19. *N*s: childhood, boys 143-147, girls 122-131; adolescence, boys 80-81, girls 80. *p < .05.

The IPB scores are essentially uncorrelated with Extraversion, but tend to be correlated in the expected negative direction with Good socialization and Emotional stability—the former, more so in adolescence for the girls than for the boys. Unexpected was the relatively large correlation with IQ and the fact that it was present only for the boys. (Some sex difference would not have surprised us, but so dramatic a difference did.)

Table 4.17 presents the correlations of the adoptees' IPB scores with the adjustment of their birth and adoptive mothers, for males and females and for the general and the specific index.

The most striking feature of the correlations in Table 4.17 is that they are only substantial for the males. Despite the failure to find IPB differences between the male and female adoptees (Table 4.15), only the males are significantly related to the MMPI indexes of their mothers. None of the twelve correlations on the right hand side of Table 4.17 is significantly different from zero, nor are those for either sex in childhood. But in adulthood, the males' IPBs are significantly correlated with their birth mothers' scores on both the broad and the specific measure of maladjustment, and with the adoptive mother for the broad measure in both adolescence and adulthood.

Again, we had not expected a sex difference of this kind, particularly in the absence of a sex difference in the IPB scores of the males and females. Could the sex difference in correlation of the IPB with IQ have anything to do with it? Table 4.18 gives the same set of correlations as Table 4.17, after statistically removing the effect of child's IQ (and just

Table 4.17
Correlations of Adoptees' Index of Problem Behavior at Different Ages with the Adjustment of Birth and Adoptive Mothers

	Males				Females			
	PI		Pd		PI		Pd	
Age	BM	AM	BM	AM	BM	AM	BM	AM
Childhood	.03	.15	.13	.02	-.09	-.13	.02	.05
Adolescence	.04	.19*	.18	-.03	.05	-.09	.12	.12
Adulthood	.22*	.23*	.40*	.04	.04	-.10	.08	.03

Note: PI = Psychosocial maladjustment Index = number of MMPI clinical scales ≥ 70; Pd = MMPI Psychopathic deviate scale; BM = birth mother; AM = adoptive mother. Ns: males 99-100 with birth mothers, 131-134 with adoptive mothers; females 82-83 with birth mothers, 114-115 with adoptive mothers. *p < .05.

Table 4.18
Correlations from Table 4.17 after Controlling Statistically for Child's IQ,
Adoptive and Birth Mothers' Beta IQs, and Adoptive Family SES

	Males				Females			
	PI		*Pd*		PI		*Pd*	
Age	BM	AM	BM	AM	BM	AM	BM	AM
Childhood	.02	.11	.09	.02	-.12	-.10	-.01	.02
Adolescence	.11	.34*	.22*	.06	.10	-.10	.14	.08
Adulthood	.26*	.35*	.38*	.20	.04	-.05	.11	.05

Note: PI = Psychosocial maladjustment Index = number of MMPI clinical scales ≥ 70; *Pd* = MMPI Psychopathic deviate scale; BM = birth mother; AM = adoptive mother. *N*s: males 79, females 66. *$p < .05$.

to be on the safe side, the effects of birth and adoptive mothers' Beta IQs and the adoptive families' socioeconomic status as well).

Although the *N*s are smaller here, because cases missing data on any of the variables are excluded, the pattern of correlations remains the same. One minor change is that the correlation with BM *Pd* for the boys at adolescence, which was borderline, is now statistically significant. On the whole, the difference between the males and females remains at least as clear after controlling for IQ and SES as it had been before.

We do not know why this sex difference is present. Perhaps it is a statistical fluke—an occasional error of this kind can be expected in a study involving as many comparisons as this one. Perhaps it is a function of a few extreme cases. As a check on the latter, we re-ran the analyses involving the IPB, dichotomizing the scales at the three ages into lower and higher scorers, as equally as the data permitted. For the adoptees in Table 4.15, the difference in childhood became statistically significant in favor of the males, but the sex differences in adolescence and adulthood remained nonsignificant. Among the correlations in the tables, there were a number of cases in which a significant correlation became nonsignificant, or vice versa, but in no case did this involve a change in sign. All of the nonsignificant correlations involving the females in Tables 4.17 and 4.18 remained so. The correlations in Table 4.16 with IQ remained significant for the boys but not for the girls. Thus, it seems unlikely that the results reported in this section were solely a function of freakish distributions. Another possibility we considered is that the scales might be biased toward males, and under-represent problem behaviors that tend to be more common in females, such as malicious gossip and eating disorders. However, this would suggest that a measure better representing such problems would have had the females scoring even higher than the males, and it would still not explain why they were not correlated with their birth mothers.

We leave this topic with the usual dictum that more research is needed, but we hope these results have at least raised questions for later investigations to address.

Drugs, Alcohol, Trouble with the Law

The outcomes questionnaire contained two items, each to be responded to by circling a number from 1 to 9:

no drug or alcohol problems 1 2 3 4 5 6 7 8 9 serious drug or alcohol problems

never in trouble with the law 1 2 3 4 5 6 7 8 9 often in trouble with the law

It will be recalled that this questionnaire was filled out by TAP children, now adults, to describe themselves, and by their parents and siblings, to describe the TAP children. The interrater reliabilities of these two items were each estimated as .86. Table 4.19 provides correlations between self-ratings on the two items and ratings by others.

Table 4.19 shows substantial agreement between self-ratings of adult problem behavior, the ratings by parents and siblings, and conclusions based on the parent interviews. The samples involved overlap, but are not identical.

The parent interview data include the adult Index of Problem Behavior coded from the interview notes and an overall rating of externalizing

Table 4.19
Correlations between Self and Others' Ratings on Problem Behaviors

	Self-Ratings	
Others' Evaluation	Drugs and Alcohol	Trouble with the Law
Parents/sibs on questionnaire		
Drugs and alcohol	.70* (275)	.60* (274)
Trouble with the law	.64* (275)	.64* (274)
Interviews		
Interviewer: Externalizing	.49* (249)	.47* (248)
Adult IPB	.51* (248)	.53* (247)

Note: Ns in parentheses. IPB= Index of Problem Behavior *p < .05

behavior across all ages made independently by the interviewer, both as described in the preceding section. The correlations for the specific items from the outcomes questionnaire—drugs and alcohol and trouble with the law—are somewhat higher than those for the more general items based on the interview, but it is apparent that the two items are highly correlated, in that the correlation of self-rating on one item and parent/sib rating on the other is nearly as high as those involving the same item. Thus, the correlations in the table provide evidence of the reliability and cross-rater consistency of the ratings of adult behavioral problems for this population. We obtained a composite score for each individual, which was the mean rating received on the item, including self-rating. The composite scores on the two items were correlated .82, and in a factor analysis of the rating scales defined a single factor, which we called Externalizing behavior, and for which we assigned a score consisting of the mean for the two items.

Table 4.20 gives the means and standard deviations on the composite Externalizing factor for offspring, classified by sex and adoptive status.

On average, the adoptees are higher than the biological offspring on this factor, and the males higher than the females—note that the last result differs from the adult IPB, for which the sexes did not differ. The average difference between the sexes is statistically significant ($p = .04$, by Analysis of Variance)—that between adopted and biological offspring falls short of being statistically compelling ($p = .13$). There is no notable tendency for the sex difference to be different between the two groups ($p = .52$, for the interaction between sex and adoptive status).

Table 4.21 shows the correlations of the child generation's Externalizing factor with *Pd* scores from the parental MMPIs, obtained some thirty years earlier—in the case of some of the birth mothers, forty or more. As you can see, in each column the offspring's Externalizing scores are significantly correlated with the *Pd* scores of the mother who gave

Table 4.20
Means and SDs on the Externalizing Factor in Four Offspring Groups

Group	Male		Female		Combined	
Adopted	4.22	(3.78)	3.33	(2.87)	3.81	(3.42)
Biological	3.51	(2.86)	3.05	(2.66)	3.30	(2.77)
Combined	4.00	(3.54)	3.25	(2.80)		

Note: Standard deviations in parentheses. *N*s: Adopted males 174, females 149; biological males 76, females 64.

Table 4.21
Correlations of Externalizing Factor with Parent MMPI *Pd*

Parent	Adopted Offspring		Biological Offspring	
Adoptive mother	.08	(308)	.19*	(122)
Adoptive father	-.02	(311)	-.01	(122)
Birth mother	.21*	(235)	—	

Note: *N*s in parentheses *p* < .05.

birth to them. However, there are no correlations with fathers, on either an adoptive or a biological basis.

Criminal Records

Most of the indices of problem behavior that we have discussed are based on self-ratings or the ratings of family members. Moreover, there are an appreciable number of individuals from the initial study for whom we have no outcome ratings at all. How do our various kinds of evidence of problem behavior stack up against an objective measure of such behavior, criminal convictions? As a check on the validity of our various indicators of problem behavior, we searched the website of the Texas Department of Corrections for evidence of criminal records. In Texas, these are public records, accessible to anyone for a nominal fee. They are limited to Texas, and thus would not cover offspring resident in other states, but the majority of the children in the study still are Texas residents. The records are limited to Class B misdemeanors and above, and so do not include minor traffic citations, parking violations, and the like. They are records based on adult offences only—they do not include possible arrests as juveniles.

In the interest of privacy, we did not record the details of offenses, but merely coded each individual into one of the following categories:

0 = no criminal record
1 = one misdemeanor
2 = two or more misdemeanors
3 = one non-violent felony
4 = two or more non-violent felonies
5 = violent crime

Table 4.22 shows the number of records found in each category.

Table 4.22
Frequencies in Criminal Record Categories

| Category | Males | | Females | |
	Adopted	Biological	Adopted	Biological
0	201	90	214	92
1	26	11	8	2
2	17	3	2	1
3	6	1	6	1`
4	4	1	0	0
5	4	1	0	0
Total	258	107	230	96
% above 0	22%	16%	7%	4%

It is evident that "no criminal record" was the finding for the great majority of the TAP offspring, and we are confident that most have simply been law-abiding citizens, at least as adults. However, this count likely underestimates the true rate of criminal convictions. For example, we know of two adopted children (one male and one female) with multiple offences who are missing from this tally because they are deceased. And another male adoptee is missing a felony conviction only because a parent struck a deal with a victim. (There were no similar discoveries from the interviews involving biological children.) As the data stand, the sex difference between the proportions with and without criminal records is statistically significant—the males have more. The adoptees of both sexes show a greater proportion with criminal records than the biological offspring, but the differences fall short of statistical significance—they are at a level where we cannot confidently reject the possibility that they might just be due to chance in sampling.

Table 4.23 shows some correlations of results from the criminal records search with other measures of problem behavior from the TAP: the self-rating of trouble with the law, the externalizing factor from the outcomes questionnaire, IPBs for adolescence and adulthood, and MMPI scores from the ten-year follow-up. Also shown are some measures of good behavior: the parent rating composites for Good socialization from childhood and adolescence and the Psychological maturity factor from the outcomes questionnaire.

Despite the fact that the criminal record data are limited to Texas—i.e., some in the zero category may be persons who have convictions else-

Table 4.23
Correlations of Criminal Record and TAP Measures of Problem Behavior

Measure	Male		Female	
	Adoptive	Biological	Adoptive	Biological
Self: trouble with law	.67*	.61*	.51*	.89*
Externalizing factor	.62*	.43*	.37*	.44*
Interview IPB—adult	.57*	.14	.26*	.12
Interview IPB—adolescent	.21*	.06	.30*	.60*
Interviewer—externalizing	.49*	.18	.36*	.13
MMPI *Pd*	.36*	.20	.15	-.08
Good socialization—child	-.11	-.21	-.05	.21
Good socialization—adolescent	-.25*	-.13	-.15	.39*
Maturity factor	-.43*	-.17	-.26*	.10

Note: IPB = Index of Problem Behavior coded from parent interview. Ns: Adoptive males 101-236, females 95-204; biological males 47-76, females 35-64. *$p < .05$.

where—the first row of the table suggests that there was considerable accuracy of self-report on the outcomes questionnaire. The substantial positive correlations in the second row of the table imply that the consensus rating by self, parents, and siblings on the externalizing factor (drugs and alcohol and trouble with the law) is also borne out by criminal records. As we move down through the table through the three interview-based measures and MMPI *Pd*, we find generally positive correlations, although the smaller biological offspring groups are sometimes exceptional. The three rows at the bottom of the table represent indices of good, rather than bad behavior, and they correlate negatively with criminal records, as we might expect, except for the female biological offspring, where the correlations are positive—appreciably so for the index of good socialization in adolescence. It should be kept in mind that the female biological offspring having criminal records constitute only four cases (see Table 4.22), and so associations within this group are probably not generalizable.

Finally, the criminal-records search permits us to make one other check on the representativeness of the respondents to the outcomes questionnaire. We sorted the TAP children into three categories: (1) those for whom we had self-ratings on the outcomes questionnaire; (2) those for whom we had ratings, but not self-ratings—these would largely be ratings by parents, since sibling ratings required mutual consent; and (3) those for whom we had no outcomes questionnaire ratings at all. Table 4.24 provides the results.

Table 4.24
Mean Record-Search Scores for TAP Participants with and without Outcomes Questionnaire Data

Outcome Study Category	Male				Female			
	Adoptive		Biological		Adoptive		Biological	
Rated by self	.23	(120)	.24	(58)	.19	(108)	.06	(47)
Rated, not by self	.61	(56)	.15	(20)	.14	(44)	.18	(22)
No rating	.63	(82)	.42	(26)	.05	(78)	.00	(27)

Note: Ns in parentheses.

The males who were non-participants in the questionnaire study appeared to have on average slightly worse records than those who participated, but the differences were not dramatic, and were not present for the females. Again, it should be kept in mind that the number of females who had any criminal record was small.

On the whole, then, there is little reason to suppose that the cases having no outcomes questionnaire ratings were drastically different in the extent of their behavioral misconduct from those who were rated by themselves and/or others, although there is a possibility that the males who participated represent a sample slightly biased in favor of conformity.

Clustering of Problem Cases in Families?

We were concerned with the question of whether problem adoptees tended to cluster in families, which could happen (for example) if the source of their problems was the attitudes or child-rearing practices of the adoptive family. For this purpose, we defined "problem adoptee" as one who met one or more of the following criteria:

1.   MMPI *Pd* T-score of 70 or more.
2.   Consensus rating on outcomes questionnaire of 7 or greater, on trouble with the law or problems with drugs or alcohol.
3.   Summed score of 25 or greater on an Index of Problem Behaviors derived from the parent interview (which represents about the top 10 percent).
4.   Parent interviewer rating of 7 or more on externalizing problems.
5.   Score greater than 1 in criminal record search.

By this standard, 24 percent (119/492) of the adoptees showed evidence of problem behavior (and 76 percent showed none). Do the problem cases cluster in families? Table 4.25 shows the evidence. It is restricted to the 192 adoptees that had at least one adopted sibling, since "clustering" in a one-child family does not have much meaning.

Table 4.25
Is There Clustering of Adoptees' Problem Behavior in Families?

Adoptee with problems	Adoptive Sibling			Percent With
	With	Without	Total	
Yes	17	42	59	29%
No	30	103	133	22.5%
Total	47	145	192	

Note: Table only includes families with at least two adoptees.

There is a weak tendency for problem cases of adoptees to cluster: if an adoptee has problems, there is a 29 percent chance that an adoptive sibling of his or hers will have problems; whereas if an adoptee does not, there is only a 22.5 percent chance of an adoptive sibling who does. This difference is not statistically dependable (by a χ^2 test) so it could merely reflect sampling fluctuation—and even if real would constitute a very weak prediction: the implied correlation coefficient is .067, which means that very little of the variation of an adoptees' problem status is predictable by the problem status of a sibling.

Even this modest degree of clustering is ambiguous. It might be that some parents are more effective than others in controlling problem behavior in their offspring—perhaps by recognizing and responding to it earlier, or more consistently. Or it might reflect a tendency of one sibling with problems to lead another astray. It might even derive from some aspect of the placement practices of the adoption agency, if some families were favored with adoptees having better prospects as judged by their family backgrounds, or other families were thought to be better able to deal with problematic cases. These were not part of the stated policy of the adoption agency, but there was some flexibility in its implementation.

In any event, two conclusions can safely be drawn: (1) the majority of adoptees did not show substantial evidence of problem behavior and (2) most of those who did were isolated cases.

3. Occupation

Most young and middle-aged US adults (at any rate, most males, and a large proportion of females) spend one-third of their daily lives in activities related to their jobs. The TAP at two points obtained occupational data. At the time of the original study we rated the occupations of the fathers in the adoptive families on their occupational status, using a modified Warner scale in which 1 was high (examples: professionals, top executives) and 7 was low (examples: unskilled or migrant workers). Later, on the outcomes questionnaire, we included two items having to do with job stability and job responsibility. (We also asked on the questionnaire for job titles, but these proved unclassifiable in a good many instances—examples: works for company X, self-employed—so we will not attempt to report on them further here.)

Adoptive Father's Occupation and Offspring Outcomes

In Table 4.26 the occupational status ranking of the adoptive father at the time of the original study is related to several child measures for IQ, personality, and problem behavior. This is done separately for adopted and biological children. In this and the following table, we have reversed the direction of scoring for occupational status, so that a high score means high status.

Table 4.26 suggests that the adoptive father's occupational status was significantly related to his offspring's IQs, at both the original and follow-up testing for his biological children, but only at the earlier time for his adopted children, although the correlation at follow-up was in the same direction. Personality and conduct measures showed negligible associations with occupational status.

Table 4.26
Correlations of Father's Occupational Status with IQ, Personality, and Conduct of Offspring

Measure	Adopted Offspring		Biological Offspring	
IQ, original study	.21*	(463)	.32*	(157)
IQ, follow-up	.10	(272)	.24*	(110)
Extraversion	-.01	(477)	.03	(161)
Good socialization	-.06	(476)	.05	(161)
Emotional stability	.02	(477)	.08	(162)
IPB, adolescence	.04	(254)	.02	(99)

Note: Ns in parentheses. IQs, original study = WAIS/WISC/Binet; follow-up = WAIS/WISC. Extraversion, etc., = mean of parent ratings. IPB = Index of Problem Behavior from parent interview. *$p < .05$.

Table 4.27 shows correlations of father's occupation with the five factors from the outcomes questionnaire (again with reversed scoring for father's occupational status).

For the most part, the directions of correlation imply that good things are going with higher occupational status, but the only statistically significant correlation is with academic achievement in the biological offspring, an association that might well be mediated by IQ. The correlations involving the adoptees, in particular, are all trivial in magnitude. In interpreting these correlations, one must keep in mind that occupational range is restricted—occupations at the lower end of the socioeconomic scale are underrepresented among adopting families—and that a considerable time gap between measurements is involved.

Job Responsibility and Stability

The outcomes questionnaire contained the following two items concerning, respectively, current or most recent job and employment history since finishing school:

little responsibility   1 2 3 4 5 6 7 8 9   much responsibility
many job changes   1 2 3 4 5 6 7 8 9   highly stable

Their interrater reliabilities were estimated as .6dsdfsd4 and .81, respectively. Table 4.28 shows the mean scores on these items for the adoptive and biological offspring.

An Analysis of Variance showed the biological offspring to be significantly more stable in their job histories than the adopted offspring ($p = .002$); there were no significant sex differences or differences on job responsibility.

Table 4.27
Correlations of Father's Occupational Status with Outcomes Questionnaire Factors for Offspring

Measure	Adopted Offspring		Biological Offspring	
Maturity	.06	(320)	.04	(125)
Successful marriage	.02	(290)	.16	(115)
Externalizing problems	-.03	(320)	.00	(126)
Closeness to parents	.09	(321)	.11	(126)
Academic achievement	.02	(321)	.25*	(126)

Note: Ns in parentheses. *$p < .05$.

Table 4.28
Means for Occupation Items in Four Offspring Groups

Group	Job Responsibility		Job Stability	
Males				
Adopted	7.71	(1.52)	6.61	(2.25)
Biological	8.02	(1.06)	7.14	(1.95)
Females				
Adopted	7.81	(1.32)	6.79	(2.18)
Biological	7.88	(1.09)	7.50	(1.55)

Note: Standard deviations in parentheses. *N*s: Adopted males 173, females 147-149; biological males 77, females 63.

Table 4.29 shows correlations of the two occupation items with the same ability, personality, and conduct measures included in Table 4.26.

In this population, neither IQ nor parent-rated extraversion is related to adult job responsibility or job stability for either adopted or biological children. Ratings of socialization and emotional stability are, however, moderately related to both occupational variables, as are adolescent problem behaviors (negatively). On the whole, the correlations seem to be comparable for the individuals in the adopted and biological offspring groups.

Table 4.29
Correlations of Adult Job Responsibility and Stability with IQ, Personality, and Conduct Measures

	Adopted		Biological	
Measure	Respons.	Stability	Respons.	Stability
IQ, original study	.06	.10	-.10	-.14
IQ, follow-up	.05	.01	.04	.04
Extraversion	.08	.02	.05	.02
Good socialization	.23*	.28*	.31*	.28*
Emotional stability	.17*	.17*	.25*	.16
IPB, adolescence	-.30*	-.36*	-.29*	-.35*

Note: Respons. = job responsibility. IQs, original study = WAIS/WISC/Binet; follow-up = WAIS/WISC. Extraversion, etc., = mean of parent ratings. IPB = Index of Problem Behavior from parent interview. *N*s: IQ, orig,: 305-308 adopted, 107 biological; IQ, follow-up: 211-213 adopted, 88 biological; parent ratings: 315-319 adopted, 124-126 biological; IPB: 221-222 adopted, 101-102 biological. *$p < .05$.

In Table 4.30 are shown correlations of the two occupational variables with the five factors from the outcomes questionnaire.

Table 4.30
Correlations of Adult Job Responsibility and Job Stability with
Outcomes Questionnaire Factors

Measure	Adopted		Biological	
	Respons.	Stability	Respons.	Stability
Maturity	.69*	.65*	.63*	.51*
Successful marriage	.41*	.56*	.19*	.11
Externalizing problems	-.45*	-.60*	-.38*	-.40*
Closeness to parents	.37*	.29*	.30*	.38*
Academic achievement	.44*	.45*	.29*	.34*

Note: Respons. = job responsibility. Ns: 289-322 adopted; 127-140 biological. *p < .05.

It is evident that ratings of job stability and responsibility are consistently correlated with positive evaluations in other areas of life and negatively related to externalizing problems. Since all of these data are from the outcomes questionnaire, the correlations are probably inflated by the so-called "halo effect"—the tendency of raters to give more uniformly positive or negative ratings to an individual than his or her actual behavioral consistency would justify. It should be noted, however, that these are not halo effects in the mind of a single rater, because the scores are composite ratings based on several raters (an average of 2.5) per individual. In general, the correlations are similar for the adopted and biological offspring; if anything, they are slightly higher in the adopted group, most notably with the happily-married factor.

4. Personal Relationships

In this section we consider items from the outcomes questionnaire related to marriage, to closeness to parents while growing up, and to having many friends.

Marriage

The outcomes questionnaire contained one item asking whether the individual in question was single, living together, married, separated, divorced, or widowed, and another item rating the "History of marriage (or similar relationships)":

very unstable and/or unhappy 1 2 3 4 5 6 7 8 9   very stable and happy

The interrater reliability of this item was estimated as .82. Table 4.31 shows the percentages of offspring in each of the six matrimonial categories, by sex, and adoptive status.

The proportions in different marital statuses are very similar in all four groups. There is, for example, no excess among the adoptees of separation or divorce, or of unmarried couples living together.

Are the marriages equally happy in the four groups? Table 4.32 gives the means and standard deviations for the "stable, happy marriage" item.

The biological offspring and the males average very slightly higher in judged marital happiness, but none of these differences is statistically significant.

The two marriage items from the outcomes questionnaire were combined into a single composite by recoding marital status into a three-point

Table 4.31
**Percentages of Male and Female and Adopted and Biological Offspring
in Various Marital Statuses**

	Male		Female	
Marital Status	Adoptive	Biological	Adoptive	Biological
Single	16	17	14	9
Living together	8	9	8	6
Married	65	60	64	64
Separated	3	3	6	9
Divorced	8	10	8	10
Widowed	0	0	0	0
Number	174	76	150	64

Table 4.32
Means for "Stable, Happy Marriage" Rating in Four Offspring Groups

Group	Mean Rating (SD)	
Males		
Adopted	6.71	(2.12)
Biological	7.09	(1.75)
Females		
Adopted	6.69	(2.11)
Biological	6.96	(2.01)

Note: Standard deviations in parentheses. Ns: Adopted males 155, females 138; biological males 67, females 62.

scale of married or widowed, single or living together, and separated or divorced. This was then reversed and combined with the happy marriage rating—the two were correlated .63. Table 4.33 shows the correlations of this composite factor with the same IQ, personality, and conduct measures reported in earlier tables for the adopted and biological offspring.

The individuals judged to be in good marriages did not differ in IQ, nor along an extraversion/introversion dimension. They were, however, rated as better socialized and emotionally stable, and had fewer adolescent problem behaviors reported in the parent interviews. These relationships were somewhat clearer for the adoptees, with larger samples, but the correlations were similar in both groups.

Table 4.34 gives the correlations of the marriage factor with the other four outcomes questionnaire factors.

Those individuals judged be happily married were (not surprisingly) judged to be more mature, to have fewer externalizing problems, to

Table 4.33
Correlations of Marriage Factor with IQ, Personality, and Conduct of Adopted and Biological Offspring

Measure	Adopted Offspring		Biological Offspring	
IQ, original study	-.04	(279)	-.04	(98)
IQ, follow-up	.03	(196)	.13	(80)
Extraversion	.02	(289)	.04	(113)
Good socialization	.14*	(288)	.22*	(113)
Emotional stability	.19*	(289)	.13	(115)
IPB, adolescence	-.19*	(200)	-.17	(95)

Note: Ns in parentheses. IQs, original study = WAIS/WISC/Binet; follow-up = WAIS/WISC. Extraversion, etc., = mean of parent ratings. IPB = Index of Problem Behavior from parent interview. $*p < .05$.

Table 4.34
Correlations of Marriage Factor with Other Outcomes Questionnaire Factors

Measure	Adopted Offspring		Biological Offspring	
Maturity	.54*	(293)	.32*	(127)
Externalizing problems	-.51*	(292)	-.30*	(128)
Closeness to parents	.21*	(292)	.07	(128)
Academic achievement	.31*	(292)	.24*	(128)

Note: Ns in parentheses. $*p < .05$.

have been more successful academically, and (at least in the case of the adoptees) to have been emotionally closer to their parents. These correlations were, if anything, higher for the adoptees than for the biological offspring.

Closeness to Parents

Two items on the outcomes questionnaire asked about closeness to parents during the school years:

very close to father	1 2 3 4 5 6 7 8 9	very distant from father
very close to mother	1 2 3 4 5 6 7 8 9	very distant from mother

For the analyses in this section, we reversed both of these so that a high score means close to the parent. Their interrater reliabilities were estimated to be .55 and .51, respectively, a bit on the low side relative to some of the other items, but still substantial.

Table 4.35 gives means and SDs for closeness to mother and to father for adoptees and biological offspring.

An Analysis of Variance revealed a significant sex difference for closeness to father (females were closer). Females were also judged to have been closer to their mothers, but the difference from the males was not statistically significant. The biological offspring were rated as having been significantly closer to their mothers than the adoptees were; the difference in closeness to fathers was of the same sort, but of borderline statistical significance ($p = .09$).

Table 4.36 shows the correlations of closeness to parents with the IQ, personality, and conduct measures used in earlier tables.

Table 4.35
Means and SDs for Closeness to Parents in Four Offspring Groups

Group	To Father		To Mother	
Males				
Adopted	5.81	(1.87)	6.22	(1.80)
Biological	6.17	(1.72)	6.66	(1.60)
Females				
Adopted	6.32	(1.92)	6.46	(1.95)
Biological	6.59	(1.65)	6.90	(1.73)

Note: Standard deviations in parentheses. Ns: Adopted males 175, females 149-150; biological males 77, females 64.

Table 4.36
Closeness of Adopted and Biological Offspring to Father and Mother, Correlated with IQ, Personality, and Conduct Measures

Measure	Of Adopted Offspring		Of Biological Offspring	
	To Father	To Mother	To Father	To Mother
IQ, original study	-.02	.02	-.16	-.25*
IQ, follow-up	-.04	-.11	-.12	-.14
Extraversion	.13*	.11*	.18*	.09
Good socialization	.11*	.24*	.06	.16
Emotional stability	.19*	.17*	.16	.19*
IPB, adolescence	-.32*	-.37*	-.07	.01

Note: IQs, original study = WAIS/WISC/Binet; follow-up = WAIS/WISC. Extraversion, etc., = mean of parent ratings. IPB = Index of Problem Behavior from parent interview. Ns: IQ, orig,: 309-310 adopted, 108 biological; IQ, follow-up: 213 adopted, 89 biological; parent ratings: 319-321 adopted, 125-127 biological; IPB: 223-224 adopted, 102 biological. *$p < .05$.

Extraversion, Good socialization, and Emotional stability tended to be associated with judged closeness to both fathers and mothers, although with the smaller number of cases the correlations for the biological offspring were not always statistically significant. The correlations of a child's IQ with closeness were more often than not negative, meaning that higher IQs went with less closeness, although only one of them was statistically significant, that for closeness to mother of the biological children. Behavioral problems were negatively correlated with closeness, as one might expect, but mainly for the adopted children, not for the biological ones. This may in part reflect the greater extent of behavioral problems in the adoptee group.

Table 4.37 gives correlations between self-rated closeness to parents and the other outcome factors. The latter were scored only from parent and sib ratings in order to minimize halo effects.

Table 4.37
Self-Rated Closeness to Father and Mother, Correlated with Outcome Factors as Rated by Others

Measure	Of Adopted Offspring		Of Biological Offspring	
	To Father	To Mother	To Father	To Mother
Maturity	.08	.16*	-.10	.05
Successful marriage	.05	.07	-.09	-.04
Externalizing problems	-.18*	-.21*	.12	.02
Academic achievement	.10	.09	.14	.24*

Note: Ns: adopted 163-183; biological 85-93 *$p < .05$.

Again, we see behavioral problems, in this case in adulthood, negatively related to self-perceived, school-age closeness, but only for the adoptees. The two other significant correlations in the table are related to perceived closeness to mothers: maturity, for adoptees, and academic achievement, for biological children.

We were curious as to the role that personality resemblance might play in emotional closeness to a parent. The measure that we had for both children and parents was the MMPI. We obtained a measure of parent-child similarity by correlating the T-scores of child and parent across the eight clinical scales of the MMPI (excluding Mf). We correlated these measures of parent-child resemblance with judged parent-child closeness, with the results shown in Table 4.38.

Table 4.38
Correlations of Parent-Child Closeness and Parent-Child Resemblance in Personality

Child Group	Father-Child		Mother-Child	
Adopted	.17*	(156)	-.02	(153)
Biological	.17	(66)	-.02	(66)
All children	.17*	(222)	-.01	(219)

Note: Ns in parentheses. $*p < .05$.

Parent-child closeness goes with parent-child resemblance in personality, it seems, but only for fathers.

Friends and Social Activity

The outcomes questionnaire contained two items having to do with having many friends and social activities in junior high, high school, and as an adult. They were, respectively:

isolated 1 2 3 4 5 6 7 8 9 many friends

few friends, little social activity 1 2 3 4 5 6 7 8 9 lots of friends & social activity

Their interrater reliabilities were .72 and .67. Although the two items were substantially correlated (.60), they did not emerge as a single factor in the factor analysis, so we will treat them separately here.

Table 4.39 gives means and standard deviations for the two items in the four offspring groups.

Neither the sex nor the adoptive-status groups differed significantly in the number of friends in junior high and high school. The biological offspring had significantly more friends and social activity as adults.

Table 4.39
Means and SDs in Four Offspring Groups for Having Many Friends in Junior
High, High School, and as an Adult

Group	Friends, HS		Friends, Adult	
Males				
Adopted	7.13	(1.59)	6.49	(1.91)
Biological	7.09	(1.45)	6.71	(1.60)
Females				
Adopted	7.13	(1.59)	6.56	(1.93)
Biological	7.42	(1.47)	7.17	(1.47)

Note: Standard deviations in parentheses. HS = in high school and junior high. *N*s: Adopted males 174-175, females 150; biological males 75-77, females 63-64.

How does the number of friends relate to other measures from the study? Table 4.40 gives the results for IQ, parent ratings, and the Index of Problem Behavior for adolescence.

Neither IQ measure was significantly related to number of friends in school or as an adult for the adoptees. For the biological offspring, the signs of these correlations were negative—higher IQs went with fewer friends—although only in the case of early IQ and current friends was the correlation large enough to be statistically significant. Extraversion, Good socialization, and Emotional stability tended to go positively with having many friends, and adolescent problem behaviors to go negatively, although a couple of the correlations fell short of statistical significance in the smaller biological offspring group.

Table 4.40
Correlations of Many Friends with IQ, Personality, and Conduct Measures for
Adopted and Biological Offspring

Measure	Adopted Offspring		Biological Offspring	
	FrHS	FrCurr	FrHS	FrCurr
IQ, original study	.04	.03	-.15	-.21*
IQ, follow-up	.01	-.08	-.08	-.14
Extraversion	.26*	.15*	.31*	.12
Good socialization	.24*	.12*	.25*	.28*
Emotional stability	.23*	.17*	.23*	.14
IPB, adolescence	-.27*	-.26*	-.19	-.24*

Note: FrHS = many friends in junior high and high school; FrCurr = many current friends and social activity. IQs, original study = WAIS/WISC/Binet; follow-up = WAIS/WISC. Extraversion, etc., = mean of parent ratings. IPB = Index of Problem Behavior from parent interview. *N*s: adopted, 213-321; biological 88-127. *$p < .05$.

Table 4.41 gives the same correlations for the outcomes questionnaire factors.

Table 4.41
Correlations of Many Friends with Outcome Questionnaire Factors for
Adopted and Biological Offspring

Outcome factor	Adopted Offspring		Biological Offspring	
	FrHS	FrCurr	FrHS	FrCurr
Maturity	.52*	.56*	.37*	.54*
Successful marriage	.34*	.37*	.13	.22*
Externalizing problems	-.37*	-.34*	-.21*	-.44*
Closeness to parents	.33*	.42*	.39*	.32*
Academic achievement	.31*	.41*	.30*	.21*

Note: FrHS = many friends in junior high and high school; FrCurr = many current friends and social activity. *N*s: adopted, 292-323; biological 126-141. *$p < .05$.

On the outcomes questionnaire, being rated as having had many friends in junior high and high school, or currently having them, tended to be positively associated with other favorable outcomes, such as successful marriage and higher academic achievement, and negatively related to the presence of externalizing problems. Offspring with many friends were also judged to have been closer to their parents. All these held for both the adopted and biological offspring, although the correlation between successful marriage and many friends in high school was not statistically significant in the biological offspring group, though still positive.

5. Maturity and Happiness

Finally, the outcomes questionnaire contained a number of items related to psychological and social maturity and personal happiness. Four items on the questionnaire formed a factor that we called Maturity. The items were:

very dependent on others	1 2 3 4 5 6 7 8 9	independent, self reliant
immature, selfish	1 2 3 4 5 6 7 8 9	mature, helpful
erratic, undependable	1 2 3 4 5 6 7 8 9	conscientious, reliable
hostile, disagreeable	1 2 3 4 5 6 7 8 9	pleasant, agreeable

The interrater reliabilities of the four items were .65, 67, 70, and .68, respectively, and the internal consistency reliability of the composite score on the factor was .91.

A single item dealt with current happiness and security:

always happy and secure   1 2 3 4 5 6 7 8 9   often anxious or depressed

This item was reversed in direction for the following tables, so that a high score means happy and secure. Its interrater reliability was .74. Table 4.42 shows means and standard deviations on the Maturity factor and the Happiness item. None of the sex differences was statistically significant. The biological children were rated as more mature and happier.

Table 4.43 gives the correlations of these outcome measures with the set of IQ, personality, and conduct measures used in previous tables.

The relationships with Good socialization, Emotional stability, and the

Table 4.42

Means and SDs in Four Offspring Groups for the Maturity Factor and the Happiness Item

Group	Maturity		Happiness	
Males				
Adopted	7.26	(1.46)	6.27	(1.90)
Biological	7.79	(.88)	6.71	(1.63)
Females				
Adopted	7.51	(1.35)	6.11	(2.08)
Biological	7.70	(1.30)	6.78	(1.52)

Note: Standard deviations in parentheses. Maturity = maturity factor; Happiness = happy and secure vs. anxious or depressed. *N*s: Adopted males 173-175, females 150; biological males 75-77, females 63-64.

Table 4.43

Correlations of Maturity and Happiness Measures with IQ, Personality, and Conduct Measures, for Adopted and Biological Offspring

Measure	Adopted Offspring		Biological Offspring	
	Maturity	Happiness	Maturity	Happiness
IQ, original study	.16*	.10	-.27*	-.22*
IQ, follow-up	.12	.02	-.14	-.04
Extraversion	.05	.07	.09	.13
Good socialization	.32*	.14*	.21*	.27*
Emotional stability	.32*	.28*	.31*	.31*
IPB, adolescence	-.38*	-.24*	-.18	-.18

Note: Maturity = maturity factor; Happiness = happy and secure vs. anxious or depressed. IQs, original study = WAIS/WISC/Binet; follow-up = WAIS/WISC. Extraversion, etc., = mean of parent ratings. IPB = Index of Problem Behavior from parent interview. *N*s: adopted, 212-319; biological 88-127. *$p < .05$.

Index of Problem Behavior are as one might expect: individuals judged
to be mature and happy were rated as well socialized and emotionally
stable, and having had fewer problem behaviors. This was the case for
both the adopted and biological offspring, although the IPB correlations
in the latter group were smaller, and of only borderline statistical significance (.05 < p < .10). Ratings of Extraversion were not significantly
related to either maturity or happiness—the correlations in both groups
were positive but low.

IQ, however, was curious. It tended to be positively related to judged
maturity and happiness in the adoptive groups and negatively related
among the biological offspring. This was most evident for IQs at the
original testing—at the time of the ten-year follow-up, although the
difference in sign was still present, none of the correlations differed
significantly from zero.

Table 4.44 shows relationships with the outcome factors.

Not surprisingly, ratings of maturity and happiness tended to be
substantially correlated with other positive factors from the outcomes
questionnaire, such as successful marriage and academic achievement,
and negatively related to the presence of externalizing problems. Also,
those judged to be happier and more mature were rated as having been
closer to their parents during their school years. All of these relationships held for both the adopted and the biological offspring. Finally, the
maturity factor and the happiness item were correlated .69 with each
other, in both groups.

Table 4.44
**Correlations of Maturity and Happiness Measures with Outcomes Questionnaire
Factors for Adopted and Biological Offspring**

	Adopted Offspring		Biological Offspring	
Measure	Maturity	Happiness	Maturity	Happiness
Maturity	---	.69*	---	.69*
Successful marriage	.54*	.63*	.32*	.44*
Externalizing problems	-.60*	-.60*	-.61*	-.60*
Closeness to parents	.40*	.42*	.40*	.42*
Academic achievement	.52*	.41*	.33*	.34*

Note: Maturity = maturity factor; Happiness = happy and secure vs. anxious or depressed.
*N*s: adopted, 292-322; biological 127-140. *p < .05.

6. Factors Related to Outcomes

Prediction of Outcomes from Childhood IQ

Our study may be able to tell us something about the extent to which childhood IQ is related to various outcomes in later life. Table 4.45 presents the relevant information for a number of variables in the study, first for all children, and then separately by sex and adoptive status. Some of these relationships have been mentioned before, but Table 4.45 permits an overall comparison.

Among the various items assessed by the outcomes questionnaire, only those specifically related to educational outcomes were predicted by childhood IQ: the level of education attained and the rating as a good student in high school. These correlations held for both sexes and for both adopted and biological children.

Curiously, there appeared to be a negative association among the biological children between childhood IQ and such positive adult traits

Table 4.45
Childhood IQ and Life Outcomes

Outcome	All	Males	Females	Adopted	Biological
Outcome Questionnaire Ratings					
Educational attainment	.28*	.30*	.26*	.29*	.27*
Good student in HS	.28*	.27*	.30*	.27*	.34*
Conscientious	.05	.10	-.00	.13*	-.23*
Job responsibility	.03	.06	.00	.06	-.06
Job stability	.05	.08	.03	.10	-.06
Stable marriage	-.04	-.02	-.07	-.04	-.07
Many friends in HS	-.00	-.01	-.02	.04	-.18
Many friends currently	-.02	-.04	-.01	.03	-.25*
Mature	.06	.10	-.01	.13*	-.24*
Happiness	.03	.04	.01	.10	-.21*
Parent Personality Rating Composites					
Extraversion	.03	.10	-.07	.02	.06
Good socialization	.12*	.15*	.08	.14*	.01
Emotional stability	.16*	.21*	.09	.17*	.12
Index of Problem Behaviors					
For adolescence	-.14*	-.13	-.14	-.14*	-.12
For adulthood	-.18*	-.16*	-.22*	-.21*	-.11

Note: Total *N*s: outcome questionnaire 378-419; personality ratings 608-610; Index of Problem Behavior, 328-332. Males, about 54% of total; adopted, about 75%. * $p < .05$.

as conscientiousness, having many friends, maturity, and happiness. This cannot be a general outcome of having a high childhood IQ, as the relationships for the same measures in the case of the adopted children tended to be positive.

Having a high childhood IQ was not generally detrimental—it went with positive parental ratings as being well behaved and emotionally stable and with fewer problem behaviors as assessed in the parent interview. These correlations were higher for the adopted children, but the signs were the same for both groups.

In short, having a higher IQ in childhood predicted favorable educational outcomes later in life and tended to be associated with favorable parent ratings for good conduct and emotional stability, as well as with fewer problem behaviors. However, with the exception of the educational outcomes, there were inconsistencies among subgroups in the extent to which these generalizations held. In particular, as we have noted before, there appeared to be some negative implications of a high childhood IQ for the biological children. Since this did not seem to be true among the adopted children, we suspect that this may reflect some peculiarity of our sample, or (less likely) of the status of biological children in families who adopt.

Parent and Child Self-Views on the Outcomes Questionnaire

In addition to having family members describe the individuals in the child generation on the outcomes questionnaire, we asked the parents to fill out a questionnaire to describe their own lives. This meant that we could look at the resemblance between parents' views of their own lives and their offsprings' views of theirs. Such correlations are necessarily ambiguous in interpretation—does a positive correlation mean similarity in the child's and parent's lives, or just similarity in the child's and parent's views of their lives? Nevertheless, it seems worth asking to what extent similarities occur, apart from how they might be interpreted. Table 4.46 presents these correlations, separately for correlations with mothers and fathers, and for adopted and biological offspring.

Table 4.46
Corrrelations between Offsprings' and Parents' Self-Reported Life Outcomes for Adopted and Biological Children

Rating	Adopted Children		Biological Children	
	With Mother	With Father	With Mother	With Father
Educational attainment	.22*	.16	.27*	.43*
Good student in HS	.18	.01	.08	.27*
Many friends in HS	-.08	-.05	.10	.28*
No trouble in HS	-.05	-.03	-.06	.03
Distance from father	-.09	.02	.02	.04
Distance from mother	.05	.00	-.01	-.02
Job responsibility	.13	.10	.12	.19
Job stability	-.07	-.16	.19	-.03
Married	.06	-.06	.24	.21
Stable, happy marriage	.08	-.23*	.17	-.18
Drugs and alcohol	-.01	.14	-.10	-.00
Anxiety or depression	.11	.15	.05	-.00
Trouble with the law	-.04	.06	-.09	-.03
Friends and social activity	.04	-.09	.14	.10
Independent	.08	-.06	.11	.15
Mature	.16	-.06	.20	.07
Conscientious	.14	.01	.05	.14
Agreeable	.04	-.08	-.10	.05

Note: HS = high school. For full rating scale, see Appendix B. Numbers of pairs: adopted, 118-137; biological, 47-67. *$p \leq .05$.

It is evident from the many small correlations in Table 4.46 that there is not a great deal of parent-child resemblance in either group. There is some modest agreement for parent-child resemblance in educational attainment for both groups, with the correlations somewhat larger on the biological side, suggesting the influence of both environmental and genetic factors. There are low, positive correlations for job responsibility across the board, suggesting environmental effects. Having many friends in high school or as adults has small positive correlations for biological pairs, but nothing for adoptive pairs, consistent with some genetic component to extraversion. No doubt, many of the correlations are limited by a lack of range among the parents: for example, by the nature of this group, most are married, and few have been in trouble with the law. For readers who may wish to examine the self-ratings in more detail, the means and standard deviations for the questionnaire items for the adopted and biological children, and for mothers and fathers, may be found in Appendix D.

Parental Antecedents of Child Outcomes

We had in our data files IQ and MMPI data for both the mothers who gave birth to and the parents who reared the adopted children, and likewise for the biological children—for whom the birth and rearing parents were the same.

We were curious about the relationship of these parental measures to offspring life outcomes. So we correlated the adoptive parents' and birth mothers' Beta IQs and MMPI scores with the five outcome factors. We obtained a large number of very small correlations, which we have published elsewhere (Loehlin, Horn, & Ernst,2009) and forbear to repeat here.

However, when we looked at these correlations from the perspective of good things in the parents (higher IQs, lower MMPI scores) going with good outcomes in their offspring (successful marriages, more academic achievement, greater maturity, fewer behavioral problems) we noticed a curious fact. The correlations in the direction of good things going with good things happened relatively often for parents and their biological children (84 percent in the case of birth mothers and their adopted-away offspring, 60 percent for the adoptive mothers and fathers and their biological children). Yet, for genetically unrelated parents and offspring, the correlations tended to be decidedly less often in the good-with-good direction (only 38 percent of the time for mothers and 42 percent of the time for fathers—with chance expectation being 50 percent). Could it be that the genes tended to lead to positive correlations between parent attributes and child life outcomes but family environments tended to lead to negative ones (at least within the narrowed range of environments found in our adoptive families)?

We fit the simple path model shown in Figure 4.1 to the correlations among parental measures and offspring outcomes, a model which attempted to capture the simple hypothesis of good things in the parent generation going with good outcomes in the offspring generation.

Initially, we fit this model to the intercorrelations of all 14 variables in each of five groups: adoptive fathers and adopted offspring, adoptive fathers and biological offspring, adoptive mothers and adopted offspring, adoptive mothers and biological offspring, and birth mothers and their adopted-away offspring. The Figure 4.1 model did not fit the correlations very well—in particular, the intercorrelations of the MMPI scales do not conform to a single factor. Adding some correlations among the bottom arrows at the left led to an acceptable fit, and allowed us to address the

Figure 4.1
Parental Measures and Offspring Outcomes.

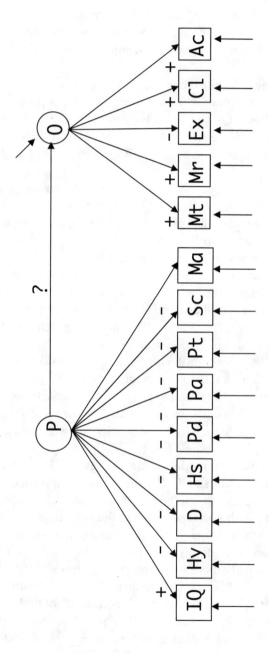

Note: Observed parental variables: IQ = Beta IQ; Hy to Ma = MMPI scales. Observed offspring variables: Mt = maturity; Mr = successful marriage; Ex = externalizing problems; Cl = closeness to parents; Ac = academic achievement. Latent variables: P = general factor among parental variables; O = general factor among offspring outcomes.

main question of interest, which concerned the horizontal arrow from P to O: Will requiring it to be equal for certain groups significantly worsen the fit of the model? Requiring it to be the same for adoptive mothers and fathers—for their adopted children and separately for their biological children—did not significantly worsen the fit. Adding the birth mother-offspring correlations to the biological groups did not either. However, requiring the P-to-O arrow to be the same in all five groups did worsen the fit appreciably, although the difference was only of borderline significance statistically ($.05 < p < .10$). The value of the arrow was +.08 for the biological groups and -.08 for the adoptive groups. Thus, favorable attributes of the parents are certainly not very highly predictive of favorable outcomes of the children in this population, but the prediction seems to be positive when genes are shared and negative when they are not.

How much prediction should one expect between favorable IQ and MMPI scores and favorable life outcomes in the *same* individuals (as opposed to parents and offspring)? For a subsample of the offspring in our study we have Beta IQs and MMPIs at the time of the ten-year follow-up, as well as measures from the outcomes questionnaire. If we fit the Figure 4.1 path model to the intercorrelations in this group we learn two things. First, the value of the path corresponding to P to O is significantly higher than that in the various parent-offspring groups, as it should be. Second, it is still far from perfect: its estimated value was +.34. We would not expect resemblance across generations to be as high as resemblance within individuals—half as high, for the action of individual genes, less than that for the effects of genetic configurations (which tend to get broken up in transmission from parent to child). Who knows what it may be for environmental characteristics? Parents and children grow up in different, but perhaps correlated, families, and parents may affect children directly in various ways.

Indeed, we would not expect an extremely high correlation between an MMPI-and-IQ-based measure of adjustment and broad life outcomes, even if both were made at the same moment in time. Thus, weak associations over time and across generations are plausible.

At least within our data, the fact that favorable parental characteristics tend to go with favorable offspring life outcomes can principally be accounted for by shared genes. In the absence of genetic resemblance, things get more complicated. Environmental mechanisms like imitation, which ought to produce parent-offspring resemblance, appear to be outweighed by environmental mechanisms like contrast or compensation, which tend to produce parent-offspring differences. Obviously much more research is necessary in order to draw firm conclusions on this point, and the special characteristics of adoptive families may need to be taken into account. Nevertheless, it is evident that studying adoptive families allows us to address some interesting aspects of why individuals turn out as they do.

5

Summary and Conclusions

1. The Story so Far

This book has described the Texas Adoption Project, a thirty-five-year study that began with three hundred families, each of whom had adopted a child from a particular Texas home for unwed mothers, the Methodist Mission Home of San Antonio, during the years between 1963 and 1971.

Initially, prospective families were interviewed by former staff members of the Methodist Mission Home, and consent was obtained for participation in the study. The response was excellent—in fact, more families were willing to be tested than the three hundred our study could accommodate. All available members of the three hundred families were given a battery of tests, either by a psychologist in a nearby city, or by a psychologist associated with the Home who traveled to reach more remote families.

The tests included an individually administered IQ test, appropriate to the age of the individual tested; a personality test from the Cattell series, for those old enough to complete a pencil-and-paper questionnaire; and, for the parents, the Revised Beta and the MMPI. Because many of the children were too young for satisfactory pencil-and-paper testing, all children were also rated by a parent (usually the mother) on a twenty-four-item set of rating scales covering a variety of aspects of personality.

At the same time, the adoption agency provided us with information from their files about the genetic parents of the adopted child. Information about the genetic fathers was usually limited to educational and occupational background, but there was considerably more information about the birth mothers. Many had been given psychological tests while

141

resident in the Home—usually an IQ test and often an MMPI. Thus, we were in the position, unusual in earlier adoption studies, of being able to relate measures of the adopted child's ability and personality to both the mother who supplied half the child's genes and the mother (and father) who provided the rearing environment.

Because in many of our families we also tested one or more siblings of the adopted child, we could compare the child to other children who grew up in the same family, but were genetically unrelated to him or her; in some families, in which the additional siblings included two or more biological children of the adoptive parents, we could compare the resemblance of biological siblings as well. Whenever there were biological offspring, we could correlate them with their parents, and compare parent-child resemblances that did and did not involve shared genes.

For the younger children of the initial study, there were problems of comparing measures given at different ages, whose equivalence might be questionable. We planned a follow-up when the children were old enough to be given the same tests as their parents, but in the meantime, we undertook a separate study of 220 families who had adopted a child from the Methodist Mission Home during an earlier period. This was before psychological tests were routinely given to residents at the home, so birth mothers were not included in this study, only the adoptive family members. Moreover, the study was to be carried out by mail, so individually administered IQ tests were not feasible, and the study used two standard personality questionnaires, the California Psychological Inventory and the Thurstone Temperament Schedule. The children in this group of families were old enough to be given the same questionnaires as their parents, and both birth and adopted children were included, thus permitting similar comparisons of family members who did and did not share genes.

We then returned to the three hundred original families, ten years after our initial testing. The children were now mostly old enough to be given adult ability and personality tests, and we approached the families again for this purpose. This time we proposed to test only the children, but our measures included both adult IQ tests and the MMPI and 16PF, plus repeating the ratings by a parent of personality traits made earlier. We were unable to reach all of the original three hundred families, and not all the children originally tested were available for retesting, but about 60 percent of the families and 55 percent of the children participated again, and a few children in these families were added who for one reason or another were not tested in the original study.

A third assessment of the main sample occurred some 12 years later, in the form of personal interviews with the parents in 167 families. These interviews focused on the children in the families (now adults)—their childhood, their adolescence, their current status. An Index of Problem Behaviors was derived for each child from these interviews for each of four periods: infancy, childhood, adolescence, and adulthood.

In a fourth phase, about five years after the family interviews, we sent a one-page questionnaire by mail to all of the children for whom we could obtain current addresses. This questionnaire attempted, within its limited scope, to gain information about outcomes—education, marriage, occupation, personal difficulties, and adult personality characteristics.

Finally, we searched the publicly-available records of criminal convictions maintained by the Texas Department of Public Safety, with two objects in mind: first, to get some idea of the dependability of self- and parental reports about trouble with the law and, second, to assess the possibility that the individuals whose cooperation we had been able to obtain in the earlier phases of follow-up might be a biased sample, underrepresenting those with problem behaviors.

2. What We Learned in the TAP

We begin by discussing our findings in very general terms; later we will consider particular areas of development, such as abilities, personality, behavior problems, and so forth.

First, one should always keep in mind that our methods are focused on the *differences* among individuals. Our results will have little to say about the universal aspects of human nature, the characteristics that all humans have in common (and in many cases share with our cousins the great apes or even with more distant mammalian relatives). With very rare exceptions, all humans are capable of fear, anger, affection, sadness, disgust, and other emotions. They learn to speak a language. They order their relationships with their fellow humans, often in intricate ways. On such issues of human nature, which are of central concern to, say, evolutionary psychologists, our study is relatively silent. But individual humans differ widely in their proneness to express fear, anger, affection, and other emotions; in their facility for acquiring and expressing their native language; in the degree of pleasure they take in their relationships with others; and in their tendencies toward dominance or acquiescence in these relationships. It is these individual differences that constitute the principal concern of our study and the province of human behavior genetics in general.

Some of these differences reflect differences in the genes, for which every human is in some respects unique, except for members of monozygotic multiple births. Some of these differences reflect differences in experience, for which every human is in some respects unique, without exception. Some of the differences in experience are a consequence of differences in genes, which tend to bias individuals in one direction or another in their encounters with the world. Some of the differences in experience are shared with other members of one's family; some are not. Some are shared with siblings but not with parents. Some reflect sheer accidents of early prenatal development. Some reflect the luck of the draw in chance encounters with the world, such as happening to meet up with a charismatic individual or a debilitating virus.

An adoption study such as ours can, in principle, sort individual differences into three categories: (1) those associated with genetic differences among individuals; (2) those resulting from experiences shared by siblings within a family; and (3) those due to everything else. We will pursue matters in more detail shortly but, broadly speaking, category 1, the genes, has fairly consistently been evident in our analyses; category 2, shared family environment, has sometimes been appreciable in childhood, but has tended to fade to insignificance by adolescence; and category 3, everything else (which includes chance in development, idiosyncratic experiences, random errors in measurement, and other factors to be discussed), has constituted by far the largest share in the observed differences among the individuals in our adoptive families.

What We Learned about Intellectual Abilities

For general cognitive ability—general intelligence as assessed by IQ tests—there was evidence that the genes accounted for a larger share of individual differences than did family environments. This was shown by both means and correlations. For means: if one compared adopted children whose birth mothers were above the group average in IQ with those whose birth mothers were below the group average, there was an average difference of about 4 IQ points in favor of the former. However, if one compared adopted children whose families were above the group average in socioeconomic status with those whose families were below the group average, the average difference was only about 1 IQ point. Now both the range of socioeconomic status and birth mother IQ are restricted in our sample, so one should not take the numbers too literally as applying to the general population, but it certainly appears that the genes were carrying more weight than socioeconomic status in explaining individual differences in IQ in our data, even though half the relevant genes for the adoptees (the birth fathers') were left out of the picture.

Correlations told the same general story. Correlations between family members—parents and children or siblings—who were genetically unrelated were close to zero, at least at the time of the ten-year follow-up. Correlations between family members who were genetically related were fairly modest, but, on the whole, larger. A curious feature of these correlations was that they seemed to be highest for pairs that had the least contact (the birth mothers and their adopted-away children) and lowest for the pairs that presumably had the most contact (the adoptive mothers and the children they reared). Based on an overall path analysis, these differences were not large enough to be statistically compelling with the sample sizes involved, but they suggest the possibility that family interaction may lead to differences more than to similarities in ability, a hypothesis that should be kept in mind in future research.

This was for overall IQ, but what about specialized cognitive abilities? To examine this question, we took scores on each of the subscales of the Revised Beta test after the variance that it shared with the other subtests was statistically removed and fitted path models to these subtest-specific scores. The results suggested the presence of unique genetic variance on some of the subtests (Formboard, Error recognition, Digit-symbol) and unique environmental variance on others (Maze, Picture completion).

A separate model-fitting analysis was undertaken to investigate IQ changes over time, based on data from the initial IQ testing and the ten-year follow-up. The results suggested that both genetic and family environmental contributions were present at the time of the initial testing and that additional genetic (but not shared environmental) influences had come into play by the time of the follow-up.

Finally, a couple of specific questions were investigated. One was whether a measure of problem-solving speed, i.e., the speed of doing problems that everyone solved correctly, would provide an independent measure of cognitive skill. It appeared that it would, to at least some degree. The other question was how well the IQs of the genetic fathers could be estimated from the available data on education and occupation. Quite well, it appeared, based on comparisons with the mothers, for whom actual IQ test scores were known.

What We Learned about Personality

There were three main sources of information about personality in the TAP. First, there were the parent ratings of their children on three occasions: in childhood, adolescence, and adulthood. (More precisely, the children were rated in the original study, the ten-year follow-up, and the time of the parent interviews, when the bulk of the children would fall within the categories mentioned.) These ratings defined the three broad dimensions of Extraversion, Good socialization, and Emotional stability. On the third occasion, ratings were added to measure the remaining two of the so-called "Big Five" as well, Agreeableness and Openness. Next, there were the two self-report personality questionnaires, the 16PF and the MMPI, taken at the time of the initial study by the parents and by the offspring at the time of the ten-year follow-up. (The MMPI had also been taken by the birth mothers, prior to the birth of their child.) Finally, there were two additional personality questionnaires, the CPI and the TTS, completed by the members of the adoptive families in a separate sample, and analyzed jointly with twin and twin-family data from other sources.

From the ratings, several noteworthy points emerged. First, the parents on average rated both their biological and adopted children favorably, i.e., above the neutral midpoint of the scales. Second, at the initial occasion, the adopted children were rated fully as favorably as the biological ones. Third, over time the ratings, though still on average favorable, became relatively less so for the adopted children. Since they clearly did not begin at a disadvantage, it seems likely that it was something about their behavior that altered their parents' appraisal. A fourth point of interest was that the negative shift for the adopted children was most notable at adolescence—by the adult rating they had risen in their parents' esteem, although still lagging behind the biological children, who tended to improve in their parents' eyes across all three assessments. Finally, these are, of course, all statements about averages. Individual children might shift up and down considerably or show different patterns for different traits, and so on.

The 16PF and the MMPI provided two kinds of information: means and family correlations. As to means, on the 16PF the adopted children averaged significantly higher than the biological children on scales measuring adventurousness, dominance, and radical attitudes. One can imagine this as contributing to difficulties with their parents in adolescence. As to correlations, the parent-offspring correlations on both questionnaires were very low in the absence of shared genes, averaging .04 and .01 for fathers and mothers with the adopted children across the 16PF scales, and .01 and .02 for the MMPI. The correlations were not very high when genes were shared, either, but they were a little higher: .11 and .12 for the 16PF, and .06, .08, and .16 on the MMPI (the .16 was the average correlation of the adopted children with their birth mothers). Midparent-midchild regressions for both questionnaires suggested that the genes were accounting for something like 20 percent of individual variation on these traits—the figure would be increased somewhat if measurement error and restriction of range were allowed for, but would still remain well below the 40 percent to 50 percent typically found in twin studies using personality questionnaires.

The third source of evidence on the genes and personality was the correlations from the CPI and TTS questionnaires in the separate sample of 220 adoptive families tested by mail. On the whole, the results were consistent with those of the main study. The average parent-offspring correlations when genes were not shared were low (.07, .04, .03, .01). The parent-offspring correlations when genes were shared were a little higher (.07, .15, .17, .09) suggesting that the genes contributed something to individual differences in personality. In this case, it was possible to combine our adoption data with data from several other studies that had used these questionnaires with identical and fraternal twins, and the children of identical twins, and to fit heredity-environment models to these sets of correlations jointly. This model fitting resulted in considerably higher estimates of the contribution of genes to individual differences in personality: 40 percent and 48 percent respectively, for the CPI and TTS. The contribution of shared family environments was estimated as 5 percent or less over the CPI scales, and was not significantly different from zero for the TTS. The presence of identical twins in the design meant that nonadditive as well as additive effects of the genes were being evaluated—models that allowed for the presence of nonadditive as well as additive genetic variance fit the data significantly better in both cases.

Finally, we did an elegant analysis that the unique data set of the TAP made possible. We looked at fifty-two families in which there were at least two adopted children with parent ratings and birth mothers' MMPIs for both. We asked the question: What were the MMPI items more often agreed to by the birth mother of the more extraverted of the two adopted children in a family (or the better socialized or the more emotionally stable)?

For extraversion, there were two items meeting the criterion of a 25 percent difference in frequency of agreement. The birth mother of the more introverted child was more likely to have marked "True" to the following statements: "Even when I am with people I feel lonely much of the time" and "I wish I were not so shy." This suggests a gene-based resemblance.

The mother of the better socialized child endorsed a number of items suggesting that she was more emotionally responsive to her environment than was the mother of the less well-socialized child and the latter agreed with several items suggestive of mildly psychopathic tendencies. Again, we seem to see the influence of shared genes.

For emotional stability, however, the results were paradoxical. The birth mother of the child rated as *more* emotionally stable endorsed items indicative of family conflict, intensity of feelings, and difficulties in relating to other people. The birth mother of the child rated as *less* emotionally stable said things like, "I wake up fresh and rested most mornings" and "My daily life is full of things that keep me interested." We really do not know what this means. One idea that occurred to us was that this might reflect a gene-based sensitivity to the environment that resulted in emotional stability in the relatively benign atmosphere of the adoptive home, but in adverse reactions in the less benign homes in which the birth mothers grew up. But we had no direct evidence about the emotional climate of the birth mothers' homes (which were predominantly middle-class), and the family interviews suggested a less-than-total benignity in a number of the adoptive homes. So we can only conclude that further research is needed to see if this result can be replicated, and, if it is, whether or not our conjecture about it is correct.

What We Learned about Life Outcomes

It will be recalled that a one-page questionnaire was filled out by the children in the study (now adults) to describe their own lives and by their parents and siblings to describe them. An individual's score was taken as the average of all the ratings he or she received on that item (self-ratings included)—the number of ratings ranged from 1 to 5, with an individual receiving on average 2.5 ratings. Several different aspects of life outcomes were addressed in the questionnaire: academic and occupational achievement, marriage and personal relationships, psychopathology and problem behavior, personal maturity and happiness. For most, we looked at differences in means between adopted and biological children, and, for many, we were able to compare the outcomes for family members who did and did not share genes.

For educational achievement, the biological children on average obtained a higher level of education than the adopted children, but the adoptees were by no means lacking in education—the majority had at least some post-high school education, and 48 percent completed college. Comparison of familial correlations suggested that both genes and family environments contributed to individual differences in educational attainment. Parents' levels of education were significantly related to the children's IQs when the children were young, but not to the children's personality traits. However, the children's educational achievement was related to their own personality traits—specifically, to good socialization and emotional stability. A rating as having been a good student in high school was related to the level of education ultimately attained, but not to the educational level of the parents. Finally—on the distinction between IQ and academic achievement—a measure of the latter, the Wide Range Achievement Test, showed less correlation among genetically unrelated sibs than did an IQ measure, failing to support a common assumption that academic achievement is more subject to family environmental effects than is IQ.

Two aspects of occupational outcomes, job responsibility and job stability, were rated on the questionnaire. The biological offspring averaged significantly higher on job stability. The difference on job responsibility was in the same direction, but it was quite small and not statistically significant.

A factor related to successful marriage showed only trivial differences between adopted and biological offspring. It was related to childhood ratings of good socialization and emotional stability, but not to extraversion or IQ.

For closeness to parents in childhood, the biological children were rated as somewhat closer than the adopted children, on average, but the differences were fairly small. Closeness to parents went with childhood ratings as well socialized, emotionally stable, and extraverted. For adopted children, closeness to parents correlated negatively with adolescent problem behavior and was uncorrelated with IQ; for biological children, the relationship with problem behavior was absent and there was some evidence of negative correlations with IQ. The implication of this latter, if real, is not obvious, particularly in light of the fact that closeness to parents tended on the whole to go with greater academic achievement, especially in the case of biological children and their mothers. Finally, were children who resembled their parents in their MMPI profiles judged to be closer to them? Modestly so, with fathers; not at all, with mothers.

There were several assessments of problem behavior in the TAP. We took the Psychopathic deviate (*Pd*) score on the MMPI as one such indicator. An Index of Problem Behavior was rated from the parent interviews. In addition, the outcomes questionnaire had items concerning problems with drugs and alcohol and trouble with the law. Finally, we obtained records of criminal convictions in the state of Texas.

The results? If adopted children were sorted into groups according to whether their birth mothers or adoptive mothers were above or below their group average on *Pd*, the sorting according to the birth mothers made a significant difference for the average *Pd* of the children, and that on adoptive mothers did not, although the differences in both cases was in the direction of mother-child resemblance. The Index of Problem Behaviors from the family interviews was significantly greater for the adopted than for the biological children in adolescence and adulthood; interestingly, the usual difference of more problem behaviors for males was not present among the adoptees. Furthermore, only for males was this index correlated with birth mother's *Pd*. Matters were a little less complex in the case of an externalizing factor from the outcomes questionnaire (that combined problems with drugs and alcohol and trouble with the law). The sex difference, males higher, was significant; the adoptees were higher than the biological offspring, although not significantly so; and the child's score on the externalizing factor was significantly correlated with the *Pd* of the mother who shared genes with the child, and not with that of the mother who did not.

Finally, the search of criminal records revealed several things. First, and not surprisingly, most of the children in the study—82 percent of the males and 94 percent of the females—did not appear in the criminal records. Second, although there were differences in both sexes in the direction of more convictions among the adoptees (22 percent versus 16 percent among males; 7 percent versus 4 percent among females) the adoptee/non-adoptee differences were not large, and fell short of statistical significance. Third, the ratings of trouble with the law on the outcomes questionnaire were in good agreement with the criminal records, as represented by correlations in the range .51 to .89 across the various sex and adoptive status groups. Lastly, there seemed not to be seriously biased attrition in our sample: the individuals lost to follow-up were not markedly less law abiding than the ones who stayed.

Further sections of Chapter 4 addressed friends and social activity and maturity and happiness. The adoptees had just as many friends in high school, but fewer friends and social activities as adults. The biological children were, as adults, rated as more happy and secure and more mature in their personalities than the adoptees. Neither IQ nor childhood extraversion predicted adult happiness and maturity among the adoptees, but childhood ratings of good socialization and emotional stability, and the absence of problem behavior in adolescence were favorable indicators. A similar pattern held for the biological children, except that a high childhood IQ tended to correlate negatively with later maturity and happiness. This was, however, less true of IQ measured ten years later in adolescence.

A final section of Chapter 4 looked at parental antecedents of childhood outcomes: Did favorable IQs and MMPIs in the parents predict favorable scores on the five outcome factors for their offspring, and did this occur for both adopted and biological children? The predictive relationships were very weak in either case, but on the whole were in a positive direction for the biological offspring, where genes were shared, and in a negative direction for the adoptive offspring, where they were not. This may tell us something about the environmental mechanisms involved in parent-child resemblance. The suggestion is that processes like imitation or identification, which would tend to lead to positive correlations, are being outweighed by processes like contrast or competition, which would tend to lead to negative ones.

3. Four Families

This book has mainly been emphasizing the cognitive, personality, and outcome dimensions along which we commonly assess individual differences. However, it is well to remind ourselves that this appraisal is based on concrete, specific individuals growing up in concrete, specific families. The following brief sketches may help give this sense. They are based on the parent interviews, but a number of circumstances and details have been altered to minimize clues to the identities of the individuals and families involved.

Family with Two Adopted Children, Small Town in East Texas—Interview with Mother and Father

Son---never got along at home or school---was spanked often---many
fights at school---grades poor in high school---in trouble
with the law for stealing and dangerous driving---frequent
truancy---graduated HS, no further schooling---aggressive,
domineering---exploits generosity of mother---now estranged

from mother---married, four children---owns own automobile business.

Daughter---excelled in everything she tried---excellent student (National Honor Society)---good relationships with parents---developed bulimia and received treatment---well now---master's degree---happily married, one child---teacher.

Family with One Adopted and One Biological Child, Central Texas City—Interview with Mother and Father

Adopted son---some rebellion in high school but outgrew it---good student---speaks well---no trouble with drugs or drinking---has master's degree in Education---very sociable---divorced---overcomes difficulty with ease.

Biological son---hyperactive child but not now---reading at age four---has a big heart---exceptional at math---practical---B.S. in chemical engineering---employed in sales---married, one child.

Family with One Adopted Child, Small Town in Texas Panhandle—Interview with Father (Mother Divorced)

Daughter---"tragic life"---screaming fits and head banging as a child ---multiple thefts even from parents---ran away often---no remorse---does anything she wants---proficient liar---constantly in trouble at school---currently on probation---never liked rules---once destroyed all her toys.

Family with Two Adopted Children, Medium-Size Texas City—Interview with Mother (Father Deceased)

Son---very gregarious even as a young child---always smiled---started piano at age six and loved it---never in trouble in school or out---A and B student---majored in music and became choral director---now in graduate school---married, two children---very involved with church.

Daughter---very shy---average student---"good kid"---no trouble in school---no school after H.S.---now married, one child, but many separations---cosmetologist then supermarket clerk now part-time receptionist.

At the beginning of one of his novels, Tolstoy says that happy families are all alike, but each unhappy family is unhappy in its own way. We beg to differ: each family, happy or unhappy, is distinctive in numerous ways, and all families, happy or unhappy, share at least some characteristics. This book has emphasized the variation of individuals along common dimensions, and the genetic and environmental sources of such variation. Another book on adoptive families might well have begun with the families and the varying configurations into which they fall. However, either approach would need to be cognizant of some of the limitations that adoption studies possess. These will be discussed in the next section of this chapter.

4. Some Limitations of Adoption Studies

One Limitation—Restriction of Range

The fact that for many traits adoptive siblings show low or zero correlations has usually been taken as evidence that the features of the family environment that are shared by siblings do not much affect the traits in question. Critics of this view have argued that the ranges of family environments encountered in adoption studies are so severely restricted that low correlations must inevitably result, even if in the unrestricted population there would be substantial correlations due to variations among family environments (e.g., Stoolmiller, 1998).

Selection in the Texas Adoption Project

Since there is little doubt that adoptive families in general and families in the Texas Adoption Project in particular are a selected group, we need to consider the effect of such selection on inferences about heredity and shared family environment from samples in which such selection has taken place. In a reply to Stoolmiller's critique, we argued that such an examination should consider the set of correlations as a whole, rather than just a single correlation, such as that between adoptive siblings (Loehlin & Horn, 2000).

In order to explore this issue further, we have carried out a simulation study. We used a two-step strategy. In the first step, we constructed a path model in which IQs were expressed in terms of genetic and environmental factors in an unselected population. We created two versions of this model, identical, except that in one, certain paths were set to values representing strong genetic influences, and in the other, the same paths were set to values representing strong influences of the family environment. (The rest of the paths were set to the same values in both models). We then randomly generated a large number of hypothetical families using each of the two models.

Then, in a second step, we drew a socioeconomically-selected subset of families from each set, and compared the means, standard deviations, and correlation coefficients of IQ in the subset with those actually observed in our data.

Readers curious about the details of the path model will find it described in detail in Appendix E. Briefly, the model specified relationships among parent, child, and birth parent IQs, mother's and father's educations, and father's occupation. It included a hypothetical variable of socioeconomic status with connections to the observed variables; it was on this variable that selection occurred. The "genetic" and "environmental" versions of the model differed in how the selection variable was connected to the parents' IQs and to the shared environments of the children. In the genetic version, the connection was mainly via the parents' genes, and these had a strong influence on the parents' IQs. In the environmental version, the connection was mainly via the parents' family environments, and these strongly influenced their IQs. Also, in the environmental model the socioeconomic variable had a greater influence on the shared environments of the offspring than it did in the genetic model.

The model was run to generate large random populations of hypothetical families—ten thousand for each version. From these, approximately 10 percent were selected from among those scoring high on the socioeconomic variable. Means and standard deviations were calculated for the IQs and the educational and occupational variables; these matched at least roughly the degree of selection actually observed in the sample. This was true for both the genetic and environmental versions of the model.

Correlations were then calculated among the observed variables in the TAP data and among their equivalents in each of the two simulated versions after the selection step. The question then was the following: For which of the simulated versions did the correlations agree best with the observed correlations?

For a number of comparisons, there was little difference. Recall that several paths, such as those between parents' education and IQs, were set to the same values in both models. But in other cases there was a difference. There were 8 instances among 29 comparisons in which there was an absolute discrepancy of .15 or more between the model-generated correlation and the observed correlation. Four of these affected both models—they presumably reflected inadequacies in the model or a poor choice of the path values shared by both versions. The other four large discrepancies all involved only the environmental version. The largest discrepancy was the correlation for genetically unrelated siblings, which was predicted to be much too high by the environmental model (i.e., .50). The actual correlation was .20, and the genetic model predicted .26. (The full list of predicted and observed correlations may be found in Appendix E.)

Conclusions about the Effects of Selection

After selection, as we have seen, the versions with relatively stronger genetic or stronger environmental paths did equally well (or poorly) for a number of comparisons; but where the predictions were substantially worse for only one, it was the "environmental" version. This does not mean that the "genetic" model or its path values were necessarily correct. But these results do suggest that, contrary to some critics, allowing for the presence of a substantial restriction of range in adoption studies of IQ does not invalidate the conclusion that the genes play a substantial role in explaining individual differences.

We would agree, however, that this topic merits further study. Our modeling has made simple linear assumptions. If there are sectors of the population that are essentially unrepresented in our samples, and if the processes of intellectual development are drastically different in these groups, inferences from adoption studies concerning the respective roles of genes and environment in such groups could be misleading. Current evidence mostly suggests, however, that U.S. subgroup differences in the structure of intellectual abilities are minimal (e.g., Carretta & Ree, 1995), as are differences in the relationships between intellectual and other developmental variables (e.g., Rowe, Vazsonyi, & Flannery, 1994). Thus, for now, it is reasonable to assume that at least the qualitative results of adoption studies of IQ will be broadly applicable in the U.S. population. Third-world populations, in which all else may be overwhelmed by the presence or absence of access to schooling or the effects of malnutrition, AIDS, or intestinal parasites may be another story and deserve separate study.

Does selection also affect other variables in the TAP, such as personality and psychopathology? As discussed in Chapter 4, adoptive parents have reduced means and smaller standard deviations on the MMPI, and so correlations involving psychopathology variables will be expected to be lowered in an adoption study. For normal personality variables, using the sample of earlier adoptions from the Methodist Mission Home, it was possible to compare scores on the scales of the California Psychological Inventory and the Thurstone Temperament Schedule with available general population norms. There was little evidence of restriction, except that the adoptive parents showed elevated means and reduced variability on traits related to conscientiousness (Loehlin, 2005), not surprising for respondents in a mail study and perhaps not for adoptive parents in general.

A Second Limitation—Nonadditive Genetic Variance

Typical adoption studies have an important limitation that we have mentioned several times in the course of this book—the genetic contribution to individual differences that they can assess is limited to the so-called additive effect of the genes involved. This is the cumulative effect of genes acting individually. By contrast, nonadditive effects of genes depend on configurations of genes. In the simplest kind of nonadditivity, called dominance by geneticists, the effect of a gene depends on the gene that it is paired with at the same locus on the chromosome. A deleterious recessive gene, for example, may have no effect if it is paired with a dominant gene, but cause trouble if it is paired with another recessive. Other nonadditive genetic effects, called epistasis by geneticists, involve interactions among genes at two or more loci, so that only a particular combination of genes may have an effect. Because a child receives a random half of its genes from each parent, genetic combinations are re-shuffled each generation, so that only their additive effects contribute to parent-child resemblance. Sibling resemblance may include some effects due to dominance, because two children stand a 25 percent chance of both inheriting the same pair of genes. However, if there is an epistatic effect that involves a number of genes, the chance of both siblings inheriting the whole set of genes becomes very small.

Behavior genetic designs involving identical twins are different from adoption studies; they can reflect the full range of genetic effects. Identical twins develop from a single fertilized ovum; they thus share genetic configurations as well as individual genes, and their resemblance reflects both additive and nonadditive effects of genes. If nonadditive genetic effects are important for a trait, designs involving identical twins, such as the comparison of identical and fraternal twin resemblance or that of identical twins reared apart and together, will tend to produce higher estimates of genetic effects than will ordinary adoption studies that only estimate additive genetic effects. Incorporating data for twins and twin families along with data from adoptive families in the CPI and TTS studies described in Chapter 3 essentially doubled heritability estimates because of the presence of data from identical twins in the model fitting. This suggests that nonadditive genetic influences are important for personality, a conclusion supported by data from a large twin-and-sibling study in Australia (Keller, et al., 2005) and a large twin-and-multiple-relatives study in the U.S. (Eaves, et al., 1998).

The presence of nonadditive genetic variance has been of some theoretical interest because it suggests that the trait in question has been subjected to natural selection—for personality traits, this would most likely be stabilizing selection, in which intermediate levels of a trait have a reproductive advantage over extreme values at either end (Penke, et al., 2007). Additive genetic variance is more rapidly depleted under natural selection than is nonadditive genetic variance, because individual genes are more closely associated with the trait when genetic effects are additive.

An alternative to nonadditive genetic variance that has sometimes been put forward to account for the greater similarity of identical twins is a greater similarity of their environments. At least three arguments can be raised against this explanation: (1) identical twins reared apart in separate families, for whom this factor should not operate, are nearly as similar as identical twins reared together in the same families (Bouchard, et al., 1990); (2) differences in the degree to which identical twins are treated alike (being dressed alike or not, for example) do not predict their resemblance in personality (Loehlin & Nichols, 1976); and (3) if sharing family environments seems to have so little effect for siblings in general, why should increasing it for identical twins make such a difference?

A Third Limitation—Genotype-Environment Interaction

In most of this book, we have been allocating the sources of individual differences into the broad categories of genes and environments, but what about "neither" or "both"? An example of "neither" is measurement error. Deficiencies in the instrument with which a trait is measured are not properly assigned to either the genetic or the environmental causes of variation on the trait. In cases where we have information about the reliability of our measures, we can usually specify or model the contribution of measurement error separately. Where we simply make a three-way breakdown into the contribution of the genes, shared family environments, and everything else measurement errors fall into the third category.

Or what about the case of "both"? Gene-environment interaction is an example. We are not referring here to the elaborate series of interactions between genes and environments that takes place in the development of any organism, including humans, but to interaction in the statistician's sense: individual differences not predictable (even in principle) from knowledge of the organism's genes, or knowledge of the environments within which the organism develops, but only from the particular combination of genes and environments involved. For example, suppose that a particular environmental circumstance is beneficial to individuals with one version of a gene and damaging to individuals with another. Knowledge of whether an individual has been exposed to this environment does not predict the outcome: it depends on which gene he has. And knowledge of the gene alone is not predictive: the outcome depends on whether or not the individual has been exposed to the environmental circumstance. Only if you know both are you in business.

In recent years, there has been a good deal of interest among behavior geneticists in the topic of gene-environment interactions. One such interaction that has been reported is that the contribution of genes to individual differences in IQ may vary with social class—that as socioeconomic status rises, the genes may make a larger contribution to individual differences (Turkheimer, et al., 2003; Harden, et al., 2007). However, this finding has not been universal (e.g., Van Den Oord & Rowe, 1997). Another example of interaction involves antisocial behavior. In an Iowa adoption study, adverse adoptive home environments predicted conduct disorder symptoms only in adoptees that had adverse biological backgrounds (Cadoret, et al., 1995).

Adoption studies play a paradoxical role in the study of gene-environment interaction. On the one hand, they provide an unmatched opportunity for the study of such interactions. Is an outcome predictable from knowledge of the biological parents (genes), knowledge of the adoptive families (environment), or only from a joint knowledge of both (interaction)? On the other hand, the limitation of range of family environments in adoptive families may preclude the discovery of interactions that would be evident over a wider range of environments.

The Texas Adoption Project does not provide much evidence for gene-environment interactions, although the large "everything else" category for most of its measures allows plenty of room for such. Table 2.8 in Chapter 2 presented the data for adopted children's IQs according to the IQs of the birth mother and the socioeconomic status of the adoptive family. There was little evidence of an interaction: having a birth mother with a higher IQ made a difference, but it made about the same amount of difference in adoptive families of lower or higher socioeconomic status.

A similar analysis based on adoptive and birth mothers' scores on the MMPI *Pd* scale yielded a similar result. Having a birth mother with a relatively high or low *Pd* score made a difference in an adopted child's *Pd* score, but there was no interaction: there was about the same amount of difference when the children's adoptive mothers were higher on *Pd* as when they were lower (Table 4.12 in Chapter 4). Of course, restriction of range could be playing a role. The adoptive mothers have relatively low means and small standard deviations on *Pd* (see Chapter 4), and one cannot rule out the possibility that over a wider range one might have observed a differential effect.

A Fourth Limitation—Genotype-Environment Correlation

Another complication involving genes and environments is that they may be correlated, introducing ambiguity as to which is producing a given effect. For example, high-IQ parents in ordinary families may provide their children with genes conducive to IQ as well as providing environments having the same tendency (many books in the home, good schools, personal example). This is called, by behavior geneticists, *passive* gene-environment correlation (there are two other kinds, *evocative* and *active*, involving others' reactions to the child's traits, or the child actively seeking out environments related to his or her abilities or temperament). When positive passive gene-environment correlation is present, favorable genes and favorable environments tend to go together and unfavorable genes and unfavorable environments likewise, and we expect to see a wider range of scores on the trait than if genes and environments were matched at random, because there will be more individuals receiving the combinations placing them at the favorable or unfavorable extremes. An adoption study provides one way of examining this. The biological children in the families receive their genes and their environments from the same set of parents, the adoptive children receive them from different sets. So we expect more gene-environment correlation in the first group than in the second, and, hence, if passive gene-environment correlation is a substantial factor, we would predict larger standard deviations among the biological than among the adopted children. Table 5.1 shows standard deviations for the group of traits used in several tables in Chapter 4: IQs

Table 5.1
Standard Deviations for Adopted and Biological Children
(Ns in Parentheses)

Trait	Adopted		Biological	
IQ, original study	11.66	(467)	11.11	(159)
IQ, 10-year follow-up	13.13	(274)	12.62	(110)
Extraversion	1.24	(481)	1.12	(170)
Good socialization	1.06	(480)	.93	(170)
Emotional stability	1.13	(481)	1.12	(172)
IPB in adolescence	6.00	(255)	3.09	(111)

Note: IPB = index of problem behavior rated from parent interviews.

at the original and follow-up testings, the three personality dimensions from the parental ratings, and the Index of Problem Behaviors during adolescence.

Clearly, there is no evidence that the biological offspring have larger standard deviations than the adopted offspring—indeed, the difference, if any, is in the opposite direction. Now, one needs fairly large samples to get very precise estimates of variation, and it is probably the case that these samples, particularly some of those involving the biological offspring, are not large enough to let us draw strong conclusions about variability differences. Such as they are, however, the differences suggest that if passive gene-environment correlations exist, they might well be negative. This may be another example of the paradoxical effects of family environment that we have noted at several points in discussing the TAP data.

What about the active and evocative varieties of gene-environment correlations? These correlations reflect the genes of the individual in question, and not those of the parents, and thus adoption studies provide no special advantage in studying them. Some would argue that, because these effects have their origin in the individual's genotype, they should just be counted as genetic effects: one of the ways that genes express themselves is through selecting or modifying their environments. However, behavior geneticists who come from a psychological background would usually want to distinguish between the effects of genes via cellular environments and the effects of genes via social and behavioral environments. Active and evocative gene-environment correlations represent ways of talking about the latter. Measurement of such correlations is simple in principle, but not easy in practice. One needs measures of genotypes and of enough environments over time to be able to trace causal sequences. As far as the TAP is concerned, some of the "genetic" effects we observe may well involve the effects of active or evocative gene-environment correlation, but a different kind of study would be required to determine this.

5. Some Implications of the Texas Adoption Project

Implications for Parents Contemplating the Adoption of a Child

Looking at the varied outcomes for the adopted children from the TAP it seems that a few cautionary remarks are in order before any general conclusions are drawn. The first is that adoption outcomes may be judged differently according to the perspectives of the different interested parties. In some cases, we observed that the mother and father rendered different judgments about their child's successes and shortcomings. Furthermore, similar objective outcomes (e. g., high school graduate) can be seen as a positive or negative depending not only on the different expectations held by family members but by standards that vary from one family to another. One relatively common disappointment for well-educated adoptive parents (the majority of our adoptive parents had college degrees) was that too often their adopted children did not attend or graduate from college.

Some adoptive parents were able to surmount their own disappointments and render judgments based on broader and more philosophical perspectives. One father said: "Even though our adopted child did not graduate from high school he is employed and stays out of trouble. He is probably better off than he would have been if raised by his biological parents." This seemed more than a rationalization. Rather it was an acknowledgment of limits combined with a sturdy evaluation of the qualities inherent in a "good life."

Certain outcomes seem less subject to individual and family variations in expectations and standards. In the interviews the prominent journalist, the PhD in the hard sciences, and the graduate student in music seemed to evoke nothing but praiseworthy comments tinged with pride from adoptive parents. Educational and occupational success seems to trump other ways of judging life's outcomes. For instance, only rarely did social and emotional limitations in a child become a matter of concern in the interview if it was clear that the child had achieved status in the educational or occupational domains. This observation probably derives from the fact that social skill and emotional stability are partially responsible for success in school and work. When we see success we are confident social and emotional sufficiency are there; when we see failure we look to social and emotional inadequacies to explain why.

Granting these differences in perspective, there was still a great variety in the outcomes in the TAP adoptive families. There were some interviews where the adoptive parents could not help but brag about their children. One couple proudly brought out a copy of a national publication and pointed to the editorial board listed on the inside. Another arranged for us, during the interview, to talk by phone to their advanced graduate student child who was due shortly to receive a PhD. Still another talked about the "perfect all-around man" his child had become—successful in business, community and church leader, loving father and husband who was also very attentive to his parents.

In order to encourage frankness we wanted to interview the adoptive parents without their child being present but one adoptee wanted to attend their parents' interview to brag about them. This adoptee had visited with her biological family and reported that she was much better off with her adoptive family. "I really have made out like a bandit," is the colorful way she put it. Her adoptive parents reciprocated her feelings.

Other adoptive parents were impressed with the resiliency of their adopted children; a father who had divorced after adopting said his child had every excuse for "turning out bad" but was, instead, "a great kid." A mother whose first adoption had become a "homeless person" was amazed to see how her other adoptee was different in "every way" in spite of bad influences from the first child.

Not all adoptive parents reacted in this way. At the end of our interview with one pair of adoptive parents the father pressed us to ask them if they would do it (adopt) again. We did ask and the answer came quickly and resolutely: "NO!" We were surprised at the timing and vehemence of his response because until that time there had been no indication of more than a usual amount of dissatisfaction with their adoptee either as a child or adult. When we tried to follow-up and solicit specific reasons for his judgment, he would only say "it wasn't worth it."

Another adoptive mother volunteered this remark: "If X hadn't been our first adoptee we never would have adopted the others."

One tearful father with two delinquent adoptees under court supervision sobbed: "How could God allow this to happen to good Christians?"

A rather grim mother said it all by informing us that she had obtained an order of protection against one of her adopted children because she had good reason to fear for her safety. The reason was a prior assault following a refusal to give, yet again, her grown daughter more money.

One reticent mother would only go as far as stating, "She has a big honesty problem."

Obviously, there are serious problems with some of these adoptees, but do we want to classify these adoptions as unsuccessful? What if one parent is unhappy but the other is less so? Such was the case for first set of parents mentioned. And what if both parents are dissatisfied but the grown child relatively content—for example, after establishing contact with less than admirable biological parents?

Recommendations?

Can we make any recommendations to parents considering adoption based on the results of this study? First, given that the birth-mother characteristics were at least as predictive of outcomes as the adoptive family characteristics, we would recommend that the adoptive parents obtain as much information as they can about the genetic parents of the child prior to making a final decision. This is not because outcomes are highly predictable from such information—far from it. The correlations we observed were mostly quite modest in magnitude. But even if the odds are only statistical, why stack them against you?

Which characteristics in biological parents seem to carry significant risks for their adopted away children? A variety of existing research—too extensive to discuss in detail here—suggests the following: serious mental illness, mental retardation, alcoholism, felony-level criminality, attention deficit disorder, and learning disabilities. We consider it prudent for prospective adoptive parents to inquire about these traits among biological parents who are giving up their children for adoption. Not that the presence of such would necessarily invalidate the choice to adopt—since the associated risks rarely exceed the 20 to 30 percent range—but foreknowledge of possibility might prove useful in dealing with some eventualities. Information on a wider array of medical and other conditions may be found in sources such as Pierce (1990).

Second, be reasonably optimistic. Most of the adopted children in our study (and in other studies of adoptions) have turned out within the normal range of abilities, personalities, and life outcomes. There are cases of individuals with serious behavioral problems, as evidenced by some of the examples mentioned earlier, but it should not be forgotten that such problems can also occur with ordinary biological children, although less frequently. To take a particular numerical example, fewer than 1 in 20 of the biological children received scores on the adolescent

Index of Problem Behavior of 10 or above; whereas about 1 in 5 of the adopted children did.

In short, our advice to prospective adoptive parents is not to ignore the statistical odds, but to remember that that is all they are. No matter how much you know in advance (and you might as well know all you can), individual children will turn out in surprising ways. And who would really want it to be otherwise?

Implications for Understanding Human Differences

We addressed this issue at an earlier point in this chapter. It is our belief that a major contribution of adoption studies to general human knowledge (as distinct from the specifics of the adoption process as such) is in learning to what extent the many differences we see in the people around us reflect differences in their genes, differences in the family environments in which those genes developed, or something else, such as sheer accident or the effects of particular gene-environment combinations.

In our study, we repeatedly found evidence that these ubiquitous differences among individuals reflect (to a modest extent) differences among their genes. In a smaller number of cases, we found evidence of the effects of shared family environment, particularly when the children were young—by adulthood, such effects often had declined to insignificance.

Much of human variation in abilities, personality, and life outcomes fell into the third, residual category: uncertain. Some of this variation no doubt represents things that happen to individuals by chance, independent of their family backgrounds or their genetic proclivities. Another part no doubt reflects the effects of particular gene-environment combinations. Studies that include a fine-grained recording of individual environmental exposures and measurement of individual responses and individual genotypes should permit progress in decreasing this area of uncertainty. Furthermore, such studies are approaching technical feasibility to a degree that we could hardly have imagined at the time we conceived the TAP. Even if technically feasible, however, a study of this kind would disturb some people on moral and ethical grounds. Is it right to know that much about anybody? Our own view is that knowledge about the sources of the endlessly fascinating differences among human beings can be used for good or for evil purposes, as can knowledge about anything else. It is our belief that in human history the good purposes have usually—although not always—won out over the evil ones, and we expect this trend to continue. We would not be devoting a good part of our own lives to the expansion and dissemination of knowledge about human variation if we did not. For the benefit of the nervous among you, we might also add that we expect that the area of uncertainty about the causes of the abilities, personalities, and life outcomes of individuals will remain very, very large for a long, long time.

Implications for Understanding Human Development

Understanding human development involves a great deal more than being able to sort the causes of human differences into broad bins like "genes," "family environment," and "undecided." Thus, an adoption study, *per se*, does not take us very far along the path of understanding human development. If you are studying the development of some aspect of human behavior, such as sociability or cognitive skill, an adoption study such as ours barely scratches the surface.

Yet, we would argue that it provides you with a very important piece of information: Where to look. It might tell you, for example, that family-to-family differences do not account for much of the variation in the particular aspect of behavior that you are interested in, so that you would be better off looking for things that happen differently to different family members, or that affect them differently depending on what genes they have. You still have the challenge of figuring out just what is going on, but in looking in the place where the action seems to be, as opposed to the place where it seems not to be, you should improve your odds of making progress.

Thus, a developmentalist should think of an adoption study or other behavior genetics study as a first step, not a final destination. After a first step, there are still many steps needed to reach a destination, but it usually helps you get there if the first step starts you in the right direction.

6. Final Comments

The study reported in this book has not left us with the belief that human abilities, personalities, and life outcomes are simple or easily understood. Far from it. In our personal interviews with the adoptive parents, and in our interactions with the hundreds of thousands of numbers that our various tests and questionnaires have produced, we have become increasingly impressed with the complexity of the situation confronting anyone who wants to understand human differences or human development. Yet, progress is made one step at a time, and as we have tried to show in the chapters of this book, we have been able to locate a great deal of modest order in this complexity.

We remind you that we have not done this alone. In the Preface you will find a longer list of names of those who have helped on the project, but we want to give special acknowledgment here to the contributions of several of them: the third member of our original group, the late and greatly gifted Professor Lee Willerman; Spencer Stockwell, Harold Burkhardt, Larry Watson, and Arthur Bouton of the Methodist Mission Home; talented and dedicated graduate students Jody Ernst, Jeremy Beer, Richard Arnold, and Gerald Turner; and finally—and above all—the contribution of the members of the three hundred adoptive families who gave liberally of their time and their insights to make this study possible.

We are confident that a new generation of researchers with an improved technology will move far beyond the level we have been able to achieve in this study, but we hope that they will find that what we have done helps them on their way. We also hope that the many thousands of people who are involved in one way or another with adoption—adoptees, families who adopt, adoption professionals—will find that our work provides them with some context for their day-to-day concerns with the adoption process and its outcomes. Finally, we hope that you, the reader of this book, have, in your own way, benefited from your encounter with it.

Appendix A

Initial Letter to Families

Text of letter from the director of the Methodist Mission Home to prospective families in the Texas Adoption Project:

Sometimes some unexpected benefits develop from just day-to-day activities!

For the last fifteen years our HOME has made a practice of providing psychological testing for most of our residents because we were convinced that this would help our counselors understand the girls' problems sooner and more accurately. For this reason alone such testing has been of great value.

Now, however, we find that this testing program provides another, and perhaps a larger benefit. I have been asked to co-operate with the University of Texas Psychology Department on an unusual Research Project which will use these test results as a basic factor in such a Study. No such Study has ever been made with such extensive data as our records provide.

The proposed Study will make a careful correlation between the intelligence and personality of the biological mother with that of the adoptive parents. Also, professional testing will be made of the children in the adoptive home. It is believed that such a Study will provide many basic facts about the relative influence of heredity and environment upon the development of adopted children.

Because your family met the minimum requirements for inclusion in such a Research Study, we are hoping you will want to cooperate with us on it. There will be no cost whatever to you in connection with this study.

Dr. Stockwell, who was in charge of adoptions at the time you became Adoptive Parents, is the HOME's representative on this Adoption Research Program—and he is looking forward to a personal visit with you and your family to discuss this matter with you and to renew his friendship with you.

Please use the enclosed self-addressed card to let us know your willingness to help us on this important matter.

Sincerely, with thanks

Rev. Harold D. Burkhardt,
Administrator

Appendix B

Rating Scales

This appendix contains three rating forms used in the TAP: a four-page form for parents' rating of their children's personality traits, a one-page form used by the interviewer to summarize the interview concerning each child, and the one-page Outcomes Questionnaire (with consent form for sibling ratings on the reverse).

1. *Personality Rating Scale.* (36-item version; the first 24 items were used in original study and ten-year follow-up).
2. *Rating Scale, Interview.*
3. *Outcomes Questionnaire.*
4. *Back of outcomes questionnaire* (consent for sibling rating).

PARENT PERSONALITY RATINGS

On this form we would like you to locate each of your children on each of the following dimensions of personality. Your oldest child (as listed on the front sheet) will be represented by the number 1, next oldest by 2 and so on. Please write these numbers above each of the horizontal lines as shown in the following example. Of course, if you have one child there will only be one entry above the line.

<u>EXAMPLE</u>

If you had actually put your children in the positions shown in the example it would have meant that you rated your second oldest child as much taller than other children his age and that your oldest is slightly shorter than most children his age. A rating of 5 would have indicated average height, so you can see that an 8 means very tall, while a 4 means slightly shorter than average.

Please remember to locate each of your children on each dimension and keep in mind that you are comparing your children to other children of the same age.

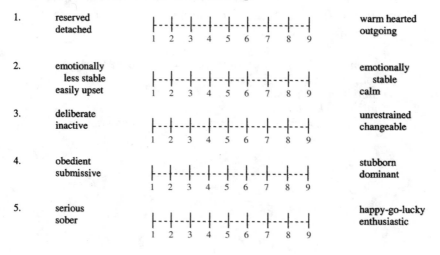

6.	disregards rules expedient	├--┼---┼--┼--┼---┼--┼--┼---┼ 1 2 3 4 5 6 7 8 9	conscientious moralistic
7.	relaxed	├--┼---┼--┼--┼---┼--┼--┼---┤ 1 2 3 4 5 6 7 8 9	tense
8.	impatient excitable	├--┼--┼--┼--┼--┼--┼--┼---┤ 1 2 3 4 5 6 7 8 9	patient subdued
9.	talkative	├--┼--┼--┼--┼--┼--┼--┼---┤ 1 2 3 4 5 6 7 8 9	reserved
10.	shy timid	├--┼--┼--┼--┼--┼--┼--┼---┤ 1 2 3 4 5 6 7 8 9	socially bold adventurous
11.	realistic	├--┼--┼--┼--┼--┼--┼--┼---┤ 1 2 3 4 5 6 7 8 9	sentimental
12.	full of zest	├--┼--┼--┼--┼--┼--┼--┼---┤ 1 2 3 4 5 6 7 8 9	restrained
13.	self-assured secure	├--┼--┼--┼--┼--┼--┼--┼---┤ 1 2 3 4 5 6 7 8 9	apprehensive insecure
14.	uncontrolled follows own urges	├--┼--┼--┼--┼--┼--┼--┼---┤ 1 2 3 4 5 6 7 8 9	controlled self-disciplined
15.	dependent	├--┼---┼--┼---┼--┼--┼---┼---┤ 1 2 3 4 5 6 7 8 9	self-reliant
16.	compulsive in following social rules	├--┼--┼--┼--┼--┼--┼--┼---┤ 1 2 3 4 5 6 7 8 9	careless of social rules

17. easygoing
    participates
    1 2 3 4 5 6 7 8 9
    critical
    aloof

18. frustrated
    fretful
    1 2 3 4 5 6 7 8 9
    unfrustrated
    composed

19. earnest
    1 2 3 4 5 6 7 8 9
    frivolous

20. worries
    guilt prone
    1 2 3 4 5 6 7 8 9
    complacent
    untroubled

21. assertive
    competitive
    1 2 3 4 5 6 7 8 9
    easily led
    accomadating

22. individualistic
    1 2 3 4 5 6 7 8 9
    likes group
    activity

23. sensitive to
    threats
    1 2 3 4 5 6 7 8 9
    unresponsive
    to threats

24. mature
    faces reality
    1 2 3 4 5 6 7 8 9
    affected by
    feelings
    changeable

25. likes variety
    1 2 3 4 5 6 7 8 9
    likes routine

26. unselfish
    1 2 3 4 5 6 7 8 9
    selfish

27. enjoys ideas
    1 2 3 4 5 6 7 8 9
    thinks
    concretely

28. wary
    1 2 3 4 5 6 7 8 9
    trusting

29.   Wide interests $\vdash--\vdash---\vdash--\vdash--\vdash---\vdash--\vdash---\vdash---\dashv$ Narrow
                          1   2   3   4   5   6   7   8   9   interests

30.   helpful $\vdash--\vdash---\vdash--\vdash--\vdash---\vdash--\vdash---\vdash---\dashv$ indifferent
                          1   2   3   4   5   6   7   8   9   to others

31.   practical $\vdash--\vdash---\vdash--\vdash--\vdash---\vdash--\vdash---\vdash---\dashv$ imaginative
                          1   2   3   4   5   6   7   8   9

32.   shows off $\vdash--\vdash---\vdash--\vdash--\vdash---\vdash--\vdash---\vdash---\dashv$ modest
                          1   2   3   4   5   6   7   8   9

33.   poetic $\vdash--\vdash---\vdash--\vdash--\vdash---\vdash--\vdash---\vdash---\dashv$ down-to-earth
                          1   2   3   4   5   6   7   8   9

34.   agreeable $\vdash--\vdash---\vdash--\vdash--\vdash---\vdash--\vdash---\vdash---\dashv$ disagreeable
                          1   2   3   4   5   6   7   8   9

35.   conventional $\vdash--\vdash---\vdash--\vdash--\vdash---\vdash--\vdash---\vdash---\dashv$ original
                          1   2   3   4   5   6   7   8   9

36.   quarrelsome $\vdash--\vdash---\vdash--\vdash--\vdash---\vdash--\vdash---\vdash---\dashv$ good
                          1   2   3   4   5   6   7   8   9   natured

INTERVIEWER'S RATING SCALE
(fill out one for each child)

Rater _____ Date of interview_____Date of rating_____

First name of ratee_____ Sex: M F   Family code_____

(1) Highest level of education completed _____

(2) Current occupational level (or that of most recent sustained employment):

Job title or description _____

_____

Level of responsibility of job:
    little or no responsibility   1 2 3 4 5 6 7 8 9   great deal of responsibility

Level of skill of job:
    unskilled labor   1 2 3 4 5 6 7 8 9   highly trained professional

Overall stability of occupational history:
    little or no stability   1 2 3 4 5 6 7 8 9   highly stable

(3) Stability and happiness in marriage (or other committed relationship):

    very unstable and/or unhappy   1 2 3 4 5 6 7 8 9   very stable and happy

(4) Presence of problems of an externalizing type (e.g., antisociality, substance abuse):

    no problems of this type   1 2 3 4 5 6 7 8 9   many problems of this type

(5) Presence of problems of an internalizing type (e.g., anxiety, depression):

    no problems of this type   1 2 3 4 5 6 7 8 9   many problems of this type

(6) Sociability

    few friends, little social activity   1 2 3 4 5 6 7 8 9   lots of friends & social activity

(7) Autonomy
    dependent on others   1 2 3 4 5 6 7 8 9   independent, self-reliant

(8) Social resposibility
    immature, selfish   1 2 3 4 5 6 7 8 9   mature, responsible, helpful

OUTCOMES QUESTIONNAIRE

RATING SCALE   Code No. _____

Rater: _____   Person rated:__Self____   Date_____

Below, describe the person being rated by filling in the blank or circling the number that best reflects your opinion. If you have no information at all concerning an item, simply omit it. If you have further comments, or need to explain any of your answers, feel free to use the margins or the back of the page.

(1) Highest level of education completed (check one): __less than HS grad; __HS grad or GED;

__1 or 2 yrs college; __3 or 4 yrs college; __college grad; __post-grad work.

(2) School adjustment during junior high and high school

poor student	1 2 3 4 5 6 7 8 9	excellent student
isolated	1 2 3 4 5 6 7 8 9	many friends
often in trouble	1 2 3 4 5 6 7 8 9	never in trouble

(3) Emotional closeness to parents: During his or her school years, was

very close to father	1 2 3 4 5 6 7 8 9	very distant from father
very close to mother	1 2 3 4 5 6 7 8 9	very distant from mother

(4) Current or most recent job (describe)_____

little responsibility	1 2 3 4 5 6 7 8 9	much responsibility

(5) Employment history (since finishing school):

many job changes	1 2 3 4 5 6 7 8 9	highly stable

(6) Currently is: __single; __living together; __married; __separated; __divorced; __widowed

(7) History of marriage (or similar relationships—omit if none):

very unstable and/or unhappy	1 2 3 4 5 6 7 8 9	very stable and happy

(8) Personal problems in recent years:

no drug or alcohol problems	1 2 3 4 5 6 7 8 9	serious drug or alcohol problems
always happy and secure	1 2 3 4 5 6 7 8 9	often anxious or depressed
never in trouble with the law	1 2 3 4 5 6 7 8 9	often in trouble with the law

(9) Current personality:

few friends, little social activity	1 2 3 4 5 6 7 8 9	lots of friends & social activity
very dependent on others	1 2 3 4 5 6 7 8 9	independent, self-reliant
immature, selfish	1 2 3 4 5 6 7 8 9	mature, helpful
erratic, undependable	1 2 3 4 5 6 7 8 9	conscientious, reliable
hostile, disagreeable	1 2 3 4 5 6 7 8 9	pleasant, agreeable

BACK OF OUTCOMES QUESTIONNAIRE

If you have brothers and sisters: Would you be willing to fill out a questionnaire like the one on the other side, describing them? ___Yes ___No ___Maybe ___Not applicable

Would you be willing to have them fill out such a questionnaire describing you?

___Yes ___No ___Not applicable

(All descriptions would be for research purposes only, and would be kept in strict confidence.)

Appendix C

IQ Test Details

Reliabilities of the Different IQ Tests

In interpreting test intercorrelations, it is important to take into account the reliabilities of the tests involved. The reliability of a test is the extent to which scores on the test reflect a stable underlying trait as opposed to random errors of measurement. If two tests each measure exactly the same underlying attribute, but measure it with error, they will not correlate perfectly. Assuming that the errors of measurement occur randomly, if each of the two tests has a reliability of .80, the maximum possible correlation between them (in the case of perfect agreement on the underlying trait) will not be 1.00, it will be .80. (If their reliabilities differ, the limit will be the geometric mean of the two reliabilities—tests that have reliabilities of .70 and .90 can correlate up to $\sqrt{[.70 \times .90]} = .79$.)

There are a number of ways of estimating the reliability of a test. Table C.1 shows the reliabilities of several of the IQ tests used in this study estimated via the internal consistency of their subscales, expressed by a coefficient known as Cronbach's alpha. It is an index of the extent to which the different subscales are all measuring something in common, which we are calling general intelligence. There is considerable theoretical debate as to exactly what it is that causes various measures of intellectual skills to intercorrelate, but something does, and alpha is an index of how well that something is being measured.

Several things are worth noting about this table. First, the reliabilities are all considerably less than 1.00. The majority fall in the range .75 to .85, but a few drop down to .60 or so. The main reason for this is a restriction of range in the IQs of the sample. Where true scores differ over a relatively narrow range, it is harder to make accurate discriminations

Table C.1
Reliabilities of IQ Tests in Various Groups

Group	VIQ α	VIQ N	PIQ α	PIQ N	IQ α	IQ N	Beta IQ α	Beta IQ N
Original testing								
Adoptive fathers	.82	291	.74	291	.85	291	.73	296
Adoptive mothers	.80	289	.68	289	.84	289	.75	292
Birth mothers	.70	51	.77	51	.84	51	.69	356
Adopted children	.75	323	.59	323	.78	323	--	--
Biological children	.81	115	.63	115	.76	115	--	--
10-year follow-up								
Adopted children	.83	260	.70	260	.84	260	.59	255
Biological children	.85	104	.63	104	.84	104	.67	93

Note: α = Cronbach alpha reliability based on intercorrelations among subscales. VIQ = Verbal IQ (6 scales, 5 for birth mothers), PIQ = Performance IQ (5 scales), IQ = Full scale IQ (11 scales, 10 for birth mothers), Beta = Revised Beta IQ (6 scales). In original testing, VIQs, PIQs, and IQs from WAIS for adoptive fathers and mothers, mostly from WAIS for birth mothers, mostly from WISC for children; in follow-up, from WAIS-R or WISC-R.

among them in the presence of measurement error. We discuss restriction of range in more detail in Chapter 5.

Second, the tests differ in reliability. The verbal and performance IQs of the Wechsler scales are each based on less information than the full test, and on the whole are less reliable. The performance IQ, typically based on 5 subscales as against 6 for the verbal IQ, tends to be less reliable than the VIQ. (Other things equal, internal-consistency measures of reliability will increase with an increase in the number of items on which they are based.) The WAIS or WISC IQs tend to be more reliable than the Beta. Partly this reflects the 6 subscales of the Beta versus the 10 or 11 of the Wechsler test, partly it reflects a more severe restriction of range on the Beta, and quite possibly the individually administered WAIS and WISC may simply be better tests.

Third, there were modest differences among the groups. At the time of the original testing, the children were less reliably measured than their parents were, although by the time of the follow-up the differences were slight. The birth mothers were anomalous—they appeared to be less reliably measured on the verbal than on the performance scales, although the reliability of the full-scale IQ was comparable to that of the adoptive parents. However, the sample that received a Wechsler IQ test was fairly small, and non-random, as a Wechsler test was sometimes given to check on a Beta IQ that seemed out of line.

Equivalence of IQs from Different Tests

Taking into account their reliabilities, to what extent can we reasonably assume that the different IQ tests are measuring the same thing? Table C.2 provides some evidence. In it are given the raw correlations r and correlations r_c corrected for unreliability, in various combinations: VIQ and PIQ from the Wechsler tests; both of these with the Beta IQ; and the full-scale Wechsler IQ with the Beta IQ. It would appear that the IQ based on the Wechsler performance scales, the PIQ, is essentially the same as the Revised Beta IQ. The corrected correlations, in fact, are slightly in excess of unity, suggesting that these tests may share specific factors as well as a common factor. This is plausible, because a number of the subtests of the two are quite similar. For all other combinations, the corrected correlations fall appreciably below unity, suggesting that the tests, particularly the verbal and performance tests, are measuring different mixes of cognitive skills. The overall IQs as measured by the Revised Beta and by the Wechsler tests are not very different, however—the

Table C.2
Correlations of IQs from Different Tests

Group	VIQ-PIQ r	VIQ-PIQ r_c	VIQ-Beta r	VIQ-Beta r_c	PIQ-Beta r	PIQ-Beta r_c	IQ-Beta r	IQ-Beta r_c	N
Original testing									
Adoptive fathers	.57	.73	.54	.70	.75	1.02	.71	.90	292
Adoptive mothers	.60	.81	.60	.77	.72	1.01	.73	.92	289-290
Birth mothers	.67	.91	.41	.59	.77	1.06	.63	.83	32-53
Adopted children	.48	.72							410
Biological children	.31	.43							145
10-year follow-up									
Adopted children	.51	.67	.42	.60	.66	1.03	.60	.85	255-275
Biological children	.47	.64	.42	.56	.70	1.08	.63	.84	93-112

Note: r = original correlation, r_c = correlation corrected for unreliability, VIQ=Verbal IQ (IQ based on verbal scales of Wechsler tests), PIQ=Performance IQ (IQ based on performance scales of Wechsler tests), IQ=Full scale IQ (IQ based on V and P scales combined), Beta=Revised Beta IQ. In original study, VIQs, PIQs, and IQs from WAIS for adoptive fathers and mothers, mostly from WAIS for birth mothers, mostly from WISC for children; in follow-up, from WAIS-R or WISC-R.

correlations are predominantly in the .85 to .90 range after measurement error is taken into account.

IQ Adjustment—"Flynn Effects"

We are also interested in comparing average IQ levels in the various groups. Comparisons of IQs across tests standardized at different times present a problem, however, due to the upward creep of IQ test performance over time that has been documented by J. F. Flynn (1984, 1987), and is often referred to as the "Flynn effect." IQ tests are renormed at intervals to deal with this drift, and the average IQ is reset to 100, but in the periods between normings, IQs creep upwards at a rate estimated by Flynn as about three-tenths of an IQ point per year for typical US IQ tests. Thus, if someone whose intellectual ability is exactly at the US average in 1975 is given a WAIS, normed in mid-1953, we would expect him to score about 6 IQ points too high: (1975-1953.5) x .3 = 6.45, or an IQ of 106. To give him the IQ of 100 that properly reflects his position as average for the population, we would need to adjust his obtained IQ downward by 6 points.

Such adjustments are necessary when comparing individuals tested at different times, or on tests for which different periods of times have elapsed since their standardization. If we want to ask, for example, whether the adopted children in our sample average higher in IQ than their birth mothers, we need to allow for the fact that the birth mothers were tested some years before their children were, and that the two groups were administered various tests normed at differing dates over a forty-six-year span. The simplest way to do this is to score all IQ tests according to their manuals and the provided norms, and then to adjust each IQ based on the interval of time between the date the test was normed and the date the test was taken. We have done this following Flynn's procedure, using a standard adjustment of .3 IQ points per year. We have also followed Flynn in his allowances for different standard deviations of tests (e.g., 16 versus 15 points) and for the different racial compositions of their standardization samples.

Adjustment of the Revised Beta IQs presented some special problems. Flynn does not include it in his table of tests. This group test was normed not on a random sample of the US population, but on a sample of male prisoners selected to match US 1940 census data on age, education, and socioeconomic status (Lindner & Gurvitz, 1946). Therefore, we have taken 1940 as the base year for the norms, rather than the date of their actual publication in 1946. Although we checked the age standardization of the test against age differences in our own sample and found good agreement (for more details, see Loehlin et al., 1997), the equivalence of adjusted Beta IQs with those of the other tests must be taken with some caution. In addition, the Beta is a nonverbal IQ test, and there is some evidence (Flynn, 1984) to suggest that norm creep may be greater for nonverbal tests.

A number of approximations are involved in these adjustments. To begin with, the norming process for tests does not take place instantaneously, but typically over a period of two or three years—we have followed Flynn in using the midpoints of these intervals for adjustment purposes. These dates can be found in Table 2.3 in the main text. We have used a uniform .3 IQ points per year for adjustments, although no doubt in a fully refined treatment this should vary a bit from time to time and from test to test. Possibly, we should have used a slightly higher figure for the Revised Beta, as a nonverbal test—there are some indications that the corrected values for the Beta average a little on the low side, but this might also partly reflect ceiling effects on this test, discussed in the main text. We have used some approximations in our own data as well. We have taken the date of testing for the original study as mid-1974, although the actual testing took place over a period of some time before and after that date (for the follow-up, we had the actual dates of testing recorded in our files, and so used those). We estimated the date of testing of birth mothers via the ages of their children, plus a little extra to allow for the fact that they were tested while in residence at the Home before the birth of their child. With the various approximations, the adjusted IQs in individual cases might well sometimes be off by an IQ point (= 3 years), but the averages should be fairly accurate—and much closer to the truth than means based on uncorrected IQs, which are often inflated by 6 to 10 IQ points due to aging norms.

Note that we are concerned here with comparisons involving mean IQs. The tests as originally scored may be quite satisfactory for correlation purposes, because correlations disregard averages, so that uniform changes in means will not affect them. There is a theoretical possibility of slight distortion with different mixtures of tests or occasions of testing, but in practice it is very slight—we have correlated IQ scores before and after Flynn correction for several of our groups, and found these correlations to be uniformly above .99, meaning that when correlations are involved, adjusted and unadjusted scores may be regarded as interchangeable. Most of our correlational analyses, including those reported in Tables C.1 and C.2 above, were in fact based on unadjusted scores, but where means are compared we use the Flynn correction.

Appendix D

Details on Self-Ratings

Table D.1 contains means and standard deviations for self-ratings on the outcomes questionnaire for adopted and biological children and for mothers and fathers in the adoptive families.

To a greater degree than fathers, mothers see themselves as having been good students in high school, having had many friends, and staying out of trouble. They view themselves as currently more conscientious and agreeable.

The adopted children, as compared to the biological children, see themselves as having been in more trouble in high school and having more problems lately, including drugs and alcohol, anxiety and/or depression, and trouble with the law.

Table D.1
Means and SDs for Self-Ratings on the Outcomes Questionnaire

Item	Adopted M	Adopted SD	Biological M	Biological SD	Mother M	Mother SD	Father M	Father SD	Sig.
Educational attainment	4.33	1.34	4.51	1.36	4.38	1.56	4.57	1.54	
Good student in HS	6.96	1.62	6.96	1.69	7.62	1.36	6.57	1.50	b
Many friends in HS	7.02	1.82	6.69	1.82	7.54	1.50	6.99	1.66	b
No trouble in HS	7.05	2.00	7.56	1.80	8.64	1.13	7.80	1.91	c
Distance from father	4.25	2.38	3.98	2.28	3.89	2.44	3.84	2.21	
Distance from mother	4.08	2.30	3.59	2.38	2.81	2.05	3.04	2.13	
Job responsibility	8.02	1.42	8.10	1.26	8.15	1.31	7.97	1.44	
Job stability	6.85	2.26	7.07	2.12	8.25	1.47	8.21	1.52	
Separated/divorced	1.46	.67	1.55	.75	1.15	.52	1.07	.35	
Happy marriage	6.98	2.31	7.13	2.02	8.17	1.47	8.30	1.16	
Drugs and alcohol	2.11	2.12	1.63	1.48	1.23	1.11	1.33	1.25	a
Anxiety/depression	3.88	2.11	3.28	1.74	2.64	1.64	2.34	1.43	a
Trouble with the law	1.59	1.46	1.26	.93	1.04	.23	1.12	.79	a
Many friends currently	6.04	2.21	6.34	1.87	7.15	1.79	7.02	1.66	
Independent	7.52	1.51	7.47	1.48	7.73	1.46	7.93	1.19	
Mature	7.60	1.32	7.59	1.31	8.22	1.00	8.02	1.10	
Conscientious	7.95	1.18	7.99	1.02	8.54	.75	8.33	.73	b
Agreeable	7.39	1.30	7.60	1.16	8.26	.80	8.03	.91	b

Note: See Appendix B for questionnaire. All items on a 1-9 scale, except Educational attainment (1-6) and Separated/divorced (1-3). In last column, significant differences by *t*-test (independent groups and matched pairs, respectively): a = adopted versus biological, b = mother versus father, c = both a and b. *N*s: adopted 198-226, biological 87-104; mothers 118-129; fathers 121-134.

Appendix E

Modeling of Selection

This appendix provides details of the simulation study mentioned in Chapter 5. The study compared the effect of socioeconomic restriction on "genetic" and "environmental" versions of a model of IQ and educational and occupational variables. Figure E.1 shows the path model used.

Figure E.1
Path Model Used in Modeling Selection

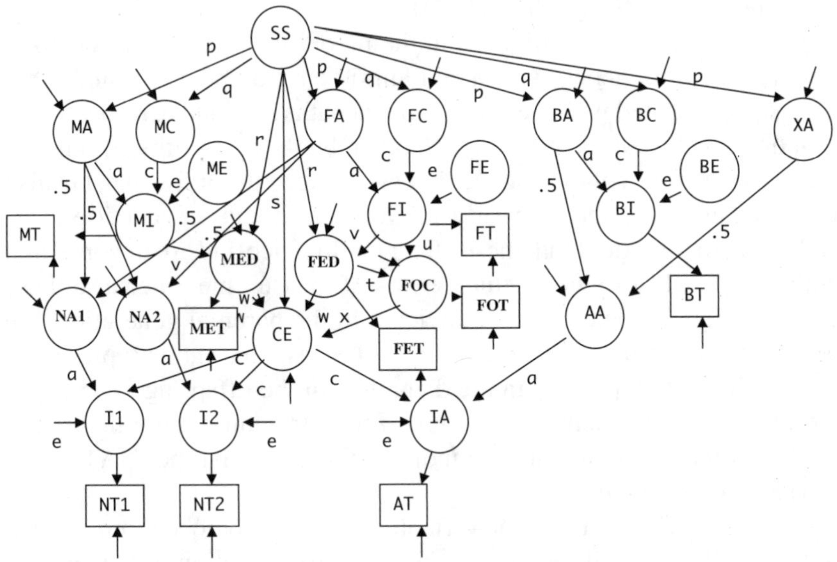

Note: For details, see text.

The Path Model

Figure E.1 shows the path model. It represents two adoptive parents, two biological children of theirs and one adopted child, and the birth parents of the adopted child. The observed variables are shown in rectangles in the diagram and identified by a final T for "test" (which includes other forms of measurement). They include the measured IQs of the two adoptive parents (MT and FT—a little less than halfway down the diagram, at the left and at the right center), the IQ of the birth mother (BT, located to the right of the diagram), the IQs of the children (NT1, NT2, and AT, at the bottom of the figure), plus three measures relevant to the adoptive family environment, those of mother's and father's education and father's occupational level (MET, FET, and FOT, about two-thirds of the way down the figure).

There are numerous hypothetical, or latent, variables in the model, indicated by the circles. Corresponding to each measured IQ is the individual's actual intelligence, indicated by an I, presumed to be imperfectly measured by the test, with a reliability equal to the square of the path $i, j,$ or k leading from true intelligence to test score, and the error of measurement represented by the short unlabeled arrow beneath each square. Imperfect measurement is also indicated for education and occupation via paths from the true variables (MED, FED, and FOC) to the measured ones (MET, FET, and FOT).

Each individual's intelligence in the model is represented as caused by three factors: genes (A), shared family environment (C), and other things uncorrelated with these two (E), via paths $a, c,$ and $e,$ respectively. A and C may be correlated with each other, but E (by definition) is not. E includes the effects of experiences idiosyncratic to the individual, but also includes random accidents in early development, nonlinear genetic effects, and so on, to the extent that these affect intelligence and are uncorrelated with A or C. (E does not include errors of measurement because these are separately modeled.) One individual in the parental generation, the genetic father of the adopted child, is not measured, and is represented only by his genotype (XA in the diagram). In the offspring generation, the family environment, labeled CE (for "common environment"), is shared by the children, but each individual has a genotype (NA1, NA2, AA) and a residual e.

At the top of the figure is the variable SS, for the socioeconomic status of the family; this will be the variable used for selection in the simulations. It is related to the genes and environments of the parents' IQs by paths p and q, to the educational levels of the parents by paths r, and to the shared environment of the children by the path s. This last path allows for possible influences of socioeconomic status on children's intelligence in addition to those occurring via the parent's intelligence, education, and occupation. Note that the diagram assumes that the birth parents are selected for socioeconomic status also; this is plausible for this particular population, but would not be the case in all adoption studies.

In the model, parents' education is a function of both their intelligence (path v) and their socioeconomic status (path r), and father's occupational level is a function of his intelligence (path u) and his education (path t). The children's shared environment is affected environmentally by the parents' education and the father's occupational level (via paths w and x), in addition to the direct influence from socioeconomic status via path s. The diagram contains many small unlabeled arrows indicating that most of the latent variables are also affected by causes other than those explicitly represented in the path diagram.

The Simulations

The path model of Figure E.1 was embedded in a computer program written in the computer language SPSS. This program produced a large number of random families in conformity with the path diagram and specified numerical values of the paths; then, in a second step, selected a subsample from among these families based on a restricted range of socioeconomic status and calculated statistics for the selected group. Ten thousand families were produced for the total population in each run of the simulation; the selected subsamples typically involved around a thousand families.

As earlier stated, two variants were used, one based on a version of the model that emphasized the genes and one on a version that emphasized shared environment. The genetic version had relatively large values of a and p; the shared environment version had relatively large values of c, q, and s. The remaining paths of the model, dealing with such matters as the extent to which education depends on intelligence or different parental factors affect the childhood environment, were arbitrarily set to values which seemed appropriate in the light of our and others' findings, and were kept the same in both versions. Because the initial simulation represented the full population, IQs were scaled to means of 100 and standard deviations of 15, and the square roots of reliabilities were assigned plausible population values (e.g., .95 for IQ).

Table E.1
Path Values Used in the Simulations

Genetic Model	Family Environment Model	Both Models
a = .8	a = .1	u = x = w = .2
c = .1	c = .8	v = .4
p = .8	q = .8	r = t = .6
s = .1	s = .3	IQ test reliabilities =.95
[q = .63]	[p = .51]	other reliabilities=.975
[e = .52]	[e = .53]	

Note: Symbols correspond to paths in Fig. E.1. Calculated path values shown in square brackets.

The path values used in the simulations are listed in Table E.1. The values for the genetic path a and the shared environment path c were arbitrarily set to .8 or .1, depending on the model. The genetic or environmental effect of socioeconomic status, p or q, was set at .8, depending on the model, and the other, q or p, solved for under the assumption that the correlation between A and C was the same across generations. (This correlation is equal to pq in the parent generation and is a function of a, p, c, q, v, r w, t, u, x, and s in the child generation). The direct effect of socioeconomic status on children's shared environment, s, was set at a small value of .1 in the "genetic" version, and to a larger value of .3 in the "environmental" one (a value of s much larger than .3, given the other path values, resulted in anomalous solutions involving correlations greater than 1.0, square roots of negative numbers, or the like).

Selections from the populations produced by these models were carried out based on the socioeconomic latent variable. Stoolmiller (1998) has modeled selection via truncation, whereby all families above a certain threshold on the selection variable are admitted, and all families below that threshold are excluded. This seems somewhat implausible as a representation of what occurs in real life. Many factors, including chance, enter into the actual determination of whether a particular family adopts a particular child, so that this event would be imperfectly associated with any single underlying variable. At best, there would be a gradual transition on such a variable, as opposed to an abrupt threshold. One might model such a transition in a number of ways; we chose a conceptually simple one of specifying two thresholds, a lower one below which a family would be excluded from adoption, and an upper one above which they would clearly be acceptable, with a linear increase in probability of acceptance between the two. We set the lower threshold half a standard deviation above the population mean on the socioeconomic variable, and the upper threshold two standard deviations higher. This criterion selects approximately 10 percent of the population. These values produce something like the observed effects on the means and standard deviations. This may seem a rather drastic restriction, but it should be kept in mind that most of it would represent the cultural and social factors that led particular families to this particular adoption agency, not choice among applicants by its staff, and that a well-above-average socioeconomic status is characteristic of our sample, whose average parental education is about 1.30 SD above the mean for the state of Texas and whose father's occupation averages about 1.00 SD above the Texas mean (Horn, Loehlin, & Willerman, 1982).

Table E.2
Observed Means and SDs of IQs Compared to Those Implied by Models Which Emphasize Genes and Family Environments

Group	Observed	Mostly Genes	Mostly Family Environment
IQ means			
Adoptive mother	112.8	115.8	115.0
Adoptive father	115.2	115.4	115.3
Birth mother	106.3	115.3	115.4
Natural child	112.5	115.6	114.5
Adopted child	112.4	115.1	114.5
IQ SDs			
Adoptive mother	10.3	12.8	13.3
Adoptive father	11.0	12.7	12.7
Bith mother	11.6	12.6	12.7
Natural child	11.5	12.4	12.9
Adopted child	11.6	12.5	13.0
SES variables, means			
Mother's education	1.24	1.33	1.31
Father's education	1.30	1.34	1.32
Father's occupation	1.02	1.00	.96
SES variables, SDs			
Mother's education	.86	.70	.73
Father's education	.80	.70	.71
Father's occupation	.76	.86	.88

Note: Observed IQs are Wechsler IQs from original study. SES variables are in standard scores based on 1970 census data for Texas, ages 30 to 49 for education, 30 to 54 for occupation.

Results: Means and Standard Deviations

Table E.2 shows that this selection results in means and SDs roughly in the observed range, for either of the two models—roughly, not exactly. For IQs, the procedure over-selects slightly on means and under-selects somewhat on SDs. For education and occupation, the means are about right for education, and the SDs a bit low; for occupation, the SDs are fairly close and it is the means that are on the high side. But the results suggest that our modeling of selection is somewhere in the right ballpark.

Results: Correlations

We will focus on a comparison of the correlations under the "genetic" and the "environmental" sets of path values. This is the comparison that tells us most about the effects of the selection on heredity and environment interpretations. After restriction of range is taken into account, do the correlations better fit those implied by a model emphasizing the genes or by one emphasizing family environment? The observed correlations and simulated correlations from models emphasizing genes and family environment, respectively, are shown in Table E.3—these are the correlations in the restricted samples.

Often the two models give fairly similar results—after all, many of the path values and the selection variable were the same in both. But on the whole the genetic version comes closer to the data. The mean absolute discrepancy between observed and modeled correlations is .085 for the "genetic" set of paths and .116 for the "environmental" set. In a number of cases, both models fit the data reasonably well. However, there are eight correlations for which there is a discrepancy of .15 or greater between the predicted and observed values. Four involve both models, and thus presumably reflect shortcomings of the overall modeling or sampling oddities in the data. These include the correlations of father's occupation with mother's intelligence and father's occupation with his education, for which the model correlations are lower than the observed ones, and of mother's education with adopted child's IQ and birth mother's intelligence with natural child's IQ, for which the model correlations are higher than those observed. The other four large discrepancies all involve the environmental model. The worst discrepancies are for the two sibling correlations, which are predicted by the environmental model to be .50 and .53, more than 20 points too high. Altogether, of the 29 correlations in Table E.3, the genetic model comes closer in 20 instances, the environmental model in 7,

Table E.3
Observed Correlations Compared to Those Implied by Models Emphasizing
Genes or Family Environment, After Selection

Vars.	Observ.	Genet.	Envir.	Vars.	Observ.	Genet.	Envir.
	Correlations				Correlations		
	Among IQs				*Between IQ and SES measures*		
MT FT	.31	.19	.17	MT MET	.50	.62	.64
MT BT	.22	.23	.22	MT FET	.43	.31	.32
MT NT	.24	.35	.28	MT FOT	.37	.20	.14
MT AT	.19	.24	.25	FT MET	.33	.30	.27
FT BT	.24	.22	.21	FT FET	.55	.67	.62
FT NT	.40	.35	.28	FT FOT	.53	.50	.47
FT AT	.17	.24	.29	BT MET	.35	.30	.34
BT NT	.03	.24	.22	BT FET	.26	.33	.31
BT AT	.32	.32	.21	BT FOT	.24	.19	.18
NT AT	.20	.26	.50	NT MET	.24	.35	.39
NT1 NT2	.27	.36	.53	NT FET	.26	.39	.39
				NT FOT	.30	.29	.32
	Among SES variables			AT MET	.14	.34	.40
MET FET	.52	.48	.48	AT FET	.22	.36	.41
MET FOT	.39	.30	.27	AT FOT	.19	.21	.30
FET FOT	.75	.58	.57				

Notes: Symbols: M = adoptive mother, F = adoptive father, B = birth mother of adopted child, N = natural child of the adoptive parents, A = adopted child; E = educational level, O = occupational level; final T = test score or measurement; 1,2 = two different children. Vars. = the two variables correlated; Observ. = observed correlation in TAP; Genet. = simulated correlation using "genetic" path values (see text); Envir. = simulated correlation using "environmental" path values.

and there are two ties. In only 1 of the 7 cases where the environmental model does better is the difference between the two more than .05 (the adoptive-mother natural-child correlation), whereas in 7 of the 20 cases favoring the genetic model the differences are this large or larger.

Our conclusion is that even after taking very severe selection into account (90 percent of the population excluded), our data are on the whole more consistent with those expected under a model emphasizing genetic influences than under a model emphasizing shared environmental ones.

Glossary

additive genetic effects. Genetic effects on a trait that represent the effects of individual genes added together.

Analysis of Variance. Statistical procedure for comparing more than two means.

behavior genetics. The science studying genetic (and environmental) contributions to behavioral differences.

Beta. The Revised Beta Examination. A primarily non-verbal IQ test used in the TAP.

Big Five. Five broad dimensions found in various personality tests and ratings in several languages; usually given as Extraversion, Conscientiousness, Neuroticism, Agreeableness, and Openness.

birth parents. The genetic parents of an adopted child.

borderline statistical significance. p-values greater than .05, but less than .10.

ceiling effect. A tendency of a set of scores to be limited at the high end.

chi square (χ^2). Statistic used for comparing the frequency of cases in two or more categories. Also used for testing how well path models fit data.

composite. A score representing a combination of scales.

correlation coefficient. An index of the degree of association of two sets of scores on the same or paired individuals. Measured on a scale of .00 to 1.00, from no predictability of one score from the other (.00) to perfect predictability (1.00).

CPI. California Psychological Inventory. An 18-scale inventory designed to measure normal personality traits. Its scales are listed in Table 3.16.

Cronbach alpha. A measure of test reliability based on internal consistency.

df. "Degrees of freedom." A quantity related to N. In path modeling, the difference between the number of observed relationships and the number of unknown paths solved for.

dichotomize. Divide into two equal groups based on scores on a trait.

error of measurement. The extent to which random errors affect a test score.

externalizing problems. Problems related to observable misconduct (as contrasted with *internalizing problems* such as anxiety or depression).

Flynn corrections. Adjusting scores for Flynn effects.

Flynn effects. The consequences of using old norms when performance on a test is changing over time in a population.

genotype. The set of genes of an individual.

genotype-environment correlation. A systematic tendency for certain genotypes and environments to co-occur.

genotype-environment interaction. Different genotypes respond differently to environment, so that the effect of environment on a trait depends on the genotype.

goodness-of-fit. How well a path model's predictions correspond to the data.

halo effect. A tendency of raters to give across-the-board positive or negative evaluations.

interaction. When the effect of one variable depends on the value of another.

internalizing problems. Problems related to emotions, such as anxiety or depression (as contrasted with *externalizing problems* related to misconduct).

interrater reliabilities. Agreement between raters, expressed as a correlation coefficient.

intraclass correlation. A correlation involving sets of scores greater than pairs.

IPB. Index of Problem Behavior. The number of problems at various ages, derived from interviewer's notes on parent interviews in the TAP.

IQ. "Intelligence Quotient." An individual's performance on an intelligence test in comparison with his or her age group, on a scale with mean = 100 and (usually) standard deviation = 15.

latent variable. An unobserved variable in a path model.

mean. Arithmetic mean—the common arithmetical average.

median. The value of the middle score when scores are ordered from lowest to highest.

midparent-midoffspring regression. Prediction of the average of offspring from the average of their parents.

MMH. Methodist Mission Home. The home for unwed mothers from which the adopted children in the Texas Adoption Project came.

MMPI. Minnesota Multiphasic Personality Inventory. A multi-scale personality inventory, originally designed to distinguish individuals with various psychiatric diagnoses from members of the general population and from people with other diagnoses

multiple regression. A statistical procedure in which scores on one variable are predicted from scores on two or more other variables.

N. Symbol for number of cases or pairings.

negative skew. A skewed distribution in which scores are spread out at the low end.

nonadditive genetic effects. Effects dependent on gene combinations rather than on individual genes.

normal distribution. A symmetrical, bell-shaped distribution of scores, in which scores at the extremes are rare, but become increasingly frequent toward the center.

norms. Criteria for interpreting test scores in relation to the population on which the test was standardized

p. The probability of obtaining a spurious result by chance in drawing a sample. p values of more than .05 (1 chance in 20) are considered to render the result doubtful.

path diagram. A model of causal relationships (represented by arrows) among a set of observed and unobserved variables (represented by squares and circles).

path model. (Or structural equation model.) Causal model of relations among variables, often represented by a path diagram.

Pd. Psychopathic deviate scale of the MMPI. A measure of disregard of society's rules and others' feelings. Originally developed to distinguish psychopaths from the general population and from persons with other diagnoses

performance IQ. An IQ based on scales of the WAIS or WISC that have minimal verbal requirements. The scales are listed in Table 2.18.

personality inventory. A personality questionnaire whose items measure a number of different personality traits.

phantom variables. Arbitrary variables introduced to clarify a path diagram.

positive skew. A skewed distribution in which scores are spread out at the high end.

r. symbol for a correlation coefficient.

raw score. An original, unadjusted score.

reliability of a test. The quality of measurement of test (on a scale of .00 to 1.00); the consistency or dependability with which it measures whatever it measures.

residual score. Part of score not predicted in a multiple regression.

response set. A systematic bias in responding to a questionnaire, such as a "halo effect."

restriction of range. Underrepresentation of scores from one or both extremes of a population.

Revised Beta. See Beta.

SD. Symbol for the standard deviation.

selective placement. A tendency of an adoption agency to match children with certain backgrounds or traits to similar adoptive families.

SES. Socioeconomic status. In the TAP, a score for a family based on the education of both parents and the father's occupation.

16PF. The 16 Personality Factors test. The adult version of a series of questionnaires designed by R. B. Cattell to measure the personality factors of his theory at different ages. Its scales are listed in Table 3.12.

skewed distribution. A distribution of scores that departs from the normal in that the scores are spread out at one end and compressed at the other.

standard deviation (SD). A measure of the amount of spread of a set of scores. In a normal distribution, about two-thirds of the scores lie within one standard deviation of the mean.

standardization of a test. Administration of a test during its development to a large sample of the general population in order to obtain standards for interpreting an individual's score on the test.

Stanford-Binet. A modification of Binet's original scale for measuring intelligence—used in the TAP for children too young for the WISC.

statistical significance. Less than 1 chance in 20 that an observed result might have resulted by chance in sampling ($p < .05$).

sten. A standardized score used by Cattell, with mean = 5.5 and SD = 2.

structural equation model. Alternative name for path model.

TAP. Texas Adoption Project, the research project described in this book.

true score. The hypothetical true score of an individual, imperfectly reflected in the observed score.

T-score. A standardized score used for the MMPI, with mean = 50 and SD = 10.

t-test. Statistical procedure for comparing two means.

TTS. Thurstone Temperament Schedule. An inventory whose scales were designed to measure several basic personality traits in a normal population. Its scales are listed in Table 3.17.

variable (as a noun). A measure that has different values over a set of individuals.

verbal IQ. An IQ based on scales of the WAIS or WISC that have a substantial verbal component. Its scales are listed in Table 2.18.

WAIS. Wechsler Adult Intelligence Scale. An individually administered IQ test for adults, consisting of a number of distinct subscales.

WAIS-R. A revised version of the WAIS.

Wechsler-Bellevue. An earlier version of the Wechsler Adult Intelligence Scale.

WISC. Wechsler Intelligence Scale for Children. Similar to the WAIS, but designed for children.

WISC-R. A revised version of the WISC.

WRAT. Wide Range Achievement Test. It has three subscales measuring achievement in reading, spelling, and arithmetic for a wide range of ages.

χ^2. Symbol for chi square.

References

Beer, J. M., & Horn, J. M. (2000). The influence of rearing order on personality development within two adoption cohorts. *Journal of Personality, 68,* 789-819.

Beer, J. M., Arnold, R. D., & Loehlin, J. C. (1998). Genetic and environmental influences on MMPI factor scales: Joint model fitting to twin and adoption data. *Journal of Personality and Social Psychology, 74,* 818-827.

Bouchard, T. J., Jr., Lykken, D. T., McGue, M., Segal, N., & Tellegen, A. (1990). Sources of human psychological differences: The Minnesota Study of Twins Reared Apart. *Science, 250,* 223-228.

Burks, B. S. (1928). The relative influence of nature and nurture upon mental development: A comparative study of foster parent-foster child resemblance and true parent-true child resemblance. *27th Yearbook of the National Society for the Study of Education, Part I,* 219-316.

Cadoret, R. J., Yates, W. R., Troughton, E., Woodworth, G., & Stewart, M. A. (1995). Genetic-environmental interaction in the genesis of aggressivity and conduct disorders. *Archives of General Psychiatry, 52,* 916-924.

Cardon, L. R., Fulker, D. W., DeFries, J. C., & Plomin, R. (1992). Multivariate genetic analysis of specific cognitive abilities in the Colorado Adoption Project at age 7. *Intelligence, 16,* 383-400.

Carretta, T. R. & Ree, M. J. (1995). Near identity of cognitive structure in sex and ethnic groups. *Personality and Individual Differences, 19,* 149-155.

Caspi, A., Sugden, K., Moffitt, T. E., Taylor, A., Craig, I.W., Harrington, H., et al. (2003). Influence of life stress on depression: Moderation by a polymorphism in the 5-HTT gene. *Science, 301,* 386-389.

Cattell, R. B., Eber, H. W., & Tatsuoka, M. M. (1970). *Handbook for the Sixteen Personality Factor Questionnaire (16PF).* Champaign, IL: Institute for Personality and Ability Testing.

Colligan, R. C., & Offord, K. P. (1992). *The MMPI: A contemporary normative study of adolescents.* Norwood, NJ: Ablex Publishing.

DeFries, J. C., Plomin, R., & Fulker, D. W. (Eds.) (1994). *Nature and nurture during middle childhood.* Oxford: Blackwell.

Eaves, L. J., Eysenck, H. J., & Martin, N. G. (1989). *Genes, culture and personality: An empirical approach.* San Diego, CA: Academic Press.

Eaves, L. J., Heath, A. C., Neale, M. C., Hewitt, J. K., & Martin, N. G. (1998). Sex differences and non-additivity in the effects of genes on personality. *Twin Research 1,* 131-137.

Ernst, J. L. (2006). *Genetic and environmental influences of maternal psychosocial and antisocial tendencies on the development of problem behaviors: A life course*

Note: This list includes publications from the TAP, whether cited in the book or not, plus other works cited.

investigation of risks and resilience. Unpublished Doctoral Dissertation, University of Texas at Austin.

Fisch, R. O., Bilek, M. K., Deinard, A. S., & Chang, P. N. (1976). Growth, behavioral, and psychologic measurements of adopted children: The influences of genetic and socioeconomic factors in a prospective study. *Journal of Pediatrics, 89,* 494-500.

Flynn, J. R. (1984). The mean IQ of Americans: Massive gains 1932 to 1978. *Psychological Bulletin, 95,* 29-51.

Flynn, J. R. (1987). Massive gains in 14 nations: What IQ tests really measure. *Psychological Bulletin, 101,* 171-191.

Freeman, F. N., Holzinger, K. J., & Mitchell, B. C. (1928). The influence of environment on the intelligence, school achievement, and conduct of foster children. *27th Yearbook of the National Society for the Study of Education, Part I,* 103-217.

Goldberg, L. R., & Rorer, L. G. (1964). *Test-retest item statistics for the California Psychological Inventory.* Eugene, OR: Oregon Research Institute.

Gough, H. G. (1957). *Manual for the California Psychological Inventory* (revised 1964). Palo Alto, CA: Consulting Psychologists Press.

Harden, K. P., Turkheimer, E., & Loehlin, J. C. (2007). Genotype by environment interaction in adolescents' cognitive aptitude. *Behavior Genetics, 37,* 273-283.

Hathaway, S. R., & McKinley, J. C. (1967). *Minnesota Multiphasic Personality Inventory; manual (Rev.).* New York: Psychological Corporation.

Horn, J. M. (1983). The Texas Adoption Project: Adopted children and their intellectual resemblance to biological and adoptive parents. *Child Development, 54,* 268-275.

Horn, J. M. (1985). Bias? Indeed! *Child Development, 56,* 779-780.

Horn, J. M., Green, M., Carney, R., & Erickson, M. T. (1975). Bias against genetic hypotheses in adoption studies. *Archives of General Psychiatry, 32,* 1365-1367.

Horn, J. M., Loehlin, J. C., & Willerman, L. (1976). Nature-nurture and intelligence: The twin and adoption studies agree. *Acta Geneticae Medicae et Gemellologiae, 25,* 195-197.

Horn, J. M., Loehlin, J. C., & Willerman, L. (1979). Intellectual resemblance among adoptive and biological relatives: The Texas Adoption Project. *Behavior Genetics, 9,* 177-207.

Horn, J. M., Loehlin, J. C., & Willerman, L. (1981). Generalizability of heritability estimates for intelligence from the Texas Adoption Project. In L. Gedda, P. Parisi, and W. E. Nance (Eds.) *Twin Research 3.* Part B (pp. 17-19). New York: Liss.

Horn, J. M., Loehlin, J. C., & Willerman, L. (1982). Aspects of the inheritance of intellectual abilities. *Behavior Genetics, 12,* 479-516.

Horn, J. M., Plomin, R., & Rosenman, R. (1976). Heritability of personality traits in adult male twins. *Behavior Genetics, 6,* 17-30.

Horn, J. M., & Turner, R. G. (1975). Birth order effects among unwed mothers. *Journal of Individual Psychology, 31,* 71-78.

Horn, J. M., & Turner, R. G. (1976). Minnesota Multiphasic Personality Inventory profiles among subgroups of unwed mothers. *Journal of Consulting and Clinical Psychology, 44,* 25-33..

Jensen, A. R. (1998). *The g factor: The science of mental ability.* Westport, CT: Praeger.

Keller, M. C., Coventry, W. L., Heath, A. C., & Martin, N. G. (2005). Widespread evidence for non-additive genetic variation in Cloninger's and Eysenck's personality dimensions using a twin plus sibling design. *Behavior Genetics, 35,* 707-721.

LaBuda, M. C., DeFries, J. C., & Fulker, D. W. (1987). Genetic and environmental covariance structures among WISC-R subtests: A twin study. *Intelligence, 11,* 233-244.

Langinvainio, H., Kaprio, J., Koskenvuo, M. & Lönnqvist, J. (1984). Finnish twins reared apart. III: Personality factors. *Acta Geneticae Medicae et Gemellologaie, 33,* 259-264.

Leahy, A. M. (1935). Nature-nurture and intelligence. *Genetic Psychology Monographs, 17*, 235-308.

Lindner, R. M., & Gurvitz, M. (1946). Restandardization of the Revised Beta Examination to yield the Wechsler type of IQ. *Journal of Applied Psychology, 30*, 649-658.

Loehlin, J. C. (1979). Combining data from different groups in human behavior genetics. In J. R. Royce and L. P. Mos (Eds.) *Theoretical advances in behavior genetics* (pp. 303-334). Alpen aan den Rijn, The Netherlands: Sijthoff and Noordhoff.

Loehlin, J. C. (1980). Recent adoption studies of IQ. *Human Genetics, 55*, 297-302.

Loehlin, J. C. (1985). Fitting heredity-environment models jointly to twin and adoption data from the California Psychological Inventory. *Behavior Genetics, 15*, 199-221.

Loehlin, J. C. (1986). Heredity, environment, and the Thurstone Temperament Schedule. *Behavior Genetics, 16*, 61-73.

Loehlin, J. C. (1987). Heredity, environment, and the structure of the California Psychological Inventory. *Multivariate Behavioral Research, 22*, 137-148.

Loehlin, J. C. (1989). Partitioning environmental and genetic contributions to behavioral development. *American Psychologist, 44*, 1285-1292.

Loehlin, J. C. (1991). Behavior genetic studies of change. In L. M. Collins and J. L. Horn (Eds.) *Best methods for the analysis of change: Recent advances, unanswered questions, future directions* (pp. 226-238). Washington, DC: American Psychological Association.

Loehlin, J. C. (1992). *Genes and environment in personality development.* Newbury Park, CA: Sage.

Loehlin, J. C. (2004). *Latent variable models: An introduction to factor, path, and structural equation analysis* (4th ed.). Mahwah, NJ: Erlbaum.

Loehlin, J. C (2005). Resemblance in personality and attitudes between parents and their children: Genetic and environmental contributions. In S. Bowles, H. Gintis, & M. O. Groves (Eds.), *Unequal chances: Family background and economic success* (pp. 192-207). New York: Russell Sage.

Loehlin, J. C., & Horn, J. M. (2000). Stoolmiller on restriction of range in adoption studies: A comment. *Behavior Genetics, 30*, 245-247.

Loehlin, J. C., Horn, J. M., & Ernst, J. L. (2007). Genetic and environmental influences on adult life outcomes: Evidence from the Texas Adoption Project. *Behavior Genetics, 37*, 463-476.

Loehlin, J. C., Horn, J. M. & Ernst, J. L. (2009). Antecedents of children's adult outcomes in the Texas Adoption Project. *Journal of Personality. 77*, 1-22.

Loehlin, J. C., Horn, J. M., & Willerman, L. (1981). Personality resemblance in adoptive families. *Behavior Genetics, 11*, 309-330.

Loehlin, J. C., Horn, J. M., & Willerman, L. (1989). Modeling IQ change: Evidence from the Texas Adoption Project. *Child Development, 60*, 993-1004.

Loehlin, J. C., Horn, J. M., & Willerman, L. (1990). Heredity, environment, and personality change: Evidence from the Texas Adoption Project. *Journal of Personality, 58*, 221-243.

Loehlin, J. C., Horn, J. M., & Willerman, L. (1994). Differential inheritance of mental abilities in the Texas Adoption Project. *Intelligence, 19*, 325-336.

Loehlin, J. C., Horn, J. M., & Willerman, L. (1997). Heredity, environment, and IQ in the Texas Adoption Project. In R. J. Sternberg and E. L. Grigorenko (Eds.), *Intelligence, heredity, and environment* (pp. 105-125). New York: Cambridge University Press.

Loehlin, J. C., & Nichols, R. C. (1976). *Heredity, environment, and personality: A study of 850 sets of twins.* Austin, TX: University of Texas Press.

Loehlin, J. C., Willerman, L., & Horn, J. M. (1982). Personality resemblances between unwed mothers and their adopted-away offspring. *Journal of Personality and Social Psychology, 42*, 1089-1099.

Loehlin, J. C., Willerman, L., & Horn, J. M. (1985). Personality resemblances in adoptive families when the children are late-adolescent or adult. *Journal of Personality and Social Psychology, 48,* 376-392.

Loehlin, J. C., Willerman, L., & Horn, J. M. (1987). Personality resemblance in adoptive families: A 10-year follow-up. *Journal of Personality and Social Psychology, 53,* 961-969.

Martin, N. G., & Eaves, L. J. (1977). The genetical analysis of covariance structure. *Heredity, 38,* 79-95.

Neale, M. C., & Cardon, L. R. (1992). *Methodology for genetic studies of twins and families.* Dordrecht, The Netherlands: Kluwer.

Nichols, R. C. (1965). The National Merit Twin Study. In S. G. Vandenberg (Ed.), *Methods and goals in human behavior genetics* (pp. 231-243). New York: Academic Press.

Pedersen, N. L., Plomin, R., McClearn, G. E., & Friberg, L. (1988). Neuroticism, extraversion, and related traits in adult twins reared apart and reared together. *Journal of Personality and Social Psychology, 55,* 950-957.

Penke, L., Dennisen, J. J. A., & Miller, G. F. (2007). The evolutionary genetics of personality. *European Journal of Personality, 21,* 549-587.

Petrill, S. A., Plomin, R., DeFries, J. C., & Hewitt, J. K. (Eds.) (2003). *Nature, nurture, and the transition to early adolescence.* Oxford: Oxford University Press.

Pierce, B. A. (1990). *The family genetic sourcebook.* New York: Wiley.

Plomin, R., Corley, R. Caspi, A., Fulker, D. W., & DeFries, J. C. (1998). Adoption results for self-reported personality: Evidence for nonadditive genetic effects? *Journal of Personality and Social Psychology, 75,* 211-218.

Plomin, R., & DeFries, J. C. (1985). *Origins of individual differences in infancy: The Colorado Adoption Project.* Orlando, FL: Academic Press.

Plomin, R., DeFries, J. C. & Fulker, D.W. (1988). *Nature and nurture during infancy and early childhood.* New York: Cambridge University Press.

Price, T. S., & Jaffee, S. R. (2008). Effects of the family environment: Gene-environment interaction and passive gene-environment correlation. *Developmental Psychology, 44,* 305-315.

Richardson, T. (1988). *The Mission Home Story.* San Antonio, TX: Methodist Mission Home.

Rowe, D.C., Vazsonyi, A.T., & Flannery, D. J. (1994). No more than skin deep: Ethnic and racial similarity in developmental process. *Psychological Review, 101,* 396-413.

Scarr, S., Webber, P. L., Weinberg, R. A., & Wittig, M. A. (1981). Personality resemblance among adolescents and their parents in biologically related and adoptive families. *Journal of Personality and Social Psychology, 40,* 885-898.

Scarr, S., & Weinberg, R. A. (1976). IQ test performance of black children adopted by white families. *American Psychologist, 31,* 726-739.

Scarr, S., & Weinberg, R. A. (1978). The influence of "family background" on intellectual attainment. *American Sociological Review, 43,* 674-692.

Schiff, M., Duyme, M., Dumaret, A., Stewart, J., Tomkiewicz, S., & Feingold, J. (1978). Intellectual status of working-class children adopted early into upper-middle-class families. *Science, 200,* 1503-1504.

Shields, J. (1962). *Monozygotic twins brought up apart and brought up together.* London: Oxford University Press.

Skodak, M., & Skeels, H. M. (1949). A final follow-up study of one hundred adopted children. *Journal of Genetic Psychology, 75,* 85-125.

Stockwell, S. T. (1966). *A history of the Methodist Mission Home of Texas.* San Antonio, TX: Methodist Mission Home.

Stoolmiller, M. (1998). Correcting estimates of shared environmental variance for range restriction in adoption studies using a truncated multivariate normal model. *Behavior Genetics, 28,* 429-441.

Stoolmiller, M. (1999). Implications of the restricted range of family environments for estimates of heritability and nonshared environment in behavior-genetic adoption studies. *Psychological Bulletin, 125*, 392-409.

Tambs, K., Sundet, J. M., & Magnus, P. (1988). Genetic and environmental effects on the covariance structure of the Norwegian army ability tests: A study of twins. *Personality and Individual Differences, 9*, 791-799.

Tellegen, A., Lykken, D. T., Bouchard, T. J., Jr., Wilcox, K. J., Segal, N. L., & Rich, S. (1988). Personality similarity in twins reared apart and together. *Journal of Personality and Social Psychology, 54*, 1031-1039.

Thurstone, L. L. (1953). *Examiner manual for the Thurstone Temperament Schedule* (2nd ed.). Chicago: Science Research Associates.

Turkheimer, E. (1991). Individual and group differences in adoption studies of IQ. *Psychological Bulletin, 110*, 392-405.

Turkheimer, E., Haley, A., Waldron, M., D'Onofrio, B., & Gottesman, I. I. (2003). Socioeconomic status modifies heritability of IQ in young children. *Psychological Science, 14*, 623-628.

Turner, R. G., & Horn, J. M. (1976). MMPI item correlates of WAIS subtest performance. *Journal of Clinical Psychology, 32*, 583-594.

Turner, R. G., & Horn, J. M. (1977a). Personality, husband-wife similarity and Holland's occupational types. *Journal of Vocational Behavior, 10*, 111-120.

Turner, R. G., & Horn, J. M. (1977b). Personality scale and item correlates of WAIS abilities. *Intelligence, 1*, 281-297.

Turner, R. G., Willerman, L., & Horn, J. M. (1976a). A test of some predictions from the personality assessment system. *Journal of Clinical Psychology, 32*, 631-643.

Turner, R. G., Willerman, L., & Horn, J. M. (1976b). Personality correlates of WAIS subtest performance. *Journal of Clinical Psychology, 32*, 349-354.

Vandenberg, S. G. (1962). The hereditary abilities study: Hereditary components in a psychological test battery. *American Journal of Human Genetics, 14*, 220-237.

Van Den Oord, E. J. C. G., & Rowe, D. C. (1997). An examination of genotype-environment interactions for academic achievement in an U. S. national longitudinal survey. *Intelligence, 25*, 205-228.

van IJzendoorn, M. H., Juffer, F., & Klein Poelhuis, C. W. (2005). Adoption and cognitive development: A meta-analytic comparison of adopted and nonadopted children's IQ and school performance. *Psychological Bulletin, 131*, 301-316.

Wierzbicki, M. (1993). Psychological adjustment of adoptees: A meta-analysis. *Journal of Clinical Child Psychology, 22*, 447-454.

Willerman, L. (1979a). Effects of families on intellectual development. *American Psychologist, 34*, 923-929.

Willerman, L. (1979b). *The psychology of individual and group differences*. San Francisco: W. H. Freeman.

Willerman, L., Horn, J. M., & Loehlin, J. C. (1977). The aptitude-achievement test distinction: A study of unrelated children reared together. *Behavior Genetics, 7*, 465-470.

Willerman, L., Loehlin, J. C., & Horn, J. M. (1979). Parental problem-solving speed as a correlate of intelligence in parents and their adopted and natural children. *Journal of Educational Psychology, 71*, 627-634.

Willerman, L., Loehlin, J. C., & Horn, J. M. (1992). An adoption and a cross-fostering study of the Minnesota Multiphasic Personality Inventory (MMPI) Psychopathic Deviate scale. *Behavior Genetics, 22*, 515-529.

Willerman, L., Loehlin, J. C., Horn, J. M., Scarr, S. & Weinberg, R. A. (1980). Examiner effects in adoption studies of intelligence. *Behavior Genetics, 10*, 431-434.

Index

8

8

8